Women in Ancient America

Also by Karen Olsen Bruhns

Ancient South America (Cambridge: Cambridge University Press, 1994, 2015)
Faking Ancient Mesoamerica and Faking the Ancient Andes, with Nancy L. Keller
(Walnut Creek, Calif.: Left Coast Press, 2010)
The Archaeology of Cihuatán: An Ancient Postclassic City of El Salvador, with Paúl
Amaroli (Lambert, Germany, 2012)

Also by Karen Stothert

"Valdivia, Machilila, Chorrera: Early Art and Artists," in *Ecuador: The Secret Art of
Precolumbian Ecuador* (Milan, Italy, 2007)
The Archeaology and Early History of the Head of the San Antonio River (San Antonio:
Southern Texas Archaeological Association, 1989)
Lanzas Silbadoras y Otras Contribuciones de Olaf Holm al Estudio del Pasado del Ecuador,
Volumes I and II (Guayaquil, Ecuador, 2002, 2007)

Women
in Ancient America

Second Edition

Karen Olsen Bruhns and Karen E. Stothert

UNIVERSITY OF OKLAHOMA PRESS / NORMAN

Library of Congress Cataloging-in-Publication Data
Bruhns, Karen Olsen.
Women in ancient America / Karen Olsen Bruhns and Karen E. Stothert.
—Second edition.
pages   cm
Includes bibliographical references and index.
ISBN 978-0-8061-4628-7 (paperback: alkaline paper)
1. Indian women—History—To 1500.
2. America—Antiquities.
3. Sex role—America—History—To 1500.
4. Social archaeology—America.
5. Feminist archaeology—America.
I. Stothert, Karen E.
II. Title.
E59.W8B78 2014   305.4097001—dc23
2014001706

The paper in this book meets the guidelines for permanence and durability of
the Committee on Production Guidelines for Book Longevity of the Council on
Library Resources, Inc. ∞

To Tom Weller and Neil Maurer,
with whom we respectively share our lives

Contents

Illustrations

Figures

Maps

Tables

Preface to the Second Edition

In the years since the publication of our first edition, the archaeology of gender has gained momentum, judging from the numerous publications, conferences, and interested participants. As a result of critiques from the margins, the practice of modern archaeology now more frequently focuses on the construction of gender differences within sociocultural systems, and archaeologists are more likely to include in their studies relationships among categories of people formerly invisible to researchers. The archaeology of sexuality and of children is now yielding fruit; and gender, age, sex, ethnicity, and class are factors that figure into archaeological interpretations.

Many scholars have observed that the feminist critique of science, and particularly the development of a feminist archaeology, have been good for the discipline and have been instrumental in peopling prehistory (Code 1991). Archaeology today is more alert to the roles of different individuals and groups in cultural processes (agency), and to making more nuanced social inferences. There is, however, room for further development. As Nelson (2004:3) has stated, one of the goals of her writing is to "convey the possibilities and ferment of gender research, research that has not yet been the leavening agent that it should be . . . in standard archaeological practice and interpretation."

In Europe and America the terms "gender archaeology" and "archaeology of gender" are now employed to designate the postprocessual, postmodern, and feminist practice that seeks not just to "find" women and others in the past, but to bring critical thinking to bear on the archaeological process of inference and on the construction of narratives about the past. The archaeologies of gender are diverse: practitioners self-consciously employ multiple lines of evidence and seek interpretations that reflect the plurality of knowledge characteristic of all societies and of contemporary researchers. They devise innovative approaches in recognition of the complexities of social relations in the past and the diverse contingencies that affect social actors. Researchers understand themselves as subjective and biased, and they expect that the individuals and social groups of the past were participants in processes characterized by conflicting motives and multiple points of view. The narratives generated by archaeologists of gender are the result of current ways of understanding the standpoint of the researcher and the factors that distort archaeological fieldwork, the interpretation of archaeological evidence, and the dissemination of archaeological knowledge (pedagogy). Today we are increasingly aware of the imaginative component of archaeological interpretation.

As archaeologists, we continue to be concerned with "finding" women in prehistory, but we are also interested in the broader goal of understanding gender systems and their operation. While our goal in writing this book has been to draw attention to women and to envision their roles in the past, we also hope to participate in the exploration of the variety of possible systems of gender, which are dynamic complexes of social relationships subject to change, negotiation, and resistance. Such systems exist in all human societies, and, like other scholars, we use ethnography to imagine the different kinds of gender relations possible in human communities, although we recognize that ethnographic data have been produced by researchers whose Western and androcentric cultural biases are now well known (Conkey 2001:351).

Similarly, we employ historical documents and direct historical approaches in order to facilitate our exploration of the identities of women, men, and others in late prehistoric societies, but we want to acknowledge here that those documents were written by individuals whose gaze was necessarily myopic given their gender, class, ethnicity, age, and social condition. We understand that we ourselves are likely to be guilty of representing the present in the past—an inadvertent sleight of hand.

In this book we are concerned with gender relations in the past, with a focus on women. We have tried not to project into the past the classic patriarchal family of Western European and Judeo-Christian traditions, and we suggest more egalitarian models that feature female and male complementarity or functional and ideological "unity." We have endeavored to avoid using the standard "division of labor by sex" and to eschew knee-jerk dichotomous thinking. We have not reified the public/private dichotomy (as universal or essentialist) but have rather envisioned women and men negotiating their participation in social arenas through time and across space. In this new edition, we have tried to illustrate the diverse strategies used in contemporary gender research.

Embedded in this book is the belief that gender is a dynamic process resulting in ever-changing social constructions that affect children, women, men, and other-gendered individuals in all societies past and present. We understand that gender roles, behaviors, and ideologies vary across time and space and are in a continual process of recreating themselves through practice as individuals and groups create, negotiate, contest, and resist in social contexts. Recent publications reiterate the commitment of gender archaeologists to the exploration of these social processes using evidence drawn from the past.

It is our responsibility to generate useful, carefully crafted narratives. It is unlikely that we observers will discover "the truth" about the past, but we do have a good chance, as Conkey and Gero have suggested, to "do archaeology differently"—to do it "better, more inclusively, more imaginatively"; the feminist perspective in archaeology is salubrious because it has resulted in critiques of archaeology, and particularly of "its hard-headed rules for a single way of knowing and its single vision" (Conkey and Gero 1997:430).

Our work falls into a category of "womanist" literature (*sensu* Joyce and Claassen 1997:1), and it was written as part of a movement to "engender" archaeology, but since our first edition, gender archaeology and the archaeology of gender have been more clearly defined (Hays-Gillpin and Whitley 1998). Today this kind of archaeology explores the social construction of gender differences through time and across space and includes numerous critiques of the concept of gender itself, probing the problem of the intersection of sexual factors along with age, race, occupation, class, ethnicity, and historical circumstances in any consideration of gender.

In terms of method and theory, we continue to espouse the appropriate use of ethnographic analogies and historical information to illuminate the archaeological record; we present case studies that examine gender through artifacts and the study of the spatial distribution of artifacts and archaeological features, including architecture and subsistence remains; and we focus on representations of human beings (art) and on skeletal remains and burials. We have been concerned with gender attribution—a method that has been central to the practice of the archaeology of gender since its inception, and we are unapologetically woman centered. These methods and practices continue to characterize the archaeology of gender even as a whole range of new approaches have emerged. Much of the research we summarize is derived from the positivist tradition and reflects the idea that knowledge about past societies can be "recovered," although many postmodernists suggest that we may "envision" but not actually "recover," since so much of extinct social context is ephemeral (Klein and Quilter 2001:6).

In this second edition we have defined gender constructs as relational and have suggested how women have been full participants in a great variety of different ways of life. Rather than sameness, we see variety: women's roles and statuses have been dynamic and interesting because of their ability to alter relationships and ideology. We have stressed how the archaeological record, when interpreted thoughtfully, reveals that there is no single "human division of labor": humans divide labor variably according to age, gender, individual ability, and class, and each system is as dynamic and responsive to contingency as any other aspect of culture in both the past and the present. It is viewed today as "idiosyncratic cross-culturally" (Costin 1996:112). It is clear that femininity and masculinity are not biologically inherent but defined and redefined by social groups through time.

Because the young discipline of gender archaeology is changing shape rapidly, we have added relevant concepts to our text and glossary; updated the references and added in-text citations; and created a new section that describes the state of theory today. We discuss the growth of many archaeologies of gender that reflect the complexity of the subject. In this revised edition we aim to raise more questions about our lives and the lives of peoples of the past with respect to gender and other dimensions of social life, including sexual identity and orientation, ethnicity, race, age, power, and class. We have tried to highlight recent methods, including studies that feature multiple lines of interpretation. It is plain that feminist theory and other critiques originating outside archaeology are reflected in the behavior of archaeologists of gender: theory has influenced their selection of research topics and data collection and shaped the narratives they generate.

However, new case studies continue to rely on the analysis of material remains, artifacts, constructions, and spatial arrangements in archaeological sites—particularly on the study of households (household archaeology)—and they maintain an emphasis on the analysis of imagery and of human remains and burials. We are committed to exploring the archaeological record with the intent of generating evidence and interpretations about the construction and change of gender relations in past societies. These case studies depend on ethnographic analogies, historical documents, and contextual analyses. This book's strength lies in presenting case studies that exemplify strategies for studying women in the past. We are highly supportive of an archaeology of gender that expands the methodological and theoretical discourse in archaeology and champions more nuanced narratives about the past. We are particularly happy that masculinist (Knapp 1998) and other perspectives are now represented more commonly in archaeology, as our interpretations grow more peopled, multidimensional, and dynamic.

Acknowledgments

No book is an individual effort; many people contributed substantially to the final document. We acknowledge with thanks all our colleagues who contributed research that has helped us envision people in the archaeological past, and we acknowledge especially Tom Weller and Neil Maurer, who have supported our efforts. We are grateful to all of those who generously contributed illustrative materials and to Alice Kehoe for her substantial contributions to the feminist mission and for her constructive criticisms of this text. We gratefully acknowledge the British Museum, which graciously waives fees for permission to publish its photographs in academic works like ours, even though we had to remove its illustration along with half of the other illustrations from the first edition in the interests of economy.

Women in Ancient America

CHAPTER ONE

Women and Gender

Archaeology is the principal means through which we understand humanity in the prehistoric past, and an auxiliary approach we use to clarify more recent human history. While the concept of humanity embodies both women and men, until recently women were underrepresented in historical narratives. Because our society uses the results of archaeological studies to validate its myths of origin, it is unacceptable to write histories that omit women and their perspectives. We must include them because women and girls constitute half of humanity, and their participation and contributions to the course of history are distinct from those of men and boys.

Human societies are made up of females and males in approximately equal numbers, and women and men of the same population overlap with respect to height and weight unless one sex is seriously underfed or otherwise stressed because of cultural practices. Moreover, observing human biological patterns leads biologists to expect similarities in women's and men's strategies in feeding and other social activities. For instance, with respect to mating strategies, Blaffer Hrdy (1981) has observed that sexual dimorphism among humans indicates that both females and males are likely to maximize reproductive success through multiple mates: they are both mildly polygamous. This lack of difference between males and females is frequently obscured by the multiplicity of values and cultural stratagems that different societies overlay onto these basic biological aspects of humanity—that is to say, gender.

Gender is a social script designed arbitrarily on the basis of a biological fact. While a person may feel that the gender system she grew up with is completely natural and universal, the arbitrariness of such systems is demonstrated by the fact that they change through time, often even within a lifetime, and are variable across space. Today anthropologists are investigating cultural constructs of gender and discovering how gender affects every individual's participation in society. Scholarly research has begun to reflect the fact that gender is a crucial factor in all social life and in history. Responsible interpretation of the past involves placing the missing half of humanity back into those scientific studies and old androcentric narratives that so often omitted women and ignored those aspects of life associated with women. Engendering the past implies creating narratives that recognize the potential for complex gender scenarios in human societies.

In the last decades, feminists have raised our consciousness about gender and history by drawing attention to the persistent pattern of exclusion of women from many valued areas of social life. This pattern is noted within the fields of anthropology and archaeology, where studies of male activities have been emphasized routinely and valued above those of women. Male behavior has defined the norm. Many inadequate narratives that pretend to describe universal human patterns have been presented as science but are really our own just-so stories. We should all be aware that other societies, past and present, have fostered different values and different stories, ones in which women's and men's roles are surprising to us, and that the historical narratives generated by other cultures are different from those of the Euroamerican and Western Asian religious and cultural spheres.

Ethnographic studies among groups relatively unaffected by European influences show that many of our supposedly common-sense ideas about the "natural and universal" division of labor are not present. Today we agree that division of labor by sex exists in some but not all cultures and that it may not take a form familiar to us. For instance, hunting, defined in our society as a quintessentially male activity, figures prominently in our scientific myths of origin, yet among many peoples it is natural for women to hunt small animals and to participate in communal hunts (Strange 1997). Cross-cultural studies reveal many examples of female hunters: aboriginal women hunt kangaroos with dogs in Australia and compete with dangerous carnivores to scavenge in eastern Africa (Kent 1998:36; Berndt 1981; Bird 1993; Hawkes et al. 1997). In North America, Chipewyan women have their own hunting grounds and, in the past, a Mimbres woman (fig. 1.1), great with child and bearing an antelope, could be a hunter (Brumbach and Jarvenpa 1997).

Figure 1.1. The painted image on this Mimbres bowl, which portrays a woman great with child and transporting an antelope, belies the stereotype of the passive, weak, herb-gathering woman. Courtesy of the Museum of Western Colorado. Cat. # G 495.

Gender interdependence may well have been a common pattern in hunting throughout human history (Bodenhorn 1990).

Both ethnographic and archaeological evidence demonstrate that patterns of human behavior are tremendously variable and often run against both Western folk wisdom and our common-sense interpretations of human nature. Sifting through the data concerning women in the corpus of male-focused scientific studies, we begin to see that many of our assumptions concerning normal behaviors are ethnocentric and untenable.

Because gender has always been a key dynamic of human life, we must consider the activities of both women and men if we hope to understand history. In the classic *Outline of Cultural Materials* (Murdock et al. 1950) is a list of over eight hundred aspects of culture that anthropologists study, and one can appreciate how behavior varies with gender as well as with time,

mode of economic production, and social organization. For example, Topic
27, "Drink, Drugs, and Indulgence," has the following subheadings:

Water and thirst
272 Nonalcoholic beverages
273 Alcoholic beverages
274 Beverage industries
275 Drinking establishments
276 Narcotics and stimulants
277 Tobacco
278 Pharmaceuticals

Investigating with an interest in gender provokes questions about how
women and men (and others) participate in these aspects of culture. Who
owns the water? Fetches it? Drinks it? What is the meaning of consumption? There are as many answers as there are groups of human beings, and
in each case women may differ from men of the same community with
respect to ideas and practices related to the drinking of water. Similarly, we
might ask, who brews the beer? In the Andean region of South America,
brewing is women's work; in the adjacent Amazon lowlands, some men brew
and women and men both drink. Who grows the tobacco? Who uses it and
when, and for what reasons? Tobacco is part of a complex of sacred, medicinal, and ceremonial practices in some societies, whereas in others it is a secular, personal indulgence. In some societies both women and men smoke, in
others only men, and in others this has changed in knowable history. Who
is the expert in the preparation and use of medicines? In Colonial North
America it was women; later, men dominated medicine and pharmacy and
forced women out, while today many women have reentered those fields.
Examining each aspect of culture with a curiosity concerning women's and
men's roles and ideologies is the key to creating a more dynamic and detailed
understanding of humankind.

What Do Archaeologists Do?

Archaeologists use systematic methods to recover, analyze, and interpret evidence from the earth in order to reconstruct social life in the past. Archaeological interpretation depends on both scientific techniques and the theories and ideologies that affect social description and history. Archaeologists
control an immense arsenal of techniques for excavating and analyzing the
remains of human activity. Today archaeological materials can be dated by a

large number of techniques, soils can be analyzed to give evidence of plants once used in the ancient context, artifacts can be analyzed to reveal the point of origin of the primary material, multivariate analysis and DNA studies of the remains of human bodies can reveal origins of the group and kinship patterns within it, chemical analysis of human remains can be used to reveal the geographic origins of individuals and their places of residence, and even feces can be tested to show both the diet and sex of the ancient person who defecated (N. Williams 1995; Powledge and Rose 1996; Sobolik et al. 1996; Price et al. 2000). The quantity and variety of information that can result from the archaeological analysis of evidence is astounding. However, the usefulness of raw data is determined by the body of theory that guides scientific interpretation.

The Role of Theory in Engendering the Past

All scientific research is governed by theory and by the specific historical and social circumstances that dictate what is useful and desirable to investigate, as well as which information should be gathered, which interpreted, and which ignored. Theory links archaeology to the wider fields of scientific endeavor, social thought, and history and makes archaeology subject to waves of fashion in the broader community of scholars. Archaeology has utilized evolutionary theory, ecological theory, structuralist and functionalist thought, Marxist models, and, most recently, postmodern feminist and critical theories.

In practice, Americanist archaeology employs an eclectic theoretical framework but always depends heavily on historical and ethnographic analogies for constructing models and making interpretations. Almost all archaeological models are formulated on the basis of the variations of human societies in history or in the ethnographic present. If there is evidence of continuity between the prehistoric and historic peoples in a region, then the direct historical approach may serve the archaeologist, although the reconstruction of the prehistoric past using models drawn from the historic period may be flawed because cultures are subject to dramatic change in Conquest and Colonial situations.

General analogical thinking is the basis for archaeological imagining, but this thinking is limited because, even taken together, the known historical cases and the entire body of ethnographic description do not cover the entire range of human cultural potential. Another problem with thinking analogically when doing engendered interpretations of the past is that archaeologists, despite their best intentions, project their own understanding of their own society onto other cultural contexts. For example, during the nineteenth and twentieth centuries, social scientists tended to view women's and men's spheres as distinct and women's spheres as being intrinsically of lesser value. Writers in the materialist scientific tradition of the industrial age have viewed women as having fewer and less interesting economic opportunities. Similarly, the social scientists who carried out the ethnographic observations on which archaeologists base their thinking frequently omitted women as sources of information, neglected to observe what women actually did, and failed to consider women as significant actors in public affairs. Anthropological research has perpetuated stereotypes concerning women's motivations, creativity, organizational capacities, political interests, and economic activities. The credible reconstruction of past societies is hampered by the uncritical use of that anthropological research, which ignores the female half of humankind. This intractable problem is exacerbated by the fact that after five hundred years of European imperialism, most of the peoples of the planet have been affected by Western concepts of gender and power.

Feminism and feminist epistemology, which appeared in anthropological fieldwork only about three decades ago, have significantly affected the androcentric culture of archaeology (Code 1991; Levy 2006; Spencer-Wood 2011; Wylie 1991), although many archaeologists continue to labor with a distorted understanding of human societies, which developed because researchers focused on those social institutions outside the household in which males often dominate. Both archaeologists and ethnographers frequently show more interest in the extrahousehold activities of the elite sectors of past societies, studying the organization of public institutions and generating an overly masculinized view of society. Both anthropologists and archaeologists have inadvertently defined women as nonparticipants. If only certain institutions are taken as the measure of employment and leadership, then female activities and groups with female participants are trivialized. This dichotomy between the formal and public on the one hand and the informal and private on the other may be an artifact of the field investigator's predisposition, not an accurate reflection of social reality.

Recent theory has opened the door to more nuanced social interpretations. For instance, the concept of heterarchy offers an alternative for imagining how power might be held in society, and the theoretical focus on agency has encouraged archaeologists to think about the actors of the past, the agents of sociocultural innovation and change, and the creators of new ideologies (Crumley 1995; Blanton et al. 1999).

While many societies in the recent past and present were or are characterized by gender-based hierarchies in which males seem to dominate many areas of human activity, other types of societies that demonstrate greater parity between women and men may have been more common earlier in history. In reality, the relationships between women and men in past and present societies are as variable across cultures as are other aspects of human behavior.

There is no single ethnographic model for the future society to which some feminists aspire, but it is useful to imagine and work toward a community life in which there is sexual equality and a division of labor without an ideology that stereotypes as important the social, political, and economic activities of one sex and as trivial those of the other sex. The aspirations of contemporary women find support in anthropological evidence: ethnographic studies show social contexts in which women form work groups and alliances that operate independently of men, and they show economic networks managed by women that control materials, create opportunities, achieve political goals, and meet challenges.

For people of Western cultural heritage or those converted to the cultural and religious ideologies of the West, it is difficult to imagine women in any of these ways. Nevertheless, in the past there were societies in which women's economic contributions were valued and celebrated by the society at large. Before colonization, in many parts of the world there were institutions that fostered women's economic networks outside the household. Women in such societies engaged in reciprocal exchanges and mutual assistance outside their immediate family groups. Because such societies persist even today, it behooves archaeologists to consider the proposition that similar organizations existed in ancient contexts and that material remains could well reflect gynocentric organizations.

Anthropological models provide archaeologists with grounds for making interpretations that differ fundamentally from those based on Western Asian and European ideological systems. It is imperative that archaeologists consider alternative models of sex roles and relations rather than relying on what has been termed the "direct ethnocentric approach" (Bruhns 1991:420). Thus, in the reconstruction of past societies, archaeologists might draw on appropriate models from historical and contemporary non-Western societies in which there is a greater parity between the sexes than that which has existed in the public sector of Euroamerican society. One model of parity can be derived from ethnographic studies of foragers among whom there is no marked division of labor along sexual lines, and where sexual hierarchy is not very important because no individual systematically makes decisions for anyone else. Such models need to be considered as archaeologists interpret the remains of past foraging societies and imagine how these societies became more complex.

Another model of parity can be seen among the historic Iroquois and Huron, groups in which sex roles were clearly marked and differentiated, but not obviously ranked. In such societies, women and men are believed to be very different, but both make key economic contributions, both have equivalently valued roles, and both exercise power. Women and men in these societies control their own sexuality and labor, and both have strategies for achieving their self-defined goals: they both participate in making decisions, allocating resources, and negotiating social values. Interdependence between the sexes in these societies is high (Venables 2010:21–57).

The study of these societies presents us with alternatives to androcentric interpretations. In order to write a responsible prehistory of America, it is imperative to adopt an engendered viewpoint, putting women and men alike into the narratives of the past. To understand social dynamics and social change, we must model how the two sexes are assigned economic activities and how they create serviceable ideologies and origin histories, negotiate leadership, and manage change. What women and men did in any particular past cultural context cannot be assumed, because women's and men's roles are not fixed but vary with time, space, and culture. The activities and roles of women and men should be assessed case by case as the archaeological record is interpreted. Even when the evidence for such reconstruction is thin, scholars may still productively and responsibly imagine the lives and values of all individuals.

New Archaeologies for Studying Gender

Recent research demonstrates that archaeologists of gender are focused on honing their thinking, refining their research strategies, and improving the narratives they generate. The following synopsis of some influential statements of method and theory that have appeared in recent years draws attention to diverse archaeologies of gender and to some recurrent subthemes that have emerged. New theories constitute the underpinnings of current research in gender archaeology and provide food for thought.

The discipline of gender archaeology flourishes in a context of various kinds of postprocessual thought, such as neohistoricism, idealism, neo-Marxism, and contextual archaeology (Trigger 1989). Feminist thought is an important source of theory that has guided both interpretation and practice in gender archaeology.

Recent publications on the archaeology of gender are characterized by diverse feminist perspectives and a willingness to entertain alternative approaches to generating knowledge about the past. As gender research has matured, archaeologists have discovered a variety of ways to "connect empirical archaeological study with theoretical resources and arguments" (Conkey and Gero 1997:416). These authors believe that gender archaeology is changing the practice of archaeology for the better, but Nelson (2004:3) remarks that gender research has not yet become "the leavening agent that it should be . . . in standard archaeological practice and interpretation."

The Problematics of Studying Gender

Central to most discussions in gender archaeology is some definition of the concept of gender, but there is little consensus (Conkey 2001:341–345; Nelson 2004:3–4; Joyce and Claassen 1997:4–5). Most writers emphasize the "constructed character of gender" and how humans are capable of developing myriad diverse systems and arrangements (Nelson 2004:5–8; Gilchrist 1999; Klein and Quilter 2001). Most agree that gender refers to the social construction of relationships among people of different sexes, but postmodern thinkers reject the stability of sex and gender as categories and emphasize that class, race, and ethnicity may in fact be more important categories (Conkey and Gero 1997:417–418; Conkey 2001:354). Later in prehistory, class is often more important than gender in shaping the lives of individuals, and most observers agree that the feminist movement has been fractured by the fact that race, ethnicity, and class divide women into groups with sometimes conflicting interests (Joyce 2008).

Archaeologists have recently taken responsibility for informing their readers about how gender roles, behaviors, and ideologies vary across time and space. Today, raising consciousness about gender and thinking critically about other constructs such as ethnicity, sexual orientation, race, age, and class are characteristic of archaeology and other fields of study, including anthropology, history, history of technology, art history, and sociology (Nelson 2004:4).

Feminist Postmodern Critique

Gender archaeology today operates within an "explicitly feminist framework" (Conkey and Gero 1997:411, 427–428). Archaeological practitioners are now aware of embedded androcentrism; committed to modeling societies composed of persons who differ by gender, class, ethnicity, sexuality, age, physical capacity, and so forth; less enamored of universalist, essentialist, and reductionist explanations; less concerned with origins, and more with differences; less concerned with hierarchy; more committed to understanding unique standpoints, diverse agents, and nuanced interpretations; and more accepting of alternative ways of knowing. In addition, feminist archaeologists are engaged in doing research differently and bringing about change: this involves rooting out entrenched biases, raising consciousness about agency in the production of knowledge, and creating respect for a diversity of practices and results. Perhaps their most radical (and yet obvious) suggestion is that archaeologists report "multiple interpretive judgments and evaluations at each nonreversible step of investigation" and that they "coordinate multiple strategies and objectives of different co-investigators into the research of nonrenewable archeological resources" (Conkey and Gero 1997:429–431).

Feminist Pedagogy

Because of the feminist critique of science and because of changes in archae-ology in the last twenty years, many archaeologists in academic contexts have become committed to new strategies designed to stimulate critical thinking in our students and in society: our aim is to communicate to the consumers of archaeological interpretations more believable and responsible narratives (Nelson 2004:40–41; Adovasio et al. 2007). Several recent works deal directly with teaching archaeology and can be seen as contributions to feminist ped-agogy (Romanowicz and Wright 1996; Conkey and Tringham 1995; Gero 2000).

Changing Archaeological Practice

Postprocessual archaeology is characterized by a number of approaches, which Duke and Wilson (1995:10–13) identify as "contextual" and which attempt to take a more emic attitude with respect to evidence. These approaches include variously archaeologies of social power, neohistoricism, idealism, neo-Marxism, cognitive archaeology, and so forth. In the postprocessual ferment there is "a resurrection of skepticism, a rejection of positivist assumptions" (Kehoe 1995:25).

Conkey and Gero (1997:424) ask archaeologists to reposition them-selves with respect to "the complex web of theory, data, and archaeological practice." They are concerned that much of the available literature (includ-ing our book) treats gender but does not "reconfigure" archaeology in any way. They encourage practitioners to draw on new resources and tackle new problems.

Archaeologists of gender are relying less on historical and ethnographic sources for analogues, while placing greater emphasis on contextual evidence as a basis for interpretation and inference (Gilchrist 1999:39, 53). It is very common for gender archaeologists to adopt "multiple lines of evidence" (including biological and iconographic sources) to investigate and describe the complexity of past social processes. For example, Brumfiel (1996a) recognizes "official versus popular imagery" of females; other authors recognize "multiplicity," "tension and contradiction," and "hegemonies and counter-hegemonies" in the archaeological record (Gilchrist 1999:53; Hollimon 1997).

Scholars have also used evolutionary models to argue how gender systems changed in human history. They envision the transformation of relatively egalitarian social relations of earlier prehistory into the hierarchical ones of more recent times. By understanding gender as an evolutionary process, some scholars have successfully engendered archaeology (Conkey and Gero 1997:418–419). An evolutionary pattern seems to be apparent in this book, but we do not intend to imply a simple, linear development. All through history, and today, we observe both tendencies toward the creation of hierarchy and the persistence of egalitarian and heterarchical social relations in the same society. Today, as in the past, the process of historical development may be perceived as idiosyncratic and serendipitous.

In Europe, gender archaeology has emphasized symbolic representations of gender, with focus on the individual's body, gender identity, and sexuality in art, space, and grave goods (Gilchrist 1999:54–108). In contrast, American archaeologists have been more concerned with gender roles and the sexual division of labor, and Americans, Scandinavians, and Australians have espoused more "explicit feminist political objectives" (109–149).

One of the results of critical thinking about prestige and power is that the issue of women's leadership roles is being framed as a question to be researched in each social setting (Nelson 2004:108). In Nelson's chapter on power and prestige, she opines that "archaeological evidence shows the constructedness of leadership and denies that it is universally male" (105); she also argues that "serious study of gender in the past is inseparable from the gender negotiations of the present" (5–8).

Power is a recurrent theme in feminist thought. Archaeologists like Nelson are now addressing issues related to the unequal power relationships between men and women in our culture, although this may not be a necessary condition of human life. The feminist critique with respect to power and prestige is a tool to free scholars to test hypotheses about gender relations in the past that do not simply recapitulate what we know from our personal experience growing up in the late twentieth century (Nelson 2004:18–33).

In gender archaeology today, masculinist as well as feminist perspectives are represented in the discourse about power, and the practice of gender archaeology has been influenced by "queer theory," which promotes the study of difference, but without hierarchy (Voss 2000; Blackmore 2011). Scholars like Gilchrist seem to be less concerned with "hierarchical power and differential prestige between men and women" and more interested in understanding gender differences as the "social and symbolic metaphors that create the complementarity between men and women that is necessary for the functioning of a particular society" (1999:8).

The creation of the concept of female agency has been important in reinterpreting "androcentric narratives of the past" and in promoting the idea that female individuals can "bring about innovation or social transformations" (Gilchrist 1999:xiii). Furthermore, "if gender itself is taken to be produced by the goal-oriented actions and performances of individuals or groups, this opens the door, even within archeology, to reassessments of everything from technology . . . to sculptural choices . . . to apparently simple artifacts, such as the pins and spindle whorls . . . to food preparation" (Conkey and Gero 1997:420). What this means for archaeologists is that we should be thinking about the people who made or used the artifact, as well as their intent and their goals.

Archaeologists, following the idea that gender is neither natural nor inherent in individuals but rather is generated by "repeated performance" (Butler 1993), have recently found it convenient to think about performers and the material evidence of their performances. Sometimes scholars identify instances of the creation and contestation of gender identity in the archaeological record, as well as "inconsistencies and mutabilities in orthodox sex and gender categories" (Gilchrist 1999:13–14, 57, 82; Conkey and Gero 1997:420–421).

Gender archaeology is characterized by methods and theories of knowledge concerning gender relations of production, gender identity, gender representation, and the experience of gender including new interests in the study of the body, sexuality, and "gendered lifecourse" (Gilchrist 1999:30). Recognizing that "sexuality is socially managed" means that archaeologists

Women in Ancient America

can look for evidence of how this aspect of behavior has been promoted, resisted, repressed, and channeled (Schmidt and Voss 2000:21–22). This line of thinking, which has also given rise to a new discipline called "body studies," has encouraged archaeologists to interpret human bodies in cultural contexts as communicating cultural, social, and political information (Nelson 2004:142–144). Joyce's (1996, 2002, 2005, 2008) work exemplifies how the body is an appropriate focus for archaeological interpretation. Archaeologists are also paying more attention to children, in a continuing effort to people the past (Baxter 2004; Sofaer Derevenski 1997).

Gender archaeology has introduced individuals and groups of actors onto the stage of prehistory. These agents, the creators of the archaeological record, disappeared in the universalizing generalizations and evolutionary frameworks that characterized some archaeological interpretations, such as processual theory that privileged "adaptive systems" (Kehoe 1995). Contemporary scholarship restores people to the narratives about prehistoric societies, and feminists and postmodern theorists have introduced gender, class, and factions as important agents in cultural change (Brumfiel 1996a; Conkey and Gero 1997:422). For instance, feminist historical archaeology has enriched our understanding of how women achieved the "Transformation of American Culture by Domestic Reform Movements" in the late nineteenth and early twentieth centuries (Spencer-Wood 1996:397–446).

In sum, archaeologists of gender are promoting ways of thinking that topple the old frameworks and result in new perceptions of the human past. There seems to be a growing appreciation for women and men, not as victims of power systems but as individuals who use their flexible biological capacities to create culture and produce stunningly diverse sociocultural manifestations. If humans manage to survive on our planet another 10,000 years, we imagine that our descendants will generate another dazzling range of diversity in that time.

Studying Women and Men Archaeologically

If men are knowable in the archaeological record, women must be knowable as well. Finding women and men in the archaeological record depends on the skill and imagination of archaeologists, but they can be identified with greatest confidence through the study of human physical remains and the analysis of art. Human skeletons reveal what ancient individuals were like and they enable anthropologists to ascertain ancient diet, activities, health, and histories. The investigation of relationships between skeletons and tomb offerings and other cultural contexts results in hypotheses about gender roles, kin patterns, and other aspects of culture. While the excavation and analysis of human remains has been interdicted in North America because of the beliefs of some Native American groups, such research is welcomed by people in most Latin American countries. In another approach to the identification of women and men, the study of art helps archaeologists flesh out a picture of the past because artistic representations of people communicate ideas about their economic, political, and religious activities.

The Interpretation of Physical Remains

Human remains are best preserved by extreme aridity or by constant cold or wet conditions, situations that are rare. In most sites only bones and teeth are preserved for archaeologists, and their recovery is impeded by decomposition, vandalism, scavenging, and cultural practices associated with the disposal of the dead.

Given a fairly well-preserved skeleton, researchers can tell the sex of the deceased, and they can address questions about the health and mortality of women, men, and young people, or members of particular social groups. The proper excavation of human skeletons involves the measurement of the bones while they are still in their original position, the identification of the osteological materials by a specialist, the sampling of soil from around the body for pollen and phytolith analysis, and the fine screening of burial soils to recover small bones, fragments, and fetal remains. The collection of samples for DNA and chemical analysis is also indicated (cf. Ubelaker 1989; Bass 2005; Ortner 2003; Matisoo-Smith and Horsburgh 2012).

Because humans are sexually dimorphic, skeletal remains may be identified by sex. Female pelves are wider and more bowl shaped than male ones, and the sciatic notch is relatively open in females and closed in males. Similarly, the preauricular sulcus on most female skeletons is marked by a pronounced groove. Finally, the proportion of the ischium to the pubis is distinct for males and females. With respect to each of these features, the difference between males and females is a matter of degree, so one can be confident of an identification only by evaluating several features. Females tend to be more gracile (slighter) and males more robust, although there can be considerable variation in individual size within a population. Female skulls and mandibles normally are smaller, their orbits more rounded, the supraorbital ridge less marked, the mastoid process less massive, and the nuchal crest unmarked by heavy muscle attachments. Again, these are matters of degree within a given population and one cannot use any one feature to tell sex with certainty.

It is difficult to tell females and males apart on osteological evidence alone until they reach sexual maturity (between ages twelve and fourteen). Various approaches have been suggested to sex the remains of young children, but these have not generated much confidence. DNA analysis will, of course, give genetic sex, but it is not always available owing to cost and to the unhappy facts that ancient DNA may not be preserved and that many archaeological remains may become contaminated during burial or excavation.

Archaeologists also study physical remains in order to determine individuals' age at death. This is the first step toward answering questions about whether men and women had different mortality profiles. Aging children's skeletons is relatively easy since the eruption rates of teeth are fairly standard across our species. One can determine the age of the child at death by observing which teeth are developed, but determining the age of adult skeletons depends on the wear and general state of the teeth, the closure of cranial sutures, the amount of ossification in the long bones, and wear and tear on the skeleton. This allows adults to be sorted into age categories with some confidence, although there may be problems in dealing with non-modern populations, as work with populations of known age at death has indicated that the "oldest old" are skeletally much younger than their actual age (Perls 2004; Hammond and Molleson 1994).

Many factors impinge on human life expectancy: these include genetic propensities that affect survivorship, the prevalence of parasites and disease, the quality of diet, and other cultural practices (like warfare). Gender is often a significant factor in determining the life expectancy of individuals in particular societies because females and males have different life experiences.

In studying ancient skeletal populations, researchers identify certain bioindicators of stress that can be useful in the reconstruction of women's and men's lives in a particular time and culture. Malnutrition and episodes of severe illness will leave clear skeletal indications. Common osteological indicators of stress are porotic hyperostosis and cribra orbitalia, which cause lesions of the cranium. Affected persons probably suffered from one of several anemias. Studies of prehistoric populations in Mexico and Central America have shown that this condition occurred among agricultural peoples whose staple crop was maize and whose diet did not include beans or animal protein. Maize-dependent populations may be characterized by a high incidence of porotic hyperostosis among children three to five years old. The first period of great risk for the new generation is just after birth; the second is at weaning, when anemia may contribute directly to ill health and inhibit the digestive system from absorbing nutrients at just the time in which the weanling is being exposed to parasites and microbes in the food and water. Ancient children with evidence of severe porotic hyperostosis often show lesions of the bone indicating the presence of infection as well. In traditional societies throughout the world where both anemia and infections are common, weanling death rates are high.

Harris lines and enamel hypoplasia are other common indications of episodic stress, including a number of nutritional problems and diseases. Harris lines are traverse marks that can be seen in X-ray photographs of the growing ends of human long bones, and enamel hypoplasia produces visible, horizontal grooves or lines on the teeth. Both types of lines are caused by growth resuming after a period in which development was slowed or stopped because of disease, malnutrition, or physical restriction.

Because bone is a dynamic system and is constantly affected by remodeling through growth, its condition is an indicator of health. Cortical thickness increases through childhood in a healthy individual and then remains relatively stable until the fourth decade of life, when bone mass decreases. Caloric and protein malnutrition can affect cortical thickness and cause premature aging of the bones. Young women who are chronically underfed will lose cortical thickness dramatically due to pregnancy and lactation. Skeletal evidence from Teotihuacán (see chapter 5) shows little infant growth in the last months of gestation, evidence that the health and nutritional status of the mothers was so poor that fetal bone development was retarded.

These and other indicators can be used to show differential stress on a population. Specific signs of aging and other skeletal modifications caused by work habits also show on bones and teeth, and these can be studied as indicators of the tasks performed by women and men. Evidences of trauma, such as broken bones and accelerated arthritis, are also useful in assessing a population. The high rate of physical trauma on the skeletons of children and male adults sacrificed in the Sacred Well of Chichén Itzá shows that they were probably slaves who were expendable because of infirmity (Hooton 1940).

There are two further traumatic indicators that are specific to women. It has been suggested that certain scars on a female pelvis may correlate with the number of a woman's pregnancies, but these scars have little diagnostic value because pregnancy does not always result in scars; moreover, these can be caused by pelvic inflammatory disease and other conditions.

Sexual assault has not often been reported from archaeological evidence, although it is known to be common in many cultural and social settings (Chadwick-Hawkes and Wells 1975). If death occurs within a relatively short time after a violent rape, distinctive physical traumas can be observed on the skeleton. The presence of this uncommon trauma could provide evidence for social customs or ideologies that involve violence against women.

Physical anthropology supplies excellent tools for the study of human remains, but osteological analysis and interpretation requires expert knowledge. Regrettably, sexing is frequently done by untrained excavators who ignore the skeleton and base their identification on cultural associations or unfounded assumptions. In the following case, despite professional identification of the ancient skeleton, some scholars were loath to recognize a high-ranking Maya woman.

The Lady of Altar de Sacrificios

The archaeological site known as Altar de Sacrificios is located on the Pasión River in the jungle of Guatemala. Excavations here in the 1960s were notable in that the team included Frank Saul, a specialist in the analysis of human skeletal remains (Saul 1972). Among the palaces, plazas, and temples of Altar were found 136 burials containing the remains of 144 people. Of the sixty-nine skeletons that could be sexed, only thirty-eight were associated with grave offerings, mainly pottery and other nonperishable artifacts. In the published analysis of the excavations, the excavators noted that sixty-one of the vessels were found in male graves and thirty-seven in female graves. Of twenty-one sexed burials in which pottery vessels protected the head of the skeleton, eleven were male and ten female; four males and three females had jade in their mouths; ten females and ten males had cranial deformation; and nine males and ten females had decorated teeth. Both of these cosmetic alterations were signs of high social status among the Maya.

From all of these data, Ledyard Smith and his colleagues (1972:59) concluded that in Maya society men were valued more highly than women. Does the evidence really lead to this conclusion? The sample of burials is small, from a single context, and in most cases neither females nor males have ceramic offerings. At Altar, thirty-three of the ceramic vessels come from two graves. In Burial 88, the simple interment of a middle-aged male, eighteen plain ceramic vessels were placed in the tomb along with a ceramic and shell necklace, several green stone and shell beads, a bone pin, an obsidian bladelet, a rotted wooden object, and a mass of red pigment near the head. This was the second most elaborate burial found at Altar. In any ranking of burials in the Maya region, this would be considered the burial of an elite person, although probably not a ruler.

The other important tomb contained two female bodies. Burial 128, a woman in her early forties, was overlain by Burial 96, a woman in her late twenties. The lady of Burial 128 was placed in a specially constructed rectangular tomb within an existing temple platform. Tombs such as this were built only for the most important people in Maya society. The lady showed evidence of an upper-class upbringing: her head was modified artificially and her upper teeth were inlaid with jade. Her offerings were far more lavish than those of any other person buried at Altar de Sacrificios. Many of the associated ceramics were elaborately decorated. Her body had been laid on a mat; a jade bead was placed in her mouth and a *Spondylus* shell lay over that orifice. Covering her head and face were fragments of a fine red painted cloth under a tripod plate. She was buried with three necklaces, of *Spondylus* beads, jadeite beads, and green stuccoed ceramic beads, disks, and pendants, the last with matching ear flares. She had another pair of jadeite ear flares and some mother-of-pearl beads, a carved and painted slate-back mirror (the reflecting surface was made of pyrite mosaic), and a small pottery mask. In addition, there was a group of broken stingray spines, four with carved hieroglyphs on them, which may have been contained in a bag that hung from her belt. Excavators found another group of seventeen stingray spines by her right knee. Three obsidian blades and a core were also placed with her and some nine hundred flint chips were found scattered in the tomb.

The Lady of Altar did not go to the underworld alone. Above her in a separate cist tomb was another woman, an apparent sacrifice. This young woman also enjoyed elite status, judging from her artificially deformed skull and her decorated teeth. She was laid on her back and was accompanied by one ceramic vessel covering her face, three other vessels, two green stone beads, and a flint knife placed near her right shoulder.

It is surmised that this young woman was sacrificed during the funeral ceremonies, as illustrated by one of the accompanying vessels. This is a polychrome cylindrical vase with a hieroglyphic inscription that dates it to A.D. 754 (Adams 1963). On the vase, the figure of a young woman, painted and decorated with symbols of sacrifice and death, is poised to cut off her own head with a knife like the one by the body (fig. 1.2). Autosacrifice of this sort

Figure 1.2. A painted vase found with Burial 96 at Altar de Sacrificios shows a young Maya woman cutting off her own head. Her face paint, blood-spotted (paper?) ornaments, and belt with "death eyes" all indicate her status as a self-sacrifice, the most prestigious type of elite Maya sacrifice. Drawn by Tom Weller after Adams (1963, color plate 1).

is known from other Maya funerary vase paintings and was, apparently, the most prestigious sort of sacrifice among the Maya.

The lavish offerings with Burial 128 and the human sacrifice accompanying her are well-known signs of royal burial among the Maya. Had there been no physical anthropologist on the project, it is quite likely that the Lady of Altar would have been identified as the "Lord of Altar," a ruler of the eighth century A.D. In fact, despite the specialist identification of the skeleton of Burial 128 as a female, several art historians later claimed that she had to be a male because of the stingray spines, which were used by the Maya to draw blood in self-sacrifice on important occasions. At Yaxchilán there are monuments showing male rulers piercing their genitals with these implements (Tate 1992; Stone 1988). In their fervor to see only male rulers among the Maya, scholars have forgotten that ancient Maya noblewomen pierced their tongues and earlobes in the same act of blood offering with the same instruments of bloodletting.

Burial 128 and its accompanying sacrifice were not given much attention in the original publication of the Altar de Sacrificios excavations. In the half century since the discovery of the polychrome vase buried with the sacrificed lady-in-waiting, it has become possible to read Maya hieroglyphs. Yet, apart from a preliminary study by Richard Adams, no further translation of the texts has been published, despite the fact that this is one of the few vases from an excavated context with good historical associations (Adams 1963, 1971, 1977).

The Interpretation of Art

Ancient art is the other major source of information concerning gender in prehistory. In order to study gender roles, women and men must be identified: the only sure way of telling the two sexes apart is by identifying realistic representations of genitalia. After the preliminary identification of female and male, it is possible to look at how secondary sexual characteristics may be represented and how features such as hairstyle, ornamentation of the skin or body, and clothing differ by sex. Many, perhaps most, human cultures do distinguish female from male in hairstyle, ornamentation, and clothing, but this must be demonstrated, not taken for granted.

Gender roles in an ancient culture may be inferred from art works that show females and males interacting. From these it is often possible to delineate what the members of this culture thought of as gender-appropriate roles or activities. However, both ancient and modern art is limited in subject matter. Maya relief sculpture, for example, deals almost exclusively with formal activities of the ruling caste: their accession, marriage, wars, and dynastic ceremonies (Bruhns 1988). The Moche artists of ancient Peru modeled and painted ceramics to represent a limited number of rituals, myths, and legends (Donnan 1975). Moreover, in many cases archaeologists and art historians lack the information necessary to translate the symbolism of ancient representations, and frequently, because much ancient art arrives in museums as the result of unscientific looting, the objects must be interpreted without the benefit of archaeological context. All of these factors limit what can be understood about gender roles from art. However, the existence of representational art stimulates and supports many interpretations of ancient cultural practices and ideologies. When the analysis of art is combined with other archaeological data, it is often possible to test hypotheses about ancient gender relations.

Finding Ancient Maya Women

The Mayan-speaking peoples of southern Mexico and northwestern Central America have constituted a distinctive cultural grouping from the earliest Preclassic (ca. 1800 B.C.) until the present day. Since the European discovery of Maya centers in the nineteenth century, scholars have been entranced with their elaborate architectural sculpture and free-standing monuments, their realistic clay figurines and polychrome pottery, and their hieroglyphic writing system (one of the two known indigenous writing systems in ancient America).

The Europeans who began to study the prehistoric archaeology of Mexico and Central America created a series of myths concerning Maya culture. Art historians and archaeologists portrayed the Maya as a simple two-class society ruled by priests and priest-kings obsessed with time and astronomy. This elite was supported by peasants who lived in the jungle, practiced slash-and-burn agriculture, and supported the ceremonial centers with their labor and devotion. This scenario was sustained by the fact that until the 1980s, only the calendrical and astronomical parts of Maya inscriptions could be read, and this false view of the ancient Maya was fostered by the identification of the figures shown in the art as priests and gods. Scholars did not identify any of the Maya figures as female despite the fact that Colonial sources refer abundantly to both goddesses and priestesses.

In the 1960s, the work of Proskouriakoff (1960:454–475) began to transform these erroneous perceptions of Maya culture. She was able to show that the stone monuments at the site of Piedras Negras were political in nature, erected by historic rulers to celebrate the events of their reigns. At the same time, excavations and looting in the Maya area, especially on Jaina Island, off the Yucatán Peninsula, brought to light many realistic clay figurines showing people in what appeared to be poses from daily life (cf. Piña Chan 1968). Among these figurines were representations of partly nude females and males. From these it was possible to recognize gender-specific clothing, and Proskouriakoff noted that some of the figurines wore garb similar to that of contemporary Maya women (fig. 1.3). Even though no one could read Mayan writing, Proskouriakoff (1961) correctly identified a female head glyph as a sign that introduced a female personage in the inscriptions on the stone monuments. Further examination of these public works revealed that certain robed figures not only shared costumes and title glyphs but had a consistent set of associations vis-à-vis other figures and certain inscriptions, now known to be expressions concerning royal accessions. Proskouriakoff's interpretation of these figures as women was supported with information from Colonial documents.

In the 1980s, Bruhns (1988) used the analysis of costumes worn by female figures in Maya monumental sculpture as a way of investigating gender roles. This study showed that women and men shared an elaborate garment

Figure 1.3. Lady Xoc of Yaxchilán. Her elaborate costume, jewelry, and high-backed sandals show that she was a woman of the highest rank, while the decorative spirals on her face perhaps refer to the ceremony in which she presents a feline helmet and a shield to a male ruler. Drawn by Wes Christensen after Lintel 26, Yaxchilán, Chiapas, Mexico.

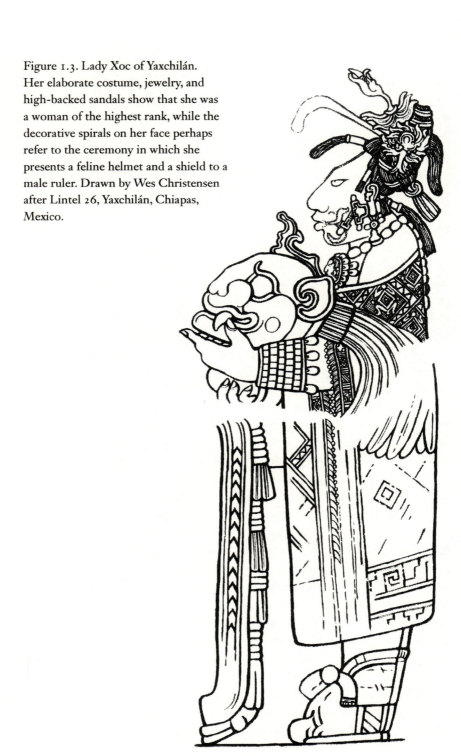

made of netting that was associated only with events such as coronation and royal marriage. Since these highly distinctive robes were restricted to rulers, if women wore them it is reasonable to identify these women as being of equal status to the males similarly dressed. Females and males also shared elaborate versions of ordinary clothing and ornaments, which appear in monuments that commemorate less transcendental events. The similarity in dress supports the idea that women and men shared many roles in public life.

Joyce (1992, 1993, 2001) has analyzed figurines and polychrome vessels with the goal of documenting the interaction of females and males, and she later expanded this to using monumental art as well. She too discovered a much wider range of activities for Classic Period Maya women than had been assumed. Other scholars (Ardren 2002; Kellogg 2005; Freidel and Guenter 2003, inter alia) have now enlarged our improved view of ancient Maya life through excavation and epigraphy, adding their discoveries of women and their deeds to the iconographic record. Thus, with the evidence of depictions of women and men executed by Maya artists themselves, and now with that of young scholars looking at the archaeological and written record from an engendered viewpoint, the modern viewer is given a reality far different from the stereotype of ancient Maya women as chattels and kitchen furniture.

The Moche of Northern Peru

The identification of women in Maya dynastic monuments was first accomplished because of Proskouriakoff's profound knowledge of Maya history, art, and archaeology, as well as her observations of the clothing worn by contemporary indigenous women. Lamentably, in much of western South America indigenous clothing has been replaced by garments of European origin, making the attribution of sex on the basis of ancient costume a dubious activity. Yet a few prehistoric cultures produced sufficiently detailed artistic representations of humans that gender roles can be appraised.

The Moche culture of northern Peru is famous for its modeled and painted ceramics featuring lively scenes involving people, animals, plants, structures, and supernatural beings that have been interpreted as representations of rituals, myths, and folklore. Vessels illustrating human sexual activity generally show the male clothed, his loose, diaper-like loincloth pulled aside to expose his penis, and the woman nude or partly clothed. The headgear, ornaments, and hairstyles of both females and males are as indicative of gender as are genitals (Larco Hoyle 1965). Moche women most commonly wear their hair in two twisted tresses and generally have straight-cut bangs. Males wear their hair cut straight across the forehead as well, but the rest of their hair is worn pulled behind the ears and hanging to the shoulders.

Because of these distinctions, it has proven possible to differentiate female from male clothing and to confidently identify the sex of players in various scenes (Benson 1988). This opens the way for the description of Moche gender roles. In the Moche ceramic world, if not in their social world, women appear as sexual partners with men as well as on their own in many other scenes. There is at least one woman commemorated in a type of portrait vessel thought to depict important people, perhaps rulers (Donnan 2004). One character, a woman with a child peeking from behind her back, may be a specific personage from folklore or legend. Women are shown in a series of vessels depicting childbirth, in which the mother is aided by an Owl Woman midwife who also appears alone or as a curer in other scenes of magico-religious practices (Sharon and Donnan 1974). Several "burial theme" vessels show a female being devoured by vultures (Donnan and McClelland 1979). Colonial documents referring to northern Peru say that this was the punishment for a doctor who lost a patient through malpractice (J. Rowe 1948). There are also female deities, identified by supernatural features (such as fangs in the mouth and belts and tresses ending in snakes' heads, common signifiers of supernatural status in Moche art), and at least one example of a series of powerful priestesses (Hocquenghem 1977a, 1977b; Hocquenghem and Lyon 1980; Holmquist Pachas 1992; Donnan and Castillo 1992, 1994). Ongoing excavations at Moche sites are revealing new evidence of female participation in governance and religion.

The ability to distinguish females and males in the ceramic art of the Moche makes the further engendering of Moche prehistory possible, although some scholars have behaved as if they knew more about Moche culture than the ancient Moche artists. For example, there is a Moche bowl that has a scene of a weaving workshop painted on it. Although the weavers have male clothing and male haircuts, they are virtually always identified as women because scholars *know* that women were weavers in the Andean culture area. This knowledge was so compelling that when *National Geographic Magazine* published an article on the ancient Peruvian city of Chan Chan, women were depicted weaving in the workshops even though the illustration was based on the famous bowl (Bruhns 1991; Moseley et al. 1973). Braids were painted onto the figures despite the objections of a (female) specialist consultant. Engendering the scholarly interpretation of the past depends on respecting the evidence and using it responsibly to create a picture that includes both female and male actors.

The Past Informs the Present

Theory is what causes scholars to ask questions and it directs them toward answers. Researchers armed with older theoretical models did not approach the archaeological record with the idea of discovering gender patterning. Only recently has new theory inspired new research goals. Postmodern and feminist theories focus on and accept gender as an important dynamic, insisting that both women and men are actors and innovators and that women too have activities important in culture and history. This body of theory causes archaeologists to take gender into account and to write a more well-balanced history by including both women and men.

Prehistoric narratives often begin with a critique of androcentric archaeology, but engendering the past also requires positive approaches, such as developing interpretations involving gender, and proposing alternative interpretations even when there may be insufficient evidence for choosing among the alternatives. Because anthropologists recognize the infinite variability in human social and cultural behavior, they are prepared to both create alternative interpretations of the past and to imagine different scenarios for the future of our own society.

Engendering the past is a service to the present. Not engendering the past allows ignorant models to persist in our minds and in public images. An engendered past serves to replace the inaccurate fictions about the past that are sometimes used in our society to validate myths about gender relations.

In the last ten years, the interest of archaeologists has shifted from finding women in the archaeological record to the problem of describing gender relations in the past. This is important because it seems likely that we will never appreciate the great variety of gender systems until we can reliably infer the ones that emerged and disappeared during the long prehistoric period. Contemporary women and men need to know about the past as a tool in negotiating different ideologies and practices suitable for the future. There has been great progress in defining the problem: we need to find ways to use archaeological data to illuminate ancient gender relations without essentializing men and women and without willfully projecting our norms for gender relations onto the past.

Lamentably, archaeologists have not found ways to engender artifacts without resorting to ethnographic analogy or to essentialist constructions, that is to say, generalized notions of gender drawn from dubious historical, ethnohistorical, or modern contexts. There are remedies, however: historical documents reveal a great diversity in gender systems (involving two or more genders), and the awareness of these informs the archaeological imagination and interpretation of past systems.

However, according to Pyburn (1999:193), "those studying gender in particular, continue to base their analysis and interpretations too readily on 'what we know' about gender." Pyburn's view is that "the only data likely to seriously challenge gender essentialism must come from archaeological cultures that predate the world system" (193–194). Ironically, as Pyburn says, our goal is to "construct models without essentialist preconceptions and ask hard questions," but, she continues, we use "inadequate and unresilient data," which "may severely constrain the conclusions we can draw about the past, at least for a while" (196).

However, the case may not be so grave. Alice Kehoe notes that Pyburn is wrong and that historical data from documents do permit more precise analyses of diversity in gender systems than do archaeological data alone. In her opinion, the former offer opportunities to avoid the overgeneralizations and assumptions about gender roles that have characterized archaeological interpretations in the past (Kehoe, pers. comm. 2012).

The following chapters describe research that explores the diverse social and cultural experiences of ancient American people, narrating a story about how women participated along with men in populating the Americas and in developing and managing social, economic, political, and religious systems. Examples are drawn from North and South America (maps 1 and 2) and from all periods of American prehistory (table 1).

Map 1. Locations of archaeological sites and cultures in North and Central America that are mentioned in the text. Drawn by Tom Weller, redrawn by Vicki Trego Hill. Copyright © 2014 by The University of Oklahoma Press.

Map 2. Locations of archaeological sites and cultures in South America that are mentioned in the text. Drawn by Tom Weller, redrawn by Vicki Trego Hill. Copyright © 2014 by The University of Oklahoma Press.

Table 1. *Periods in American archaeology*

Eastern North America

Paleoindian	18000 B.C. (?)–7000 B.C.*
Archaic	7000 B.C.–1000 B.C.
Woodland	1000 B.C.–A.D. 900
Mississippian	A.D. 900–A.D. 1600
Historic	A.D. 1600–present

Southwestern United States

Paleoindian	18000 B.C. (?)–7000 B.C.
Archaic	7000 B.C.–100 B.C.
Basketmaker, Ancestral Puebloan, Hohokam, Mogollon, & Mimbres	100 B.C.–A.D. 1450

Mesoamerica

Preceramic / Archaic	8500 B.C.–1800 B.C.
Formative / Preclassic	1800 B.C.–A.D. 150
Classic	A.D. 150–A.D. 950
Postclassic	A.D. 950–A.D. 1521
Colonial	A.D. 1521–A.D. 1822

Colombia

Preceramic	8000 B.C.–3000 B.C.
Formative	3000 B.C.–A.D. 1
Chiefdoms / Regional Development	A.D. 1–A.D. 1531

Coastal Ecuador

Preceramic	8500 B.C.–4700 B.C.
Formative	3500 B.C.–300 B.C.
Regional Development	300 B.C.–A.D. 800
Integration	A.D. 1150–A.D. 1531
Colonial	A.D. 1531–A.D. 1820

Peru

Preceramic	9500 B.C.–1800 B.C.
Initial	1800 B.C.–900 B.C.
Early Horizon	900 B.C.–200 B.C.
Early Intermediate	200 B.C.–A.D. 700
Middle Horizon	A.D. 700–A.D. 1000
Late Intermediate	A.D. 1000–A.D. 1476
Late Horizon (Inca)	A.D. 1476–A.D. 1534
Colonial	A.D. 1534–A.D. 1822

* The chronologies of the prehistoric periods are based on uncalibrated radiocarbon dates.

CHAPTER TWO

The First Women in America

Modern archaeological studies of sites inhabited between approximately 18,000 and 8,000 years ago have enabled archaeologists to expand their understanding of the earliest Americans, the Paleoindians. New archaeological evidence has resulted in a shift away from the traditional emphasis on stone tools and hunting in the description of Paleoindian lifeways. New, engendered interpretation permits both scholars and the public to see the female members of Paleoindian society, not just the male hunters.

Evidence from Siberia and the Americas indicates that Paleoindian women, men, and children started making their way into the New World from Asia as early as 18,000 years ago. These first Americans were fully modern humans, *Homo sapiens sapiens*, bringing with them flexible and successful cultural adaptations that enabled them to thrive in severe climates. The far north was rich in resources, including large terrestrial herbivores, fish, and birds—animals that provided both food and the primary materials for clothing, tools, and shelter. Although Paleoindian sites are often poorly preserved, archaeologists have recovered stone and bone tools, some food remains, an occasional burial, and vestiges of shelters. By inferring from this evidence and developing models based on ethnographic analogues between Paleoindians and cold-adapted hunters and gatherers who lived in America and Asia in the historic period, archaeologists have challenged the older interpretations of early American life.

Figure 2.1. *Man the Hunter*, an artist's conception of Paleoindian hunting, perpetuates the stereotype that this was the master behavior of the earliest male inhabitants of America. Painted by John C. Dawson. Courtesy of the Natural History Museum of Los Angeles County, Section Rancho La Brea, Cat. # 2849c.

Deconstructing the Old Model

The idea that Paleoindian life was dominated by male hunters and their stone projectile points has been popular for a long time. The people who entered America at the end of the Ice Age were first recognized because their distinctive stone tools were found with the bones of extinct Pleistocene mammals. Before radiocarbon dating was available, archaeologists concentrated their efforts on these kill sites rather than on habitation sites because the ancient bones were irrefutable evidence that these sites were very old. Kill sites then became the basis of the popular view that the first inhabitants of the Americas were almost exclusively male hunters (fig. 2.1). More recently it has been shown that habitation sites of equal antiquity reveal evidence of a much broader range of activities than was known from kill sites alone, offering excellent opportunities to deconstruct the old model and build an engendered view of early American life.

Because of the kill site focus, Paleoindians were stereotyped as big game hunters who subsisted on late Ice Age mammoths, giant bison, horses, and

similar large species. One of the best known scenarios for the rapid peopling of the Americas is that these "efficient" hunters attacked unwary
herds of animals that had never seen humans, drastically reduced the
available population, and then moved onward to repeat the slaughter (P.
Martin 1973). This view, which focused on aggressive male hunters, was
based on kill sites with diagnostic projectile points, most of which were
located in the ancient grasslands of the North American West. The focus
on projectile points discouraged the serious study of the simple flake tools
meant for cutting tasks, also found in kill sites (Gero 1991). Researchers
were discouraged from looking for variation in the archaeological record
and from modeling other aspects of daily life, including women's activities,
as women, it was said, did not hunt. Logically, of course, finding tools in
association with animal bones does not necessarily indicate men hunting.
These remains could equally indicate persons of either sex butchering after
a communal hunt, or even a scavenging event, both behaviors well attested
to in the ethnographic record.

Early Paleoindian studies mimic the narratives about early human ancestors in Africa and Asia, where the concept of "Man the Hunter" dominated
scholarly thinking about the distant past. Hunting, an upper-class activity in
Europe, has figured as a hypermasculine activity in explorers' tales and other
manly fantasies. In its simplest form, the "Man the Hunter" myth holds that
all human progress was due to men hunting animals with the stone tools they
made (Taylor 1996; Washburn and Lancaster 1968). Since scholars accepted
hunting tools as both the cause and the evidence of human progress, they
placed scientific emphasis on the study of projectile points thought to be
designed to pierce the hides of large animals.

This line of thinking was fostered by early anthropological studies of
Inuit (Eskimo) and Cree hunters, historic peoples who lived full time or
seasonally in tundra and boreal forests. These people were erroneously held
to be "living fossils," providing evidence of how the earliest Americans had
survived in a similar environment. Anthropological studies, done by males
and focused on male activities, provided a model for Paleoindian studies in
which males hunted and women processed food. Other women's activities
were ignored and women and their work were devalued by anthropologists.
Ethnographers, because of their interests, and often their lack of linguistic
capacity or proper age and marital status, were also shut off from the larger
picture, so they focused on the "moment of kill" and not on the more meaningful technical and symbolic aspects of hunting, which often serve to stress

the fundamental interdependence of women and men in hunting activities (Bodenhorn 1990). There is also good reason to think that northern peoples may not always be appropriate analogues for Paleolithic people: all ethnographic records concerning them date to after they became specialized in harvesting animals in order to sell their skins to Europeans. Contact with Europeans caused women to lose status and roles because many traditional social institutions disappeared as the population was decimated by disease, and because interaction with missionaries and traders caused groups such as the Chipewyan, Inuit, Cree, and other boreal hunters to adopt misogynistic attitudes along with new technologies (Brumbach and Jarvenpa 1997; Brumbach et a1.1982; Jarvenpa 1987).

Newer research on living hunter-gatherers has begun to change the earlier androcentric views by including women and their activities as objects of study. These studies have highlighted the importance of resources other than large mammals in foragers' subsistence systems. For example, aquatic resources were important to all Arctic and Subarctic groups and were almost certainly important to the earliest Americans. Fishing in rivers, lakes, and the ocean, gathering shellfish, scavenging beached whales, and collecting kelp and other sea vegetables were probably important subsistence activities in the past, as in more modern times. Bird trapping and egg collecting and the gathering of berries, mosses, and edible ferns in the summer were all crucial to the economies of the northern peoples and would have been important to the first immigrants into unglaciated central Alaska.

In many hunting societies, women are responsible for much of the exploitation of water and land resources, employing traps and snares for small mammals that are an important everyday source of food. Even the classic compilation of ethnological studies *Man the Hunter* (Lee and DeVore 1968), which did a great deal to promote the myth that hunting was the human master behavior, demonstrated that the bulk of the food consumed by modern subsistence hunters is gathered, not hunted, and the authors concluded that almost everywhere below the Arctic Circle people gather or used to gather for a living. This idea has finally infiltrated Paleoindian studies.

Thirteen years after *Man the Hunter, Woman the Gatherer* was published (Dahlberg 1981). In this book, anthropologists reassessed women's activities among historic and modern foraging groups and applied those assessments to stories about early hominids. This engendering of the early human record is important to American archaeologists not only because it provided a feminist critique of the previous model, but because it offered the opportunity of including real people and social dynamics (including gender relations) in the interpretation of early prehistory.

Today we reject the limited view of the past that focused on men, giant beasts, and projectile points. Recent studies of sites in diverse environments have proven that Paleoindians, most of whom lived below the Arctic Circle, ate a varied diet and enjoyed a richer material culture than previously thought. New research, informed by contemporary ethnographic studies and by developing feminist perspectives, presents a broader picture of the past, featuring more actors and more activities.

Early Women in Ethnographic Perspective

The first groups who moved into the Americas, whether by land or by water routes, were cold-adapted peoples who depended on the efforts of both women and men to survive. Everyone's labor was needed to meet the challenges of the long, cold northern winter and to satisfy needs for food, clothing, shelter, and food storage. Although we should not project our division of labor onto this group, a gender-based division of labor may have existed among early Americans. Social scripts vary, but in most contexts females and males are encouraged to take on certain tasks assigned by sex, and people then cajole and coerce their kin (mothers, sisters, fathers, brothers, spouses) into doing the work that is expected of them.

Ethnographic data from recent cold-adapted peoples suggest that men benefit when women make clothing for them. This is a grueling and time-consuming process that begins with preparing the animal skins and terminates in a wide variety of protective garments for heads, hands, feet, and bodies. Garment production requires specialized labor, meaning that the women receive lengthy training and gain high status from their skill in producing beautiful and useful clothing (Frink 2005).

These women find it advantageous to have men bring home the raw materials and to produce some of the primary tools they require in their work. Men often undertake the economically and personally risky business of hunting animals while women convert meat into food for immediate consumption and for storage against the barren season and transform hides into clothing, bedding, containers, and tents. Together, women and men manage social and biological reproduction, integrating their respective contributions in creative and flexible ways.

Ethnography shows archaeologists some of what cannot be seen in the archaeological record, illustrating dramatically that it is impossible to infer exactly what ancient life was like because human behavior is variable and people are "set in their ways" only for the short run. People change as new challenges arise. As the first Americans entered the new continents and occupied new environments, the particular activities of women and men had to have been negotiated on a continuing basis in response to new situations.

Archaeologists think that the first Americans lived in small kin-based groups without formal leaders. Within families, decisions can be made by consensus. Lacking evidence, such as artistic representations of human beings, we have no idea how the Paleoindians negotiated roles or leadership or how these early peoples thought about femininity and masculinity. In later times, North American Indian societies showed considerable flexibility in their construction of gender categories. It seems safe to assume that some tasks were divided along sex lines and that others were divided according to age and personal preference. It also seems likely that the tasks necessary for subsistence were assigned in a complementary fashion within family groups, and that women and men controlled their own activities. Gender complementarity is deeply rooted in surviving Native American societies. Native Americans often created gender differences within a social system that featured complementarity and interdependence. That later there developed many nonegalitarian variations on this theme does not negate it as a basic organizing principle in Native American societies.

Ingalik Gender and Material Culture

The artifacts and other remains found in Paleoindian sites were used by women and men, adults and children. But archaeologists want to know more specifically who made them, who owned them, and what customs and ideologies governed their use. Cross-cultural comparisons demonstrate the complexities of artifact systems, so it is not always clear how to interpret archaeological remains. We can get a hint of the richness of even "simple" hunting peoples, however, by looking at historic cold-adapted peoples such as the Ingalik, or *Deg Hit'an*, an Athabascan people of Alaska (Osgood 1940). They are not fossilized remnants of Paleoindians, being as unrelated to the ancient peoples as any other twentieth-century group. Nevertheless, some of the features of Ingalik cultural adaptation may be similar to those inferred for the Paleoindians and, as such, are of interest in trying to flesh out the meager remains of the ancient peoples. For example, their primary foods and sources of materials for artifacts were all wild species, and their manufactures involved hand labor and individual skills applied to locally available raw materials. Because Ingalik manufactures were embedded in a complex system involving gender, it is tempting to infer similar gender ideas for the Paleoindians.

Ingalik material culture, meticulously documented by Osgood (1940), carried a nonmaterial ideological element, as does material culture everywhere. This can be shown by the traditional Ingalik artifacts listed in table 2. These were made by men and women for themselves, by women for men, by men for women, by adults for children, and even by children for other children. These items, even though we lack tallies for things made by women for other women and girls, demonstrate the depth of engendered relationships within Ingalik society. Artifacts served not just as aids to material living, but as means for achieving social cooperation and interdependence. Although men made more things, women's manufactures often involved a greater investment of time and skill. Compare an awl, made by a man for a woman, with a parka, made by a woman for a man. Men made more things, with which women made more complex things.

Table 2. *Items used by historic Ingalik People*

	Used by men	Used by women	Used by children or anyone	Total
Made by women (33%)*	14 (15%)	40 (43%)	39 (42%)	93 (100%)
Made by men (62%)	98 (57%)	56 (35%)	19** (8%)	173 (100%)
Made by women and men together (5%)	2 (14%)	1 (7%)	11 (79%)	14 (100%)
Total items	114	97	69	280

Note: Analysis by Karen E. Stothert based on ethnographic descriptions published by Cornelius Osgood (1940).

* Of the 280 items in the sample, this percentage was produced by the makers indicated.

** Seven of these items were made by men exclusively for boys.

The loci of production of male and female manufactures were also different. Men worked out of doors or in a men's ceremonial house, whereas women worked in their smokehouse in the summer or in winter houses with other women. This traditional spatial separation was linked to the idea that an individual of one sex might contaminate or be damaged by specific items associated with the other sex. The two sexes were differentiated in myriad ways, including the production of cordage. Because women and men made lines from different materials, it was necessary for both to seek out members of the opposite sex to acquire the kind of line they themselves did not make. The system required and reinforced mutual interdependence between women and men.

Gender distinctions also characterized Ingalik ceremonial regalia and acts: women were associated with dentalium shell and men with ocher. Women's and men's ritual activities were largely separate, expressing the idea of the distinctness as well as the interconnectedness of the two sexes in much the same manner as the more mundane material culture. Separation afforded individuals of both sexes the power to control their own activities.

The Ingalik show us one way in which even "simple" societies work out complex systems in which their members participate in the business of living. The differentiation of tasks and the artifacts that are associated with these tasks are accompanied by a model of integration. The Paleoindians certainly organized their social lives in a variety of ways to meet local challenges. We cannot claim that any Paleoindian band was organized exactly like the Ingalik, but this case serves to remind us about the potential complexity of ancient scripts, including the importance of gender dynamics, in those systems. With this awareness we can then approach the archaeological record in a less simplistic manner and arrive at a better understanding of what the surviving material culture really represents.

Deconstructing Clovis Hunters

The quintessential Paleoindian hunters were the ancient Clovis people of the Western Plains, first identified on the basis of their distinctive stone projectile points, which were sometimes found in direct association with the carcasses of now-extinct elephants. Clovis points have inspired hyperbole: one author believes that "it may not be too strong a statement to say that the Clovis projectile point is the first piece of flaked stone weaponry in the world that was well-designed enough to allow a single hunter a dependable and predictable means of pursuing and killing a large mammal such as a mammoth or a bison on a one-to-one basis" (Frison 1993:241). This scenario is a romantic fantasy. It is unrealistic that lone individuals would willingly take on an elephant or any other large beast. In contrast, some scholars have suggested that the

Clovis peoples were scavengers. Reality may lie in the middle. Archaeologists believe that teamwork was required to kill large Pleistocene animals: for example, Jean Auel (1985), in *The Mammoth Hunters*, envisions men, women, and children cooperating in the woolly mammoth hunt, although she (speculatively) creates men as the directors of the enterprise.

Surely the hunt was important to the Paleoindians, and hunting stories, embellished with derring-do and great feats, were told around campfires at night, but these tales probably celebrated cooperative labor and not the prowess of individual males. In real life, hunting is often done by a team of specialists or by large organized groups of adults, including children as lookouts. The goal of all, of course, is to provide a living for the group.

Recent studies have redefined Clovis people as diversified foragers, living in small groups and creating large sites only by multiple reoccupations across the centuries. While meat was surely important to them, they had strategies for harvesting many wild animal and plant species. These sites were slow to be recognized as Clovis by archaeologists because they lacked the diagnostic extinct megafauna and specific types of projectile points. Advances in dating technologies and the input of archaeologists trained to look beyond male hunters have changed Clovis archaeology. Archaeologists working in lower latitudes, like the southern Great Plains, have interpreted the Paleoindians as generalists who lived in a wide variety of environments during a period characterized by environmental changes at the end of the Ice Age. Remains of plants and small animals are evidence that the first North Americans processed resources other than Pleistocene elephants and giant bison. The highly variable stone tool kits, only occasionally including diagnostic projectile points, show us that Paleoindians everywhere harvested and processed a wide variety of plants, extracting from them fibers for containers, clothing, and tools. Based on analogies with recent temperate foragers, one can imagine women managing these plant-processing technologies. This alerts us to the idea that Paleoindian women would have been as independent, skillful, and self-directed as their later Native American sisters.

According to recent scholarship, Clovis people chose to situate their camps and to move them seasonally in order to satisfy many criteria. Hunting was only one of several factors considered in determining settlement location (Bonnichsen and Turnmire 1991; Johnson 1991; Lepper and Meltzer 1991). In southern Mexico, the ancient people of the Tehuacán Valley expressed their desire for company by locating their sites near stands of prickly pear fruits and mesquite beans, which were abundant in the spring

(Flannery 1986). The sites of the historic Western Mono of the Sierra Nevada of California were pegged to the requirements of women's subsistence activities, particularly acorn procurement, processing, and storage (Jackson 1991:301–325). According to Jackson, settlements and their locations were determined by the work of the women who built the storage silos and owned the stone mortars used to grind acorns.

Important insights are present in a recent model that accounts for the dramatic appearance of Clovis sites all over unglaciated North America between 11,500 and 10,800 years ago. Surovell (2000:501) uses "a mathematical model that estimates the cost of raising children for mobile hunter-gatherers" and concludes that high mobility and high fertility were compatible. He argues that Clovis people moved their residential base camp frequently to avoid the escalating costs of living at a long-term base camp. Specifically, the key factor in determining the costs of child rearing is the "logistical mobility of women or how much energy a woman invests in feeding the child until it is independent." One can imagine that camp was moved when women began to complain about the burden of walking farther and farther from camp on a daily basis to collect resources that had been depleted locally. Surovell concludes that in a "homogeneous environment hunter-gatherers can minimize child-related transport costs by moving residential base camps as frequently as possible" and that "for a patchy environment, longer duration occupations would in fact become optimal" (501–504). The aching backs and feet of Paleoindian women would have signaled time to move. Another interesting result of frequent mobility is intriguing: "Frequent movement of base camps must have permitted short foraging distances around base camps. Under these conditions, Paleoindian children would have been relatively inexpensive to raise, and fertility could have been quite high. The model suggests that rapid colonization of the Americas was very possible as frequent movement of base camps would have allowed early hunter-gatherers to move long distances across the landscape while actually minimizing daily walking distances" (504). The rapid peopling of America by Clovis people can then be explained in part by high mobility and high fertility. They may have achieved "long-distance migration with minimal costs," thus facilitating the maintenance of social relations, and especially mate seeking (505). Big game hunting may also have lowered the cost of child care (permitting people to stay in one camp for a while). It is curious that frequent camp movement is not the same as being "highly mobile":

Clovis people may actually have walked less than later Archaic "pedestrian foragers," who lived in a more densely populated world (505).

This emphasis on women's work departs from the old models in which hunting was the master behavior that explained most aspects of culture. Recent interpretations place women back into the Paleoindian culture as active participants in the negotiation of the way of life of the group. Women's work in some environments was probably the reliable economic strategy that underwrote the more risky activities often associated with men.

Paleoindian archaeology has been dominated by projectile points—their morphology, technology, and distribution. Rethinking projectile points is part of the process of balancing the androcentric view of the earliest Americans. Some scholars now believe that many projectile points were hafted as cutting tools and that they functioned for a variety of purposes, thus making it more likely that they were used by women as well as men (Kehoe 1987).

It is also possible that Clovis and other elaborate points had ideological functions. It has even been suggested that Clovis technology was spread as an emblem of male identity associated with a men's cult (Storck 1991). This scenario imagines men producing these fancy bifaces as a way of celebrating their societal role, and perhaps as a way of drumming up enthusiasm for a risky activity. In this case, women may have avoided contact with these artifacts, fearing that female power might interfere with the functioning of the points. Still, if the Clovis points also functioned as knives, an equally reasonable interpretation of their ideological value would be that they were symbolic tools first presented to a girl on, say, the occasion of her first menses or some similar important coming-of-age event. Ideology does not need to be androcentric.

This positing of an ideological function for stone tools reflects the still-strong focus of researchers on stone tools. Yet it is unlikely that stone tools occupied as central a place in Paleoindian life as archaeologists imagine. Now scholars are paying more attention to the diverse artifacts manufactured by Paleoindians and to sites that were oriented to many different kinds of resources. One of these is the Gault Site in central Texas, where a wide variety of plant and animal resources were exploited by Clovis women and men at the end of the Ice Age. Engraved pebbles found at this site are today the earliest examples of art in America (Collins 2002, figs. 7 and 8). Attention to these other aspects of Paleoindian production has provoked the deconstruction of "Man the Hunter" as the focus of early American history.

Engendering Stone Tools

The humble, unretouched stone flake, which is easily manufactured by anybody from the age of four on, is the most abundant and earliest evidence of ancient Americans. Because male archaeologists dominate in the study, interpretation, and replication of lithic artifacts, and because of our modern gender prejudices about tools, many scholars believe that lithic technology was a male domain going back to Adam, a premise that is assumed, but not proven. Abandoning this prejudice, Gero (1991) has reinterpreted stone tools in a more balanced gender perspective, taking us beyond "Man the Toolmaker."

Since there is ethnographic proof that women make and use stone tools, and since biological strength is not a constraining factor in their manufacture, it would have been inefficient for ancient women to have relied on men for the production of adequate cutting edges. Although Gero (1991) concedes that exactly who made what, where, when, and why is subject to great variation across time and space, she engenders lithic artifacts by assuming that the remains of women's activities will be found "on house floors, at base camps and in village sites" where women gathered and worked (169).

The most common artifact in these contexts is the technologically simple utilized flake, a preeminently expedient tool, easily manufactured and used for most chores. These flakes are normally devalued by archaeologists, perhaps because of their technical simplicity, possibly because they are associated with women. There should be, of course, no stigma attached to making and using cheap and efficient tools, and Gero argues that women may well have crafted finely worked stone tools as well. After all, women produced high-status objects in many ethnographic cultures in the New World. Because gender systems are very complex and respond to many factors, we expect variation in the past. Neither stone nor metal has been identified exclusively with a particular sex.

Stone projectile points dominate the written archaeological record of the Preceramic Period, but most tools in the Paleoindian tool kit were not fluted bifacial points, but scrapers, knives, choppers, and utilized flakes. These, as Gero (1991) has demonstrated, are the backbone of any stone tool kit. In the new, holistic picture of Paleoindian life, based on understanding the total tool kit, it is now possible to infer the wide range of food sources utilized by the Paleoindians and the locations of the activity areas once inhabited by both women and men.

The Buhl Woman

More than 10,500 years ago, a woman, seventeen to twenty-one years old, was buried along the Snake River in southern Idaho. Isotopic analysis of her well-preserved remains suggests that she lived on a diet of meat and fish; radiographic study of her bones suggests that she suffered periods of nutritional stress in childhood. Dental examination reveals teeth heavily worn from chewing food bearing abrasive grit, possibly derived from the consumption of food processed with stone grinding equipment. The grave goods associated with her body offer a glimpse of this woman's world: they included "a large stemmed biface, an eyed needle, and a bone implement of unknown function" (Green et al. 1998:437). The stone biface belongs to a type widely associated with Paleoindian sites in the Great Basin and the Northwest; at least some women had access to high-tech lithic equipment. The bone needle, similar to others found in Paleoindian sites, must have been indispensable for survival in the cold north. The unmodified penis bone of a badger is a curious grave offering. This animal was not known to have been eaten by Paleoindians, so this particular bone may have functioned as a talisman. The incomplete bone artifact is intriguingly adorned with a series of evenly spaced "distinct incisions or notches," which could be glossed as decoration or as evidence of record keeping (451).

Paleoindian Living Sites

The investigation of numerous Paleoindian living sites has shown that from the very beginning of the human occupation of the Americas there was variation from locality to locality in the exploitation of plant and animal species. Themes of diversity and variability have begun to replace simple hunting models. For instance, archaeologists now infer variable economic, technological, social, and ritual roles for Paleoindian women and men, and they expect great variation in the social construction of gender roles in each ancient group because they appreciate how female and male activities respond to the exigencies of regional and local conditions. The following early sites have been chosen for review because they clearly demonstrate these variations in economic and social adaptations. We cannot know for sure which activities were performed by women and which by men, but communal work, equality, and sharing may be inferred in the following communities.

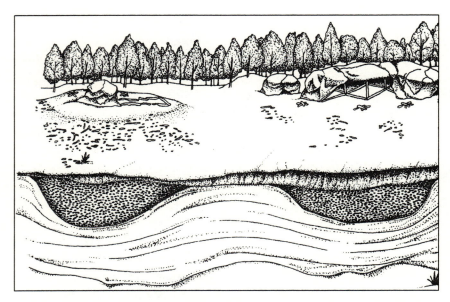

Figure 2.2. Reconstruction of the Paleoindian village located in a peat bog at Monte Verde in southern Chile. The excellent preservation of houses made of skin and wood and other organic remains enlarges our view of Paleoindian life. Courtesy of Tom Dillehay.

Paleoindians of Southernmost South America

One of the earliest known Paleoindian sites is Monte Verde, dated to about 12,000 B.C. and located in the cold forests of southern Chile (Dillehay 1996, 2000). This site is especially important because both excellent organic preservation and thorough reporting make it possible for us to imagine the activities of women and men at the site. As with the bodies in the Danish bogs, organic material was preserved by waterlogged peat along the creek where the ancient inhabitants built a village of some twelve wood, skin, and sod houses and a larger communal structure (fig. 2.2). Several houses had small clay-lined pits for fires inside, and large, presumably communal, hearths for cooking or for conviviality were located outside the line of houses adjacent to the large structure.

Evidence of wood and skin working in the vicinity of the houses was preserved by the peat, and activities such as cooking and eating were indicated by remains in the houses and around the communal hearths. The animal

  Women in Ancient America

bones recovered around hearths and in middens included the remains of seven mastodons, killed elsewhere and transported back home in pieces. Plant remains were abundant: seeds, fruits, berries, various leaf vegetables, and tubers and rhizomes, among which were wild potatoes. The variety of plants suggests that Monte Verde was a permanent settlement, not a seasonal one. Wooden mortars and grinding stones indicate that plant processing was important. There are also remains of nonedible plants, including leaves and seeds of several species still important in the native pharmacopoeia. Archaeologists recovered only a few bipointed projectile points among the relatively abundant stone tool remains, and grooved stone balls were found, hinting that bolas were used for hunting small and medium-sized animals. Presumably the mastodons were "hunted" by the tried-and-true method of driving them into the bog, where, mired and immobilized, they were killed. Butchering may have depended on the use of hafted flake tools, several of which were preserved in the habitation site. These show that unprepossessing flakes were important cutting tools in a location where both men and women worked.

Comparative Data from Warmer Regions

In the warm and semiarid Tehuacán and Oaxaca Valleys of southern Mexico, a series of regional surveys have yielded detailed information on ancient society and economy (Marcus and Flannery 1996). For thousands of years, the ancient inhabitants of this region moved seasonally through a series of different ecozones. Their movement and the size of the group at any given time of the year were tied to the availability of key plant staples that formed the major portion of their diet. The animals hunted were medium- to small-sized, including deer, tortoises, mollusks, insects, and rabbits. The fact that projectile points are rare in these sites supports the idea that the ancient procurement strategies included trapping, clubbing, and communal drives in addition to hunting with spears. Coxcatlán Cave (Puebla) and Cueva Blanca (Oaxaca) preserve the remains of many gophers, tortoises, rabbits, rats, a few white-tailed deer, and fox. This last may have served as food and provided pelts for clothing (Flannery 1976, 1986).

Because their diet was not dominated by meat, the yearly foraging schedule of these early Mexicans was not dictated by male hunting (Flannery 1968). In the spring, when the huge stands of prickly pear cactus bore fruit and the mesquite bushes along the river course were heavy with sweet bean pods, people would gather together in multifamily groups to consume food and trap a few rabbits. Remains of traps have been found in their sites. In Oaxaca, one of the earliest known structures in America, a dance floor, is evidence that families socialized and enjoyed performing ritual activities in their spring camps (Drennan 1976).

In early summer this community probably broke up into smaller family groups that moved into the higher valleys to forage in the wild grasses, including the ancestors of maize and amaranth, and to gather ripening fruits from scattered avocado and zapote trees, which bear abundantly in good years. By September, however, these resources would have begun to play out, and groups split up further to move into the higher hills where they gathered acorns and hunted white-tailed deer. Within a few months, as the cold dry season advanced, resources supported only nuclear or small extended families. In this meager season people survived by consuming the hearts of agave, which require lengthy cooking in an earth oven, and eating whatever birds, insects, or plants they could find until spring came once more. Under such conditions everyone's labor is valuable, and the survival of the group depends on the expertise of every forager. This yearly subsistence pattern suggests social complementarity and equality.

Paleoindians of Temperate Regions

Indian Creek, a deeply stratified Paleoindian site in south-central Montana, was occupied from late winter through early spring (Davis 1993). It was utilized for some thousands of years, people coming back each season much as they did in the Mexican sites. The largest animal hunted at Indian Creek was the bison, but far more common in numbers and in contribution to the diet were small animals: marmots, prairie dogs, voles, and jackrabbits. The excavators suggest that preferentially collecting fat-bearing small animals may have been an adaptation to the hard times of late winter. A Paleoindian trap was found in Wyoming in the 1980s (Frison et. al. 1986). Indian Creek has preserved evidence of numerous domestic activities as well as abundant refuse from stone working. Although the excavators identify the stone refuse as the result of males making and maintaining stone tools, more than 85 percent of the total stone tool inventory consisted of scrapers and knives, which they admit is evidence of women working in the site as well. This kind of sophistry is altogether too common in discussions of Paleoindians and other early human groups and serves to impress modern social values on peoples who were, obviously, quite different in lifeways and ideologies (Gero 1993).

Other Montana sites reflect similar foraging activities focused on small animals, while sites with good organic preservation show that plants formed an important part of the diet. Barton Gulch, to the southwest of Indian Creek, has the remains of earth ovens, another technique of transforming plants and animals into food. Barton Gulch has also yielded bone needles and other bone implements, grinding and pounding tools, scrapers, knives, and a great many utilized flakes (Davis 1993). All of these implements suggest that numerous different activities were being undertaken by the women and men in this site.

In the northeast sector of the United States, sites vary considerably in size, and some of the better preserved indicate that people were living in small portable or quickly constructed shelters, perhaps like the wigwams or tepees of later peoples. One of the few well-published sites with substantial plant preservation is Shawnee-Minisink in the upper Delaware Valley of Pennsylvania (McNett 1985). During the Paleoindian Period this area was a transitional zone between the boreal pine forest and the preboreal spruce and fir forest. Shawnee-Minisink was apparently a late summer and early fall camp to which two families returned year after year. They worked outside around the fireplace and probably used their shelters for sleeping and storage. Most tools were scrapers of various sorts, knives, spoke shaves, hammerstones, cores, and debitage. A single Clovis point/knife was found.

Plant remains around the shelters included amaranth, chenopods, smartweed, winter cress, and a host of fruits including blackberries, hackberries, grapes, and hawthorn plums, all rich in vitamin C. The unidentified fish remains found in their refuse indicate that the Paleoindians of Shawnee-Minisink may have caught salmon, an important seasonal food of foragers in many colder zones. Hunting seems to have often been a secondary activity in much of the eastern woodlands, where many peoples were forest gatherers, supplementing their plant diet with fish, birds, rabbits, and an occasional deer or mastodon. That the Shawnee-Minisink people hunted caribou is suggested by the site location, not by actual bone remains.

Family Structure, Gender, and Work

Archaeological evidence suggests that the basic unit of Paleoindian social life was the small family group in which nuclear family ties were the most important. For the people of Tehuacán and Oaxaca, the nuclear family was the basic subsistence group, especially during the hardest parts of the year. Thus strong affective ties and cooperation between the members of this minimal human social group would have been crucial in ensuring the survival of all. Shawnee-Minisink shows two families living side by side during one season of the year. If Monte Verde was a permanent village, as the excavators suggest, then the possibility exists for greater separation of activities, perhaps along some lines similar to the Ingalik model, where material culture was strongly engendered to promote cooperation and mutual dependence among women and men, young and old.

A gender-based division of labor is not inevitable or fixed but a flexible model designed by people to meet their current needs. The archaeological record makes it difficult to identify female and male activities, so archaeologists have to make serious efforts to avoid ethnocentric interpretations of evidence and to eschew the old stereotypes of women's work and men's work. Because hunting is romantic and masculine in the minds of European scholars, it has been given elevated importance in interpretations of Paleoindian life, devaluing other activities that were fundamental to prehistoric cultural systems. This perspective has changed with the realization that the conversion of animals and plants into food and the consumption of food are crucial and ideologically charged activities in all sociocultural systems. Food preparation is often, although not inevitably, women's work. Hearths and burned bones and vegetable remains show that meals were prepared and consumed. People invested skill, knowledge, and hours of time to produce meals that were nutritious, satisfying, and even enjoyable. Meals then, as now, symbolized and reinforced the basic structures of social life in the minds of individuals.

Who did the cooking and who did the snaring? The assignment of activities may well have varied with the group and the context. The Paleoindian evidence does not indicate that women and men were set against each other in antagonistic interest groups of the kind that have characterized some historic societies. It seems likely that cooperative and flexible family interactions characterized their lives, and we can be sure that the labor of women as well as that of men is reflected in the archaeological record at Paleoindian sites.

The women who lived in these Paleoindian habitation sites may have made clothing—we know that in modern times skin working is frequently women's work. The transformation of raw animal skins into processed hides that are soft and supple enough to wrap around the body requires laborious cleaning and scraping, and the stretched skin probably requires treatment with urine or other substances. In temperate and Arctic climates, skin working was essential to the survival of the group because skins were the basic material of both clothing and shelter. Only at Monte Verde do skin shelters survive, but we can imagine that similar shelters were an essential part of the equipment of many peoples moving through North and South America.

When the archaeological record preserves remains from a wide range of activities, these usually include the manufacture of items from skin and from plant fiber: clothing, carrying equipment, netting, cordage, and basketry. Small impressions in clay of twined netting have been found at a 27,000-year-old site in Czechoslovakia; rope was found in somewhat later contexts at Lascaux in France (Pringle 1998). In the New World, fragments of twined sandals or bags have been found in terminal Paleoindian contexts on San Miguel Island off Santa Barbara, California (Connolly et al. 1995). In Peru, at the highland Guitarrero Cave, new radiocarbon dates indicate that the inhabitants were processing plant fibers and making mats and cordage between 10,100 and 9800 B.C. (Jolie et al. 2011). Coiled basketry was being made by the inhabitants of Huachichocana Cave in Argentina around 7000 B.C. (Fernández Distel 1975). Paleoindian tool kits include many bone tools for skin working, twining, and coiling that must have been wielded frequently by women. The success of early Paleoindians in surviving and multiplying in the Arctic environment suggests that they must have had adequate clothing. Paleoindians living in the tundra and the taiga would have had to cover their bodies because of life-threatening cold much of the year and masses of biting flies and mosquitoes in the summer. There could have been no hunting in Maine, the Great Plains, or Chile without clothing. Artists' renditions of cavemen clad only in crude skins covering the genitals are silly.

No substantial pieces of clothing have yet been found in Paleoindian contexts. Excavations at the Russian site of Sungir, north of Moscow, have provided evidence for ancient garments, reconstructable because of their beaded decoration (Hadingham 1980:75–77). One suspects that "waders" like those worn by a Sungir male or leggings and moccasins with some sort of shirt or parka-like garment were worn by all the late Ice Age peoples of northern Eurasia. Many Native American groups preserved this sort of skillfully made clothing into the historic period.

Art and ritual were probably important in Paleoindian life, but there are no figurines, engraved plaques, or decorated tools from American sites. The box turtle shells reported by Redder and Fox (1988) from the tomb of a Paleoindian adult in the Horn site (Texas) might have been rattles used in dances and ceremonies, but the only known Paleoindian artwork is the sacrum of an extinct camelid found in the Valley of Mexico, carved into the form of an animal when the bone was fresh (Bárcena 1882). Although evidence of personal ornaments is lacking, it seems likely that Paleoindians wore bone toggles, buttons, or other sewn-on ornaments common in the European Paleolithic. We can be sure that the Euro-Asian women and men who walked or paddled into America brought with them the mythology, music, dances, and religious practices of their forebears.

In the Americas, hallucinatory states were achieved through rhythmic drumming and chanting, but one characteristic of historic and contemporary Native American religious practices, and one that seems to have great time depth, is the use of psychoactive substances of plant origin. Furst (1976) has summarized the evidence of mescal beans (the psychoactive red seeds of the Texas mountain laurel, *Sophora secundiflora*) in Archaic and Paleoindian contexts in caves of the Southwest and in northern Mexico, and snuffs containing dimethyltriptamine have been found in Archaic contexts in northern Chile. Late prehistoric people contributed tobacco to the Old World at the end of the fifteenth century.

The religious use of mind-altering substances may well have come from Siberia with the first peoples (Brekham and San 1967). Later, many Native American groups developed detailed knowledge of the chemical properties of medicinal, hallucinogenic, and poisonous plants as they explored each new environment of the New World. Curiosity and self-interest were probably important motivators. Paleoindian women, who, like recent foraging women, may have been specialists in plants and plant collecting, probably took up the challenge of discovering useful plants as their family moved into a new region.

In America today, female participation in rituals using hallucinogens is quite restricted, but contemporary Huichol women on pilgrimages chew hallucinogenic peyote cactus buds, and, of course, the Mazatec shaman María Sabina, who used hallucinogenic mushrooms in her rituals, is famous in psychedelic circles (Furst 1996; Wasson 1974). Evidence from the archaeological record includes ceramic figurines from West Mexican tombs dating to between 500 B.C. and A.D. 300 that depict females, perhaps shamans, in trances or preparing peyote (Furst 1965, 1978; Goldstein 1988). In the past, throughout the Americas, women have taken important healing roles and have often engaged in high-status divination, two important foci of hallucinogenic drug use (Glass-Coffin 1998). Because women were often knowledgeable with respect to plants and their uses, they likely participated in the ubiquitous rituals involving psychotropic plants, even if they did not always ingest concoctions themselves (Langdon 1992).

At Home in the Tequendama Rock Shelter

The rock shelters of Tequendama yield abundant evidence of the earliest inhabitants of the Sabana de Bogotá, a swampy plain located high in the mountains of Colombia (Correal and van der Hammen 1977). The drier parts of the plain and hills around the Sabana were forested and the swamps provided resources including fish, mollusks, and turtles. Excavations in one rock shelter revealed a number of superimposed living floors where people prepared food and carried out other productive activities shielded from cold wind and rain.

Fires were built in a well-lit portion of the rock shelter, where they served as the center of activity. Two hearths were found in the earliest excavated levels and more in later ones. The pattern of remains indicates that the kitchen waste of the earliest occupants of the rock shelter accumulated a little way from the hearths, mixed with the debris from a variety of tasks performed there. Little plant material was preserved, but the excavators carefully documented the distribution of animal bone and artifacts on the old cave floors. Stone tools were manufactured just two meters east and southeast of the hearths, where cores were found and where hide working and other tasks were performed beneath the rocky overhang.

The people of Tequendama brought food, water, and fuel from outside to be processed, cooked, and consumed in the cave, where they also manufactured and repaired wooden tools, worked skins and fibers, and assembled clothing. Members of a family carried out the work necessary for subsistence and comfort, but we cannot specify who performed each given task. Perhaps women engaged in stone working and made the bone tools they themselves used. The majority of the tools recovered are knives and scrapers, including abundant unretouched flakes, which might have been used by anybody. Bone tools and perforators are evidence of the manufacture of clothing, bags, cordage, and baskets. Grinding tools indicate that seeds and other plants were important in the diet. Most of the animals represented in the midden are small, such as species of rat, rabbit, armadillo, guinea pig (first hunted and later domesticated at the site), skunk, and deer. The proportion of small to large animals suggests that the people were collectors who snared and netted as often as they hunted. Stone projectile points were not used by these Paleoindians.

Although Correal and van der Hammen (1977:181) identified Tequendama as the home of specialized deer hunters, the occupants of the cave performed many different activities and consumed a wide variety of food.

The map of the spatial arrangement of artifacts and food and other debris on the cave floor helps us envision the human group that produced the archaeological record. They were not all men, and we need not conjure a cartoon version of men hunting while women hide idly in the rock shelter. Extrapolating from historic and contemporary hunting and foraging peoples, we speculate that women provided the bulk of the food consumed. Because the labor pool was small, women (like men) flexibly undertook whatever work needed to be done.

One can imagine older women and men by the fire working and chatting, while vigorous adults tote heavy loads up the slope and children and infants help or play. During the day adult women collect food, including trapped animals and birds. Later, everyone processes the foodstuffs contributed by women and men. Women, with the help of girls, invest long hours in other productive activities that require years of training and the skilled use of tools and materials, and females as well as males engage in solving problems such as healing sick and injured family members, developing plans for a ceremony, and finding mates for maturing offspring. In this reconstruction of the deep past, when people return to the cave in the evening for food and the company of their kin, women and girls appear in the center of the scene, not as the shadowy peripheral figures of artists' conceptions (Gifford-Gonzalez 1995).

Engendering the Deep Past

The archaeological record of Paleoindian societies affords little art and few burial assemblages from which archaeologists can argue about gender roles, yet we know that both women and men participated in the peopling of America. By analogical argument, an interpretation of Paleoindian women that is consistent with archaeological evidence can be made using ethnography, imagination, and a critical perspective. Because stone tools dominate the corpus of remains, their interpretation led to androcentric reconstructions of the past, but this is changing. Scholars like Gero (1993) and Sassaman (1992a) have demonstrated that both women and men made and used those stone tools. Scrapers, knives, choppers, and humble utilized flakes, as well as a few elegant, fluted, bifacial projectile points, are evidence of the range of economic activities that made life possible in ancient America. In the new, holistic picture of Paleoindian life, based on understanding the total tool kit, the wide range of productive activities and food sources, and the location of habitation sites, Man the Hunter does not appear alone.

CHAPTER THREE

Women in the Archaic

Following the Paleoindian Period, people progressively intensified their foraging activities, focusing on a wide range of resources. The dates of this Archaic way of life are not fixed because in local areas it developed at different times and persisted variably: for 8,000 years in some parts of North America, for only a few millennia in other regions. Archaic cultures, as originally defined, lacked permanent architecture, ceramics, and food production. Based on analogy with recent foragers, Archaic societies are believed to have been characterized by low population densities and small egalitarian social groups in which both men and women achieved high status as providers of foodstuffs, as healers, or in other roles.

Archaic peoples were descended from Paleoindians and it is likely that the skill and knowledge accumulated by Paleoindian women became the foundation of the way of life of later, less mobile Archaic groups. Some anthropological studies have suggested that males dominate in situations of migration but parity is established with sedentism (Mazel 1989:121). The pattern of broad-spectrum foraging characteristic of many Archaic peoples provided a situation in which women may have negotiated equal social power. As Archaic people settled down into areas where an array of resources was harvested, women may have continued to exercise control over their own working conditions and over the distribution of the food they produced, a situation that meant greater economic power. Under some circumstances, foraging adaptations culminated in women's innovation of new food-producing systems based on the cultivation of plants.

Early broad-spectrum foraging in the eastern forests of North America involved changes in lithic technology that may reflect evolution in the division of labor between women and men. According to Sassaman (1992b), the archaeological record reflects the progressive reduction of high-risk hunting (presumably by men) in favor of more reliable subsistence activities, including the more intensive exploitation of plants and other nonmobile resources like fish and small animals (accessible to women, children, and men). This shift correlates with a reduction in the production of specialized hunting equipment and an increase in the production of more expedient tools (formerly classified by archaeologists as useless debitage from the manufacture of "real tools"). Archaic sites are characterized by large quantities of technologically simple flakes, which were produced easily and used to process foods and create an expanding inventory of material culture. Feminists such as Kehoe (2005) initiated the analysis of flakes as expedient tools that were as valuable as projectile points to the women who made and used them. Sassaman (1992b:71–80) demonstrates that women became much more visible in the archaeological record because of their increased activity in the production and use of stone tools, and later, pottery.

Later in the Archaic, as people in the eastern United States grew more sedentary, formal tools were produced with less and less frequency. Fancy bifacial projectile points lost their prominence, although in late prehistory men continued to perform rituals involving these tools. According to Sassaman (1992a:258), this suggests male resistance to technological change.

Archaic Burials: Gender and Status

Some Archaic people buried their dead in cemeteries. This permits us to reconstruct aspects of prehistoric gender and status behaviors. In fact, some of the strongest engendered interpretations in New World prehistory come from the study of burials.

Status refers to the relative position of individuals in society. In our society this means ranking on a socioeconomic scale and involves distinctions between high-status individuals and low-status ones over whom others hold power. In contrast, under egalitarian conditions there is relatively little exercise of authority over others, although social differentiation and different statuses do exist. The old and the young may differ with respect to role, emblems, and access to goods, just as women will differ from men; talented people may be assigned leadership roles in limited contexts and elders can be expected to be more central in decision making, but hierarchy is not a necessary dimension of social organization in all cases. Women's status is variable among hunters and gatherers.

Hayden and his colleagues (1986) have defined several indicators of female status that vary greatly among societies and are difficult to identify in the archaeological record. Some of their indicators of high status for women include female voice in domestic decisions, female control of children and of food they have procured, female ownership or control of the dwelling, female voice in interband affairs, and the possibility of female leaders. Status is interpreted as low if females are frequently beaten or poorly treated, if they are excluded from ritual activity, if (in hunting societies) their participation in hunting is limited by taboos, if there are myths of former female control of males, and if there is a belief in the inferiority of females with respect to males.

This research on ethnographic foragers has shown that the status of women of childbearing years in both the domestic and political spheres is strongly related to the frequency and severity of environmental crises. Hayden and his colleagues conclude that under conditions of stress men force heavier workloads on females. This may alleviate local stress because the women act to control their fertility by resorting to infanticide. Women's status increases, according to Hayden (1992), and their workloads ease only after menopause. This cultural pattern, observed in many foraging societies, suggests that adaptation may be achieved at great cost to women. However, Hayden has shown that women's status in ritual domains is variable and not controlled by techno-environmental factors. Furthermore, women's status may be high in the absence of adverse conditions. The presence of warfare may reduce women's status, but if the men travel great distances and leave women in charge, the reverse may be true.

It is important to emphasize that female status has been observed to vary dramatically among foraging societies. And, as circumstances change, so do social patterns. It is unwise to generalize any interpretation: women's and men's statuses are changeable. In the archaeological record we expect to confront diversity and uniqueness.

The assessment of comparative status for women and men in society is difficult because they frequently do not participate in the same activities. Women and men may not compete for the same things as they do in modern Euroamerican society. It is unproductive to define high status only in terms of the spheres open to men. In some societies sexual segregation means that women and men have different spheres: in their own sphere women may have considerable autonomy, make their own decisions, and achieve respect via competent performance. At burial, women will be interred with goods important and relevant to them and men may be buried with other goods that are not comparable to female things.

The Chinchorro Archaic Tradition in Chile

Between 9,000 and 2,000 years ago, along the desert coast of northern Chile and southernmost Peru, the Chinchorro people exploited cold-water marine and adjacent terrestrial environments, eating sea mammals, fish, shellfish, and seaweed, as well as land plants and animals. Good preservation in their coastal habitation sites and cemeteries facilitates our interpretation of the roles of women and men (Arriaza 1995a, 1995b).

The following partial list of their material culture helps one imagine the productive activities of both women and men. They possessed many wooden artifacts including spears and spear throwers as well as needles; bone items such as compound fishhooks, *chopes* (tools to process shellfish), and decorated flutes; vegetable fiber bags and pubic covers; reed mats and baskets; bags and loincloths twined out of camelid hair; prepared and decorated bird and mammal skin garments; stone net weights, mortars, and knives; seeds used in rattles; cactus thorns used in fishhooks; human hair cords; feather headbands; sea lion teeth; unfired clay figurines; disk-shaped shell artifacts; and red, white, and green paint.

Some early Chinchorro foragers were generally healthier than the later agricultural people in the same area (Guillén 1992; Allison 1984; Arriaza et al. 1988). Their skeletal remains show that women and men had a good life expectancy for that period in history: if they survived childhood their average life expectancy was twenty-five years, although some individuals lived to be fifty or more. Guillén's (1992) study of Chinchorro cemeteries found little evidence of pathology in the skeletons. This is normal for foragers living in small groups and eating well. It has been suggested that the high number of instances of auditory exostoses in males is an indication of a sexual division of labor in which men spent more time diving in cold waters, thus becoming more susceptible to ear infections and hence developing this condition. However, women, even when diving, do not form auditory exostoses with the same frequency as males, making it difficult to say whether Chinchorro women as well as men were diving. Eighteen percent of the male skeletons showed fractures in their lower back regions, evidence of frequent accidents in the rough, rocky waters.

Allison's (1984) work showed that female skeletons had unnatural facets on their ankle bones, a condition caused by the habitual bent or squatting position of women cleaning shellfish. This may be evidence of an ancient division of labor. Women were also affected by spinal arthritis, found in a third of all their skeletons, and one in five women suffered from compression fractures in the spine, due to osteoporosis, perhaps aggravated by multiple pregnancies. Forty percent of all people suffered from severe infections that damaged their leg bones.

In another study of fifty-one Chinchorro individuals from about 2000 B.C., Allison (1984) observed some deterioration in health: 86.4 percent of the adults had Harris lines, evidence of nutritional stress; 86 percent of the children had lines; and the twelve women in the sample showed 50 percent more lines than males. These numbers may not accurately reflect the differential health status of women and men but simply the fact that Harris lines more often disappear from men's bones, as these are heavier than those of women and more likely to be remodeled in their lifetimes. Nevertheless, women are often subject to greater nutritional and disease problems during pregnancy, and the poor health of mothers can cause prenatal lines in the tibiae of their children. At the Morro 1 site, investigations concluded that most health problems occurred in children between seven and sixteen years old and among young women, who would have had greater nutritional requirements due to pregnancy, parturition, and nursing infants (Arriaza et al. 1988). Generally, however, there is a pattern of good dental health and no evidence that either women or children were differentially harmed by social or cultural practices of the sort that became common later in history.

Chinchorro ritual life focused on artificial mummification. In its most elaborate form, the bodies of children, women, and men were first defleshed and eviscerated, and the bodies were then reassembled using artificial supports of wood; stuffed with plants; coated with clay, tar, and paint; and festooned with ornaments and wigs (Guillén 1992; Arriaza 1995b). Not all people were so prepared: many were simply interred, but among the elaborate mummies there is a slight preponderance of children, from miscarried fetuses to near-adults. The preparation of mummies was a way of preserving and venerating the dead, and mortuary ceremonialism probably had multiple social functions. In societies in which there is little differentiation between the public and the domestic spheres, ceremonialism makes possible the integration of kin groups. During burial ceremonies, some South American

Indians strive to achieve ethnic and family solidarity, which facilitates decision making by consensus, thus avoiding political hierarchy.

A 4,000-year-old cemetery in Morro de Arica contained seventeen Chinchorro individuals who were evidently part of a single kin group. Sixteen artificially mummified bodies were interred along with a male body that had been naturally preserved by the arid environment. All were dressed in a similar fashion, each with a loincloth of wool cords or reed fiber. Most were wrapped with leather cloaks. There were no food offerings and all had had their heads removed before burial. Guillén (1992) analyzed the grave goods by sex and concluded that (aside from clothing) most artifacts were related to the extraction and processing of marine resources. Six mummies had net bags used to hold fishing gear: two were associated with a male, one with a female, and three with individuals of undetermined sex. Cactus fishhooks and a compound fishhook were found with two male children and one fetus of undetermined sex. Other fishing gear elements were lines, weights, *chopes*, and a knife, associated with three male children and three mummies of undetermined sex. None of the female mummies had such tools, although some of the unidentified mummies could be female. The available information suggests that offerings of fishing gear were suitable for males. However, Allison (1984) reports that in northern Chile women were buried with harpoons, fishhooks, and lines, as well as with elaborate turbans, and he suggests a sexually undifferentiated society. Artifacts associated with both male and female skeletons included reed brushes decorated with transverse red bands, bags containing colored clays used cosmetically, and tiny stones individually wrapped in skin.

The development of cemeteries in the Archaic Period has been explained on the grounds that people were more sedentary and concerned with controlling territories and access to particular resources. For thousands of years, the Chinchorro clearly prepared these mummies to be viewed and to be kept around for some time: many mummies show signs of repeated moving and repair. Later, the bodies were deposited in cemeteries not far from residential areas. This could be evidence of ancestor worship or a cult centered on kin members: the larger the group of mummies displayed, the more visually strong the claim of the family to territory and nearby resources. Only later, as the local people became agricultural, did they adopt funerary practices that involved the disposal of individuals in personal tombs.

In another interpretation, Rivera (1995) suggests that competitive, individually oriented Chinchorro bands achieved better social integration among themselves by practicing group-oriented mortuary rituals. By communally preparing selected dead, the Chinchorro people counterbalanced individualistic or family economic activities and reduced competition. This kin-based religious activity, while ritualizing themes of communication with ancestors and, perhaps, fertility, would have permitted the recognition of part-time leaders and created a focus of community identity.

The function of ancestor worship among ancient Andean peoples is well documented in the ethnohistoric and ethnographic literature. The Chinchorro people may have propitiated female and male ancestors in order to ensure growth and fertility: the ancestors received homage because they were thought to protect the welfare of the community. In many nonmodern groups, communication with the dead and other rituals are widely seen as validating the territorial claims of the living.

La Paloma in Desert Peru

La Paloma, a site on the desert coast of Peru dating to 5000–2500 B.C., has excellent preservation of habitation remains and burial features (Benfer 1984). The Palomans exploited the resources of the coast and the nearby hills, which, bathed by fog, supported lush vegetation and large animal populations. They also cultivated plants, such as squash, beans, and gourds. A decrease in the stem diameter of firewood through time may indicate that the environment was being degraded.

Palomans lived in reed houses and were usually buried in a flexed position, wrapped in mats and accompanied by a few simple offerings, below the floors of the houses. A few special group mortuary facilities, including an infant burial house, have been identified, but all burials were recovered in or near houses, probably showing the importance of the household in the social organization.

This kind of small kin organization is favorable to both women and men because when decision making takes place at the level of the family, everyone's personal concerns can be taken into consideration. The burial of a twenty-five-year-old male and a twenty-four-year-old female (Burials 51 and 52), located in the earliest levels of the Paloma site, shows the equality of the sexes: the two people had similar wrappings, and he was buried with several cut shell amulets, while she had twenty-five bone beads (Quilter 1989).

With respect to gender relations in the late phases of the occupation of Paloma, Quilter observed that female burials had fewer grave goods and that males appear to have had higher status than females. Furthermore, Quilter suggests that sedentary life results in the limiting of women's autonomy and influence. The evidence, however, can lead to another interpretation: that the Paloma burial data show gender parity and suggest that age was a more important factor than sex in accounting for variation among burials. Quilter's cluster analysis identified three major groups of burials, but there was no significant clustering in any of the three on the basis of gender. Of the seventy-six burials studied, the most elaborate were those of infants and small children.

It is difficult to see how the small differences between the number and kind of artifacts found in male and female burials could translate into difference in status. A simple tally of associated items (counting each as one, without respect to size or quality) indicates that males have a higher average number of offerings only if you omit the beads and amulets associated with the woman and man mentioned above. It seems risky to assert an overall superordination of men over women when there is so little variability among the graves.

Difference in status between males and females cannot be inferred from evidence like Burial 159, the most elaborate burial at Paloma. A seventeen-year-old male was laid under a cane structure and covered with several mats, accompanied by many funerary offerings. His death was violent: his left leg was missing, and cut marks on the pelvis suggest that a shark removed it. This grave is special not because it contains a male skeleton, but because of the manner of death.

There is very little expression of special status in the Paloma remains. Although a few exotic items such as a monkey bone, tropical seashells, and obsidian were acquired, the Palomans did not accumulate or manufacture any obvious luxury goods, and even beads seem to decrease in frequency through time. These people may not have invested surplus production in elaborate ceremonial activities, and the site was abandoned before coastal people intensified their fishing and cotton-growing activities and embarked on the course of social and cultural intensification that led to the construction of monumental architecture and other dramatic changes in lifeways.

A physical analysis of two hundred Paloma skeletons demonstrates that the ancient people were healthy by preceramic standards, although they suffered from tuberculosis and carcinomas as well as frequently broken foot bones, osteoarthritis of the spine, and back problems. Apparently, everyone performed hard physical labor. Studies of the hair found in some Paloma graves showed sharp differences in mineral composition, suggesting seasonal variation in diet.

The excavators see population increase through time at Paloma, and they believe that people at the site were healthier, taller, and better adapted later in history. According to Benfer (1990), life expectancy increased through time, and the incidence of tooth wear, Harris lines, and cribra orbitalia decreased, although hypoplastic lesions were fairly common in all periods. The relative numbers of fetal and infant burials decreased over time, perhaps indicating an improvement in living conditions.

There are some curious patterns in the burial evidence from Paloma. Almost twice as many adult females died in their thirties as died in their twenties. This contrasts with the expected pattern of premodern societies, in which high female mortality occurs among women in their twenties due to pregnancy and childbirth. Moreover, there are at least twice as many non-infant male skeletons as female ones. Benfer has suggested that this might be evidence of a social strategy: in an effort to control population size and growth, the ancient people may have postponed marriage and practiced female infanticide. It is not surprising that the Palomans tried to control their population using strategies often used in history, but it is hard to believe that there were twice as many men as women, so we expect that there are other explanations for the recovery of more male skeletons. One wonders if polyandry was practiced at Paloma or if there was an unequal marrying out of the village by women.

Benfer has made an effort to show that division of labor by sex was dynamic at Paloma. He noted that sexual dimorphism in musculature was marked in the skeletons of the early Paloma population, suggesting that males and females did very different activities, and that men were very robust. Later, women increased their muscle mass by more vigorous and prolonged activity, while men showed reduced amounts, probably reflecting reduced mobility and less hard work. The major changes in the shape of both men's and women's upper arm bones may reflect more intensive maritime tasks such as netting small fish or intensified gardening and food processing.

Trace element analysis has revealed a convergence in male and female diets from the early to late occupations of La Paloma. In the early period, men and women exploited, and apparently consumed, different foods. Later, there was a decrease in the availability of wild plants and fur-bearing animals, and with increased sedentism, the investigators infer an increased emphasis on fishing and cultivating plants. In this later period, men, helped by women and children, may have fished and hunted marine animals, while women processed products of the sea and worked gardens with the help of children and men.

A glimpse of the ancient gender roles of the Palomans comes from an analysis of the burials. Females were more frequently interred on their right sides and males on their left than might be expected in a random distribution. Quilter (1989) hypothesizes that projectile points, flakes, and miscellaneous tools were associated with male activities and that grinding stones were associated with preparing foods at home, but he found only a very weak statistical association between males, hunting, and small processing tools, and between females and grinding stones.

In actuality, all adult burials had very similar ranges of artifacts. In making gender activity attributions, one must remember that in small communities women and men cannot afford to be inflexible about who does what. Five female skeletons and four males were associated with bone tools used in manufacturing nets, cordage, and other textiles. Quilter speculates that men used these artifacts to repair fishing nets and tackle and that women made house mats and clothing, although, as he notes, gifts to the dead may not reflect the activities of the deceased person (as archaeologists often assume). Twined *junco* reed mats were very common at Paloma, as were fine twined textiles of agave-like plant fiber that served as clothing and head coverings. The Palomans also made bags of knotted netting, fish nets, and twined baskets. Making and repairing fishing gear must have required a great amount of energy and care; net and hook manufacture was time consuming, although we have no real evidence concerning who did what tasks.

During the long occupation of Paloma, there were significant sociocultural changes. Animal fur and hides decreased in quantity through time at the site, while textiles increased (MacAnulty Quilter 1976). This may reflect both degradation of animal resources and changes in labor allocation. A shift from hunting to more intense fishing by males, resulting in a shortage of hides, might have necessitated the investment of more effort in plant fiber collecting and processing, and increased investment in textile production. Such a change would have had a gender component: if the processing of animal hides and the production of plant fiber textiles were both women's work, then female workload might have been altered. Did women press for this change because they found textile production more convenient? Or did they resist the change because it required increased effort on their parts? Later in prehistory, in much of Peru, weaving was often associated with women. It is possible that the women of Paloma undertook the manufacture of textiles because, compared to skin garments, textiles were more expressive of women's skill and pride. Did the development of textile production offer women more independence—an area of productivity in which they were relatively autonomous and creative? Was it more efficient for women to harvest reeds and bromeliad plant fiber to increase their productivity than to try to intensify efforts to snare sea birds and trap rabbits? Were men happy that women no longer demanded a steady input of skins? Ultimately these speculative questions may be pointless if men as well as women made textiles, as was often the case later in Andean history.

The Archaic Las Vegas People of Ecuador

The preceramic Las Vegas people were broad-spectrum hunters, fishers, and gatherers adapted to an ecologically complex tropical coastal environment with a high biotic potential (Stothert 1985, 1988). They added plant cultivation to their subsistence system around 7000 B.C. (Stothert et al. 2003). The largest Las Vegas site may have been occupied permanently or revisited seasonally. It also served as a preferred burial place in the later Las Vegas period.

Study of the skeletal population shows the Las Vegas people to have been typical of early collectors and farmers, with none of the degenerative diseases associated with intensive agriculture. Life expectancy was more than thirty years, somewhat more than the later agricultural populations of coastal Ecuador.

The remains of 192 individuals from the main Las Vegas site show clear gender-related practices in disposal of the dead. Males were buried in a flexed position, generally on their right side and with their head toward the west or southwest, toward the setting sun or the open sea. Often a shell "pillow" was placed under the head; offerings included stone flakes, a cobble tool, or a conch shell. Adult women were buried in a similar way, but their heads were oriented in every direction, with a slight preference for the northeast. Women's grave furniture included shell dishes, stone knives, and cobble tools. Regrettably, fibers and gourds, surely used for shrouds, clothing, and containers, were not preserved. Age differences in burial practices are reflected in the relatively shallower graves of subadults, who were buried flexed on their left sides with their heads to the east or southeast.

Among the primary burials there were no significant differences in the distribution of grave goods by sex or age. However, females (74 percent of nineteen burials) and subadults (78 percent of nine burials) were more likely to have durable offerings than males (only 56 percent of nine burials). Secondary burials were common and provide evidence that mortuary ritual continued long after the death of an individual. Small bundles contained the reburied bones of eight men, seven women, and six children. Often only a few body parts, or selected bones of several individuals, were included in these burial bundles. The bones of the dead evidently had special meaning for the ancient people.

In three large, circular ossuaries, adult males and females were about equally represented, and there were subadults as well. Among the communal offerings in one of these ossuaries was a cache of twenty-six selected polished pebbles, interpreted as a shaman's charm stones. These may have served to protect the individuals in the burial.

Ubelaker (1980, 2003) identified the sex of 118 adult Vegas skeletons: 53 percent were female and 47 percent male. In contrast to this general parity, among the 26 adults of known sex recovered in primary burials, only 31 percent were male and 66 percent were female. This sexual imbalance in the primary burials indicates that females apparently received or remained in primary burials more frequently than males: males may have been exhumed and kept elsewhere more often than females. It is clear that the remains of women and men were manipulated differently—evidence of different statuses or contrasting roles for female and male ancestors vis-à-vis their living descendants. Of some importance is that the single individual found buried under the threshold of an early Las Vegas shelter was a female over forty-five years old. This may suggest the importance of this female ancestor.

The most provocative Vegas burial, known as the "Lovers of Sumpa," is that of a twenty-year-old female, buried in the normal flexed posture, embraced in the tomb by a twenty-year-old male arranged in an amorous pose (fig. 3.1). They apparently died together or within a short time of each other. Their relatives arranged them in the tomb and placed several large stones over the bodies, perhaps to keep them from returning in search of their loved ones or as a gesture of magical protection. Such burials may have signaled extraordinary deaths.

In late Vegas times, there is evidence that the people increased their dependence on fishing, began taking a broader range of shellfish species, and added more domesticated plants to their diet. Gardening may have increased the productivity of the river bottoms and expanded the variety of reliable

Figure 3.1. The bodies of a young man (*left*) and a young woman, both twenty years old at death, were interred together between 7,000 and 8,000 years ago in southwestern Ecuador. Because of the position of the bodies, they are known as the "Lovers of Sumpa" and have been popularized as the Preceramic Adam and Eve. Photograph by Neil Maurer.

local resources. Men may have expanded the hours invested in fishing while the women invested progressively more labor in gardening.

Evidence of bottle gourd, squash, root crops, and primitive maize were found in Las Vegas soil samples dated to the phase when burial ceremonialism was at its height. Because women are associated with plants, it seems logical that they were the ones tending the gardens and creating new domesticated species. Their careful husbandry and selection produced the genetically engineered species so important in the diets of their descendants.

Perhaps the Vegas people intensified both the cultivation of plants and fishing as responses to population growth, drier conditions, or changes in the coastline by 6000 B.C. Alternatively, women and men may have adopted new economic strategies because of escalating social needs: participation in burial ceremonialism and trade requires surplus production. A polished stone ax found in pristine condition in the tomb of a Las Vegas woman buried between 6000 and 5000 B.C. is evidence of long-distance exchange. No other axes have been found in Las Vegas sites, so the burial artifact was not local; rather, it is very similar to axes common in preceramic sites near Talara in northern Peru. The woman buried with the ax may have traveled to Talara, or received the ax from a trading partner, or acquired it only as a burial offering. The lack of use wear indicates that it functioned as a token or talisman, and not as a cutting tool.

Regardless of what motivated change in Vegas society, the founding of the cemetery at Site 80 likely had the practical effect of facilitating social connectedness. The creation of elaborate mortuary rituals and other commemorative activities could have provided opportunities for cooperative labor and might have increased the size of the functional kin group, making it more capable of defending its territory. As this group organized to carry out rituals, it may have developed more elaborate social mechanisms that conferred economic benefits by permitting larger task groups or supporting economic specialization by sex, domestic unit, or family group. Change and attendant social adjustment would have affected the lives of both women and men.

We see the Las Vegas people through a veil, because the majority of their material culture has not been preserved. But the evidence shows us healthy, enduring, egalitarian people in benign ecological conditions. Life seems to have been good for both women and men, who innovated new technologies (plant cultivation) and new social mechanisms (burial ceremonialism) to meet changing needs.

Change in the Archaic

Cultural change involves people making choices that in turn create conflicts in all areas of their lives. New activities have to be accommodated. Today and in the past, sex roles and, ultimately, gender ideologies change as individuals undertake new tasks. At the same time, changes in production result in the changing symbolic value and meaning of particular products. Social arrangements will be reorganized to handle new productive activities or in response to the loss of customary ones, and diets will be modified as well as tools, cooking, and so forth. Many apparently small changes may add up to a major historical trend. History is made by women and men making small adjustments that result in the evolution of sociocultural systems. This is an aspect researchers need to consider as they seek possible explanations of change.

Several studies in North American Archaic cultures show us some situations in which the causes of cultural change can be inferred.

Archaic Adaptations in California

Hunter-gatherers thrived in the Central Valley of California from early in prehistory until the time of European contact. Archaeological data from about 2500 B.C. until A.D. 1450 show a pattern of subsistence change as acorn consumption increased and salmon fishing replaced deer hunting. Gender played a crucial role in the life experiences of both women and men as their activities changed dramatically through time.

Dickel and his colleagues (1984) have suggested that as a dietary dependency on acorns developed, birth spacing decreased and local populations grew. This change must have radically altered the lives of women. At the same time, there was increased adult mortality. Although the researchers did not see evidence of differences in female and male mortality, they hypothesized that young adult females were dying at a higher rate due to the risks of more frequent childbirth. There is evidence of heavier mortality in later Archaic periods for unweaned children from the time of birth until two years of age, which is attributed to the loss of their mothers. The researchers' interpretation of the paleodemographic information, based on the aging and sexing of skeletons from Central Valley Archaic cemeteries, indicates that overall subadult survivorship increased through time while adult survivorship decreased.

The changes observed in the Archaic reflect the choices of generalized foragers who were sparsely settled in the Central Valley in the early Archaic Period. Progressively, they redefined their economic strategies, focusing on a reduced number of plant and animal species. By the late Archaic, these foragers were emphasizing acorns and salmon and were living in more stable settlements. Population size and density increased and people adopted various kinds of cultural activities that anthropologists normally associate with early agricultural peoples.

This shift, like many other important changes in history, was linked to changing material conditions resulting from women having more babies. The cultural changes in the Central Valley probably involved greater emphasis on gendered labor, as assigning labor by sex is one form of specialization, one way to achieve greater output. Among the historic California Indians, acorn processing and storage was women's work. Women may have resisted the shift to acorn processing because it committed them to the heavy, tedious labor of detoxifying acorns. On the other hand, they might have been willing to undertake the processing and storing chores because the labor could be carried out in company with other women, because the new subsistence strategy solved some perceived problems of food shortages, and because it relieved them of the burden of moving camp so often. One wonders if men were happy with an intensified focus on salmon. Was this an activity of choice or were they pressured by women and children to forgo deer hunting because fishing was especially reliable and productive?

Dickel and his colleagues (1984) suggest that the subsistence shift toward specialization may have resulted from a series of prolonged and stressful dry periods. Under these conditions, people probably perceived that acorns were productive and reliable, so they increased their exploitation of this food source. Focusing on acorns then resulted in a more sedentary lifestyle to facilitate their processing and storage. This innovation may have been linked to population increase caused by reduced birth spacing, a situation often seen when mobile people become sedentary. According to Dickel, the ancient people may have chosen to exploit resources that involved heavy labor investment as their circumscribed valley became overcrowded.

A study of skeletal pathologies indicates considerable biological stress among the Central Valley Archaic people. Subsistence change did not result in better health for the people; in fact, data from early, middle, and late Archaic skeletons show that although acute stress decreased, chronic stress increased, presumably due to inadequate nutrition and disease. This pattern of change in health that accompanied the development of specialized collecting in central California is analogous to the changes seen in the shift from foraging to agriculture in other regions. Dickel and his colleagues

(1984) believe that the Archaic people may have been creating a new system in response to perceived health problems: they worked out a system to decrease the seasonal lack of food (acute stress), which may have been perceived as a cause of morbidity. They achieved resource stabilization but may not have perceived the costs of increased infant and maternal death, and the likelihood of overall higher mortality due to increased population density and disease.

One of the most important aspects of the female role in history is each woman's potential to reproduce. This is sometimes under the control of women themselves, but sometimes it is under the control of male relatives (or even the state). In addition, societies develop a variety of both conscious and unconscious mechanisms to control the fertility of women. This area of choice and policy is not only of personal concern but is one of the major dynamics of human history. Babies may translate into population growth, demographic pressure, competition for resources, conflict, techno-economic change, and sociopolitical evolution. In the California Archaic, individual women must have made decisions that resulted in a greater number of pregnancies: they decided to have sex sooner after a birth since they were more sedentary and no longer worried about carrying more than one small child; they chose to wean sooner onto acorn gruel, thereby increasing the probability of ovulation and pregnancy; they opted to keep a baby that more-mobile families might have let die. When mobility is decreased, energy demands on adult women decrease, which may allow them to keep up their fat levels, thus increasing fertility. More children may have been desirable to help with the labor-intensive activities involved in acorn and salmon processing. Relatively sedentary people often slacken the onerous controls on fertility normally practiced by mobile foragers. In this way, the decisions made by individual women or families had revolutionary consequences for history: higher fertility meant progressive subsistence change and contributed to persistent stress. Increased mortality in later Archaic periods may not have been obvious to the people because it was not directly tied to lack of food.

Cultural change in the Archaic surely involved negotiations between women and men as they chose new strategies that required innovative commitments of time, labor, and technology. We know from ethnographic descriptions that entire families cooperated in harvesting acorns in one season; that women took responsibility for processing acorns and building and managing storage facilities for that staple; and that men invested energy and time in salmon fishing. One underlying concern would be settlement location, which evolved with changing subsistence strategies. Women's interests and voices were surely heard because settlements and their locations needed to be tailored to acorn processing and storage as well as to hunting and fishing.

A number of interpretations of Archaic peoples in California have drawn attention to the importance of women's work in food production (not just reproduction) and to the role of women as actors in ancient cultures. In the Sierra Nevada, Late Archaic acorn-eating people were interpreted based on analogy with the ethnographically known Western Mono and other acorn-dependent Indians (Jackson 1991). Jackson showed that women's food production activity was the key factor in community decisions about subsistence behavior, social and economic relations, and settlement location. The late prehistoric Indians were characterized by a settlement system involving the creation of bedrock mortars and storage silos, which facilitated women's labor and production. Jackson suggests that the archaeological distribution of sites responded to women's social and resource needs. Within the big winter campsites, Jackson identifies groups of mortars around the houses and main midden area, where both men and women worked and left debris, and other mortars fifty meters away, interpreted as women's areas. This exclusive space may have been balanced by men's sweat lodges, which in the historic period were located a little distance from the main camp. In the summertime women may have dominated the small, high-altitude sites, where men may have spent less time. In these camps there were no isolated mortar facilities.

Jackson (1991) points out that historic period Western Mono people were matrilineal, a kind of social organization that confers benefits on women: they inherit rights and have substantial authority within their families. That granaries for acorn storage were the personal property of women in the historic period is evidence of their status and potential power, although men were in charge of exchange and intergroup relations and had access to surpluses generated by women.

Acorn-pounding facilities similar to the prehistoric ones were built by women in the historic period, and some have sacred and ceremonial connotations. Based on analogy it can be inferred that prehistoric groups of women spent long hours pounding acorns at sites located near water sources and stationary acorn storage facilities. These sites were very likely occupied during extended periods by matrifocal families, where a man lived with his wife and her relatives. In the historic period, women claimed rights not only to bedrock mortars and granaries but to certain trees and seed plots.

This interpretation of Archaic people draws attention to the importance

Women in Ancient America

of women's work, which produced the storable staple that sustained life for many ancient Californians. Jackson (1991) believes that the settlement system of the late prehistoric people, and perhaps their social organization, was determined by the requirements of women and their labor in acorn processing. This is a refreshing interpretation, since in most discussions of prehistoric groups men's hunting activities are given central importance. The development of new hunting technology (the bow and arrow replaced the spear thrower) was an important event in Archaic history, but so was the innovation of acorn-processing technologies, including the manufacture of bedrock mortars and the restructuring of settlement patterns.

The Shell Mound Archaic of Southeastern North America

In her studies of the end of the Shell Mound Archaic way of life, Claassen (1991) asked why shell fishing intensified during the Archaic Period and then disappeared. Her response focused on the activities of women and men and the meaning of those activities.

The Shell Mound Archaic is a cultural phenomenon restricted to tributaries of the Mississippi in the states of Alabama, Kentucky, Tennessee, West Virginia, and Illinois. Between 3500 and 1000 B.C., Archaic people, who left no evidence of permanent housing, created huge mounds of freshwater shells in which they buried humans and dogs. Human remains from these mounds showed no significant difference in health between the sexes, and while men, women, and children all had burial offerings, it is of special interest that more women than men were sprinkled with red ocher, and that ceremonial items such as medicine bags, turtle shell rattles, and flutes were found with women. Only men and children were accompanied by certain artifacts that some archaeologists think are indicative of high status.

Why did people build shell mounds in one period and then abandon the custom? Did shell fishing decline? Perhaps the weakest explanations are environmental: Claassen claims that viewing the human group as simply responsive to external change ignores the issue of human choice.

Claassen's (1991) understanding of the shell mounds grew out of a consideration of both gender and modern ethnographic cases. She argues that the elderly, infirm, and children made significant contributions to their own and their family's diet by shell fishing, although shell fishing may also have been undertaken by men for fishing bait. In ethnographic cases, shell fishing may or may not generate highly valued food, and mollusks may play a greater or lesser role in the diet.

According to Claassen's hypothesis, Archaic women allotted time for shell fishing as part of their regular schedules. She also guesses that the activity had some additional ideological or social significance. While some theorists imagine that people undertake activities such as shell fishing so as to maximize the use of their time and energy in the production of consumable energy, real people may engage in an activity because it carries prestige, because it provides social enjoyment, because it fits with child rearing, or because it allows one to realize spiritual goals.

The challenge for archaeologists is to explain the intentional creation of dense shell heaps along the tributaries of some rivers in the Midwest. One can imagine how the onset of warmer conditions and the relative sedentism of Archaic communities created a circumstance in which people, by repeated activity on the same spot, might erect mounds and create burial grounds in their traditional territories, but Claassen (1991) believes that this scenario accounts for the mounding effect only in part. Because the mounds contained high percentages of paired valves, the mollusks were probably steamed open, the meat removed, and the shells dumped on the mound. Claassen suggests that the women were harvesting mussels and drying the flesh for consumption in winter and spring. But the mounds were more than functional refuse heaps: they were thought of as ceremonial structures. In some of the mounds there are 1.2 burials per square meter, and it is significant that throughout ancient America shells frequently appear in burial contexts.

Claassen (1991) argues that the shell mound was the center of a ceremonial site, visited by large groups seasonally and preferred as a burial spot for a specific subset of community members, including many women who themselves may have been shell fishers, providers of storable protein, and perhaps religious specialists by virtue of an ideological system that associated shells with value, procreation, and death. Those buried were individuals active in reproductive and economic affairs of the aggregate social group, while others were interred in non–shell mound sites.

This interpretation sees shell fishing and shell mounding as both economic and religious activities important in women's lives. By the end of the period, the construction of shell mounds ceased; environmental change is not an adequate explanation for this change.

Some scholars hypothesize that dried shellfish meat, a storable resource, lost importance around 1000 B.C. because it was replaced by domesticated crops harvested in late summer and fall. Starchy seed horticulture, featuring chenopods, knotweed, maygrass, marsh elder, and sunflower, was growing in importance at this time. Claassen postulates that the old religious metaphors were mooted by new ideas associated with the cycle of planting, growing, and harvesting, and that the gourd replaced the shell as the most provocative fertility symbol. The daughters of important female religious specialists who had done symbolically important shell fishing and who were buried with red ocher in the mounds in the Archaic Period created metaphors more suitable to horticulture as the latter grew in importance. Claassen hypothesizes that the cause of the end of the Shell Mound Archaic may have been ideological. People decided to abandon the custom of mounding shells because the symbolism and metaphors no longer worked for them. Layers of dirt, instead of shells, were intentionally heaped on top of these mounds as they continued to serve as the residential and ritual foci of communities. People may have continued to eat mussels, but the shells were dumped in the river and lost. This interpretation is highly speculative, but it merits consideration because it models a complex social change and makes women and men active participants in cultural change.

Women's Diverse Roles

Evidence from the Archaic leads to a rejection of the stereotype that women have always done the same thing. There was a remarkable variation in women's and men's roles from the earliest epochs, as early foragers occupied every possible American environment from the Arctic to tropical forests. Evidence indicates that all adults worked hard and suffered frequently due to physical exertion, trauma, disease, and food shortages. Adults, including women, were skilled in crafts and had detailed knowledge of their natural environments, as do modern foragers. Cave paintings, figurines, and other materials hint at a rich religious life as well.

At Huaca Prieta, in coastal Peru, one burial suggests that an older woman had an important role (Bird and Hyslop 1985:70–74). Although very few people were accompanied by offerings, this woman held in her mouth the slightly chewed remains of plant material, including a flower used today in traditional healing. She also had two pouches: one of worn cattail fiber containing a gourd bottle and some plant remains, and another enclosing two gourd containers with carefully cut lids and pyroengraved decoration, objects unique in this site and unmatched in other preceramic sites in Peru. This ritual paraphernalia signals the elderly woman's status, perhaps achieved by virtue of her esoteric knowledge and talents in healing.

The Archaic way of life was enduring and admirable precisely because people were behaviorally flexible and innovative. A well-preserved archaeological record reveals that in every local history there was significant change as women and men separately and together sought to improve their conditions, minimize risk, compensate for exogenous factors, create new opportunities, or achieve less rigorous lifestyles.

Evidence from the Archaic Period also indicates relatively egalitarian conditions compared to later times. There is little concrete evidence of differentially ranked statuses for women and men, but surely female and male roles varied widely from group to group. The material culture of the Archaic is proof of the knowledge and skills of those ancient Americans, both women and men. In the Archaic, women and men produced admirable works, were buried with special offerings, and were valued members of their families and communities. Elderly women were often honored in death by the members of their communities.

Some scholars think that with growing sedentism female status may decline, or that with resource stress female status is low, but this is not a necessary pattern. In almost any context, women can negotiate spheres of control, such as in burial ceremonialism; or they can take advantage of family structures to call attention to their important roles and facilitate their exercise of authority; or they can develop productive activities and economic functions that give them influence. The rise of food production is an example of such an activity.

CHAPTER FOUR

Women and Food Production

Many prehistoric American societies made an economic transition from foraging to food production and, in some places, to intensive agriculture. As economies diversified, so did the roles and statuses of women and men (cf. Claassen and Joyce 1997). Archaeologists now have techniques to trace the development of plant and animal domestication, to investigate the changing patterns of health and disease of early cultivators, to evaluate demographic trends, and to discuss the development of more intensified strategies of resource exploitation that culminated in a variety of subsistence systems based on domesticated plants and a few animals.

In food-producing systems, people control the reproduction of the desired species. In contrast, foragers find and harvest resources produced by nature. Food-producing people invest their time, labor, and technology in manipulating plants and animals to achieve the features they want. Under some circumstances these strategies result in dramatic sociocultural changes.

There is no single cause of the food production "revolutions." Some humans, in some places, saw advantages in intensifying particular economic activities and, as a result of this, adopted more complex social arrangements. The period of development of this way of life, called the Neolithic in the Old World and the Formative in the New World, is characterized by the intensification of plant cultivation and animal husbandry, the development of crafts such as pottery-making and weaving, and the creation of larger trading networks and hierarchical social organizations.

People had many reasons for rescheduling their gathering and hunting activities and for increasing their labor investment in plant cultivation and animal husbandry. Some strived to increase the carrying capacity of the environment in order to cope with population growth or environmental degradation; others tried to minimize risk and to even out seasonal scarcity of desirable foods, or to increase production of storable food. Perhaps some women and men hoped to reduce group mobility or to increase the availability of food and raw materials (such as fiber) that could be used in trade; while still others wanted to produce surpluses that could be invested in social activities that improved individual and group viability, integration, or competitiveness. No matter what the motivations, the process of change involved both women and men working out solutions to technical and social problems.

The adoption of cultivation had a variety of social consequences and a great impact on human health. As people chose to dwell in nucleated settlements where they could take advantage of the high potential productivity of arable land, their health declined. High population density meant a dramatic increase in disease. Diarrhea and other infections and parasites, including tapeworms and pinworms, caused debilitation and prevented absorption of food, leading to malnutrition, anemia, and death. In the Southwest, dental and oral diseases were common among prehistoric agricultural people, and bones and teeth provide evidence of malnutrition that affected children and women during their childbearing years. Ancient Americans, who performed certain activities habitually, like grinding maize, were affected by tendinitis and permanent skeletal modifications including damage to their toes and ankles caused by long hours of work in a squatting position.

Developing Food Production

Food production was developed or adopted in response to localized problems in the foraging way of life. Researchers working in Mexico suggest that ancient people wished to stay together in larger social groups for longer periods each year. In order to support the enlarged group, people deliberately increased their emphasis on fewer gathered species and encouraged the proliferation of those species in convenient locations. Such activities would have destabilized the social and economic system, with differing consequences. While some mixed foraging and horticultural systems lasted for millennia, others lost stability as more intensive agricultural systems developed (cf. Flannery 1968, 1986). As women reduced their mobility they produced

Women in Ancient America

larger numbers of offspring who had to be fed. Some local groups grew and became land hungry, and their sociopolitical systems changed to cope with the management of social relations and economic tasks.

The type of food production called horticulture usually involved people using simple technology and hand labor to cultivate crops. The more labor-intensive form of food production, called agriculture, was often based on staple grain or root crops. People invested in elaborate technologies including irrigation and engineered landscapes for both types of food production.

In eastern North America, early indigenous food production was based on gourds, sunflower seeds, and other seedy and weedy plants. Late in prehistory, people acquired maize as well. In highland Mexico, agriculture was based on maize, beans, squash, fruit, and dogs, supplemented by gathered protein resources such as rabbits, birds, insect eggs, and fish. In the Andean highlands, people depended on potatoes and other tubers and roots; grains, especially quinoa and amaranths; indigenous fruits; and, ultimately, maize, combined with meat from domestic camelids, guinea pigs, and ducks. In the moist tropics, the basic foods were (and are) manioc, maize, beans, and fruit. American agricultural systems differed from those of Eurasia in that domestic animals were of lesser importance, there being few wild animal species appropriate for domestication. The exception is in the Andes, where llamas were bred selectively as pack-bearing animals and alpacas for their hair. Virtually all people had dogs, but otherwise animal food was obtained by fishing, gathering, or hunting, and portage was accomplished on the backs of humans, with watercraft, or, rarely, with dog-pulled travois.

Female Autonomy and Status

Feminist archaeology is interested in the proposition that women lost status as the Formative Period began. It has been observed, and widely quoted, that in Africa !Kung San women lost status when they became less mobile (Lee 1976). This probably did not happen in ancient America, because women's roles as providers would not have diminished with sedentism. The !Kung San may not be an appropriate analogue for modeling change in early America (or elsewhere) because those San who settled down entered systems dominated by other cultures. In these systems there was no place for traditional subsistence activities; women lost control of production and became dependent on men. Moreover, Christian missionaries, government bureaucrats, and non-San farmers were governed by religious and legal ideologies concerning the proper place of women and their activities. These ideologies, which were damaging to !Kung San women, did not exist in ancient America.

An impediment to understanding the status of early female farmers is our tendency not to recognize that women in horticultural societies frequently have spheres of activity in which they are considered fully adult, where they exercise autonomy and control, and where they can achieve high status via their performance in positions of leadership. High female status in the prehistoric record may be difficult for scholars to recognize because Western observers are culturally programmed to value only male activities and symbols of male status, whereas in many cultures an individual may attain high status through female roles, not solely through roles open to men. Furthermore, people who share in the Euroamerican cultural adaptation have become so accustomed to stratification and hierarchy that they imagine it natural to the human condition. They habitually create dualistic, ranked categories. But there are more than two possibilities in the real world. While there are many cases of domination by fathers, husbands, and brothers, it is also true that men are not necessarily or always dominant or predominant. Many societies are successfully structured around differentiated roles that are conceived as equal, contrasting, and complementary. Discussions of the comparative status of women and men in ancient American society may be unproductive because women and men did not necessarily participate in the same activities or compete for the same positions. In modern times, some feminists struggle for women to be just like men, but it is inappropriate to think that that was the case in the past. In many ancient Native American societies, the interdependence of women and men was fostered, gender complementarity was promoted by ideologies, and collaboration was enforced by division of labor.

In the transition from foraging to food production in America, the activities and relations of women and men were changed. One process of social transformation was specialization. Economic specialization in many ancient systems developed in tandem with new food-producing strategies and other productive activities, as well as with human concentration in large settlements. The specialization of tasks in human groups means that goods and other services are produced by one individual or family and exchanged for goods and services produced by other units. In this way women and men embrace different strategies and functions as specialists integrated at the family level.

The Formative way of life was characterized by developing specializations based on gender, age, and other social dimensions, resulting in a more complex division of labor that became a prominent feature of economic organization in later prehistory. Formative cemeteries demonstrate social complexity and dimensions of social differences unknown in earlier times. The location of graves, the form of graves, the treatment of the bodies, and the burial furniture indicate that individuals were differentiated by sex, age, occupation, rank, and membership in diverse groups, including kin groups.

Specialization and the greater size of some communities in the Formative created problems of organization and integration. In order for all the disparate elements of complex societies to work together, people tried many kinds of governing mechanisms: some people formed egalitarian organizations, others created hierarchical governments, and still others developed organizations with a mix of features—sometimes called heterarchy. The development of social complexity was the result of women and men who created new opportunities for themselves.

Farmers in Eastern North America

The history of food production in the Eastern Woodlands of North America has been traced through several Archaic phases, followed by three Woodland periods, characterized by pottery and change in most aspects of sociocultural adaptation. Native North American cultivation began with crops that flourished in the rich, disturbed soils around human habitations. Weedy domesticates provided containers and food and, combined with the wild resources of wetlands, made the stable occupation of base camps possible. In these camps women could conveniently shorten birth intervals, resulting in population growth.

Some researchers have suggested that domestication happened opportunistically ("naturally") as plants, animals, and humans became accustomed to each other. The weakness of this scenario is that it eliminates the need for innovators and maintains the presumed passivity of females. Watson and Kennedy (1991) developed a model that builds on the association of Native American women and plants and rejects the scholarly bias that associates women with passivity and males with activity. In their model, adult women specialized in harvesting wild plants. Because they possessed extensive botanical knowledge, they intentionally worked to improve seed size and increase the availability of desirable plants outside the area of their natural distribution. Late Archaic sites supply abundant evidence, including coprolites preserved in caves, that people were increasingly sedentary and consumed larger quantities of plants, cultivated and intensively gathered from preferred habitats near settlements.

For thousands of years this subsistence system was adequate to support some ceremonial activity. In the Middle Archaic Period along the Illinois River, people built bluff-crest earthen structures, apparently as foci for community celebrations. Cassidy (1987) describes what life was like based on burials associated with the earthen platforms: both female and male skeletons exhibited evidence of stress due to heavy work and they showed similar pathologies, including the telltale signs of periodic hunger. Despite this apparent similarity in experience, females had lower life expectancies than males at every age. By the end of the Archaic, there is osteological evidence for more differentiated gender roles: men spent more time hunting deer and women apparently spent less time gathering in the forest and dedicated more energy to tending their gardens. When pottery was integrated into social life, its manufacture, if we can judge by historic peoples, was women's work.

Subsequently, in the Early and Middle Woodland periods in the Ohio and Illinois Valleys, people lived in autonomous villages but had wide trading networks and buried some individuals under earthen platforms in elaborate tombs with offerings. This community activity, which produced the decorated artifacts diagnostic of the Adena and Hopewell mortuary cults, is evidence of growing social complexity. Adena people invented elaborate mortuary rituals and committed significant seasonal labor to building tombs and moving tons of earth to construct platforms. Children were favored with more burial goods indicative of special status, and Adena communities often buried males in central positions in the platforms, some with log tomb chambers, suggesting their roles as leaders. Adena and Hopewell art and burials indicate religious activities in which men evidently were prominent actors.

Cassidy (1987) reports that in the Ohio Valley of Kentucky, males were buried in artificial platforms and women and children in caves, showing a more pronounced differentiation of social roles than in the preceding Archaic Period. If this were the only evidence taken into consideration, one might conclude that men dominated in these communities, but such an interpretation rests on our evaluation of the two styles of burial. Cave burial may have been desirable for women for symbolic reasons. The burial data indicate that female health was slightly better than that of males and there were many healthy adults over thirty. The fact that people were mobile, occupying villages only seasonally, may have contributed to their good health.

The ceramics that marked the beginning of the Woodland Period signaled new customs in food processing, eating, and feasting. By the Middle Woodland Period, 150 B.C. to A.D. 400, ceramic vessels were part of the increasingly elaborate mortuary ceremonialism. If women made and decorated the pots, then these can be taken as evidence of female participation in the focal ceremonial activities of Woodland society.

In the Middle Woodland phase, a more pronounced sexual division of labor constituted an effective kind of specialization: women worked harder than before, cultivating crops, supporting community rituals and trade, and making pottery (Claassen 2002). Bioarchaeological evidence from this period shows more muscular women, and Claassen suggested that child labor was mobilized to allay women's increased workload. While fertility increased in this period, the substitute of child caregivers for mothers may have caused higher childhood mortality.

In the Midwest, the Adena and Hopewell mortuary complexes are examples of cultural elaboration involving wide trading networks and extraordinary art. In all areas, males were buried in or under earthen platforms with more frequency than females, and, where comparative data exist, the males in platform burials tended to be larger than males buried in other contexts. But there is no clear picture of female subordination: women from presumed elite tombs showed little difference in health profiles from nonelite women, and in one case, a young woman and man were buried together under a platform at the Hopewell site with a tremendously rich array of exotic and precious items, including copper ear spools (Seeman 1979).

Adena and Hopewell mortuary behavior may have had many social functions. In one interpretation of charnel house rituals, Seeman (1979) suggested that feasting with the dead stimulated hunting activity and achieved a wider distribution of foodstuffs, particularly meat supplied by male hunters. Hopewell women must have supported and encouraged this ceremonialism because it benefited them and their children. This interpretation is supported by the analysis of strontium in human bones, which shows little difference in male and female diets at this time. Evidence of increasing warfare in the Woodland phases and some worsening of childhood health suggests that people were competing for scarce resources, so perhaps potential warriors and war leaders were defined as especially important members of society and they received exotic burial offerings that archaeologists interpret as valuables. In the Midwest this burial focus on male elites disappeared between A.D. 400 and 500.

Endemic syphilis appeared by the Middle Woodland Period, affecting both women and men. The overall prevalence of syphilis was about 50 percent during this time, considerably greater than in Archaic times, and must have affected health and fertility substantially. With the expansion of long-distance travel and trade, diseases like syphilis became widespread. Exchange may have been an integral part of family economic activity, so that family members had roles in both production and trade. In historic times in lowland South America, women and men developed part-time craft specialization in order to participate in exchange relationships. Perhaps some women were traders themselves or joined male family members on expeditions, as in ancient Mesoamerica. While in ethnographic cases it is usually men who participate in ceremonial exchange and create economic and social networks that benefit the whole group, women often engage in the utilitarian exchange of domestic surpluses, adding an important flexibility to family economy. Both ceremonial exchange that stimulated nonaggressive male interaction and utilitarian trade that satisfied practical needs were very important.

DeBoer (2001) proposes an interesting hypothesis concerning women and "trade" in native North America. Researchers have noticed that weapons and utilitarian implements tend to be associated with male burials, while ornaments of shell and bone are found in women's graves. This has been ascribed to women displaying objects given to them by males; in other words, the woman is an object of display and status for the male, who presumably is the one involved in trade and other extramural activities. However, DeBoer reminds us that gambling with dice is associated with women throughout North America and is a part of Native American lifeways. Women generally socialized with other women while gossiping, and they gambled, which often involved the jewelry of the loser. In this way, objects could travel very speedily across space. Members of the Lewis and Clark expedition observed iron axes, forged fourteen months before at Fort Mandan, that had moved over a thousand miles along the trade networks linking the people of the Middle Missouri and the Nez Perce of Idaho. Gambling may have been the mechanism of diffusion: someone always loses at dice (216). DeBoer suggests that the appearance of "foreign" ornaments in female burials should be considered the result of women gambling successfully, arguing that ornaments are not gifts from men but rather a woman's own display of prowess and luck.

During Middle Woodland times in the Lower Illinois Valley, people showed gains in nutrition and health compared to Late Archaic people, and there was no significant difference in bone strontium between females and males, suggesting that their diets were similar. By Late Woodland times, male and female activities had changed. Males were eating more meat, perhaps because organ meat was consumed from animals killed away from home or perhaps due to ideologies about appropriate food for making men warriors. Competition for deer hunting territories is likely since the faunal evidence shows a decline in deer consumption and a relative increase in the use of fish and mussels. At the same time, women began to show more robust bones and muscles, a trend that continued into Mississippian times. However, women were shorter in stature relative to males than they had been earlier. This indicates an ever-greater participation of women in cultivation and suggests that they were fed poorly in their growing years. By the time of first European contact, virtually all agriculture was done by Native American women. Men hunted, made war, and traded while women farmed, thus facilitating, and indeed underwriting, all the rest (Buikstra 1984).

Despite the Victorian dictum that ladies should not sweat, most human societies assign grueling, laborious tasks to both sexes. In many places, women are thought to be as appropriate as men for carrying large loads, and some female skulls show grooved foreheads from habitual use of a tumpline to move heavy loads (fig. 4.1). In fact, burdening women with hard physical labor is an excellent birth-control strategy, more effective than moral restraint.

Figure 4.1. A Casas Grandes vessel demonstrates how prehistoric women used a tumpline to bear a burden basket and suggests the longevity of a certain posture: the woman sits with her legs straight in front of her, as do traditional modern Puebloan women. Courtesy of the Witte Museum, San Antonio, Texas.

Maize was present in the Eastern Woodlands by 1800 B.C. but it became significant only much later, when the Northern Flint variety was developed. Its spread after A.D. 800 must have been the result of the purposeful investment of skill and knowledge in agricultural experimentation and selective breeding that resulted in a species that became the staff of life for eastern Indians. This crop was the basis for the development of chiefdoms along the Mississippi, and it was the ancestor of modern hybrid corn. In the view of Watson and Kennedy (1991), women developed this revolutionary agricultural technology. After A.D. 800, in the Late Woodland and Mississippian phases, maize became progressively more important in diets and there was rapid cultural change and growth in some settlements. That women were farmers is shown in their skeletons, which present more arthritis of the left arm and spine than do those of earlier Woodland females. Maize necessitates much more hoeing and other hard labor than earlier indigenous cultivars. The maize-based diet brought worsening childhood health, probably due to the less healthy village environments. Human crowding and competition is indicated by evidence of Late Woodland and Mississippian warfare (Milner et al. 1991). The result of the progressive development of agricultural systems was that the late Mississippian Period people did not suffer from nutritional diseases or seasonal stress, but Cook (1984) argues that disease load, the result of infections common when people congregate without adequate sanitation, affected them negatively.

The major health problem of Mississippian times was tuberculosis—a disease exported directly along trade routes into interior America. The founding of Cahokia, the only major urban center in aboriginal North America, brought a large enough population together, in crowded and unsanitary conditions, to support this disease. Cahokia's population is estimated at between 25,000 and 50,000 by A.D. 1200. Without clean drinking water and controlled sewage removal, even well-fed people were vulnerable to disease.

Female size and nutritional status fluctuated in later prehistory. Along the Georgia coast, where neither agriculture nor foraging was physically demanding, the skeletons of the late prehistoric population show a reduction in body size, robustness, and mechanical stress. But in many regions, from Middle Woodland through Mississippian times, females exhibit a progressive increase in the development of the deltoid tuberosity (where the main shoulder muscle is attached to the bone that affects arm abduction). Bridges (1991) found that some Mississippian female skeletons show increases in personal strength indicative of a major increase in workloads. This increased strength of women's arms and legs was due to agricultural work and to other chores like pounding corn, carrying water, and making pottery. Male skeletons showed little evidence of change in activity after the Archaic.

As human groups proliferated and grew in size, emphasis was placed on resources that were dependable, easily stored, and nearby (Buikstra et al. 1986). The Mississippian subsistence strategy at some sites focused on riverine bounty and agriculture, while deemphasizing deer and nut crops. At great cost to female maize farmers, the community sought to avoid seasonal shortages, but health was compromised as dental disease increased due to a sticky carbohydrate staple and as people coped with infections and epidemic diseases.

What explains the increasing investment of labor on the part of female farmers, the exaggeration of the gender-based division of labor, and the dramatic differential health status among Mississippian people? Aristocrats pressured people to work to feed a larger population and to contribute to expensive sociopolitical activities, such as supporting elites, importing elite symbols, and building giant earthen platform complexes. Contact with Mesoamerica and new ideas concerning ceremonialism and tribute may have been a part of this major shift in agricultural emphasis. Communities were seeking ways to compete with their neighbors for what must have been perceived as limited resources, and women and men were rendering portions of their production to the elite while also producing surplus to negotiate alliances, marriages, and peace accords.

One can imagine serious-faced elder women in villages and towns making the decision to commit more labor to the production of larger surpluses of food. They discuss the importance of supporting men in their travels and trade, which bring the benefits of foreign alliances; they speak of the necessity of engaging in warfare and undertaking religious activities to ensure community well-being. The advantage of food production is that, compared to gathering, it can be more effectively expanded through technological innovation and intensification of labor investment. The women making decisions about food production would have been aware of the costs to themselves, but they probably did not have much choice because of the needs of their extended families and the tribute payments owed to elites in chiefly centers.

The decision to intensify maize production 1,000 years ago had a tremendous effect on women's work and women's health (fig. 4.2). It also may have affected women's status, which, by the time of first European contact, was definitely subordinate to that of males in most of the horticultural societies of the eastern United States. Nevertheless, women's efforts in domestication

Figure 4.2. A sixteenth-century woodcut shows Native American women processing corn: one grinds with a metate, another prepares tortillas on a griddle, and a third wraps tamales in leaves. Drawing after Girolamo Benzoni, *La Historia del Mondo Nuovo, Libro Primo*, "Modo di fare il pane," 1572. Ad instante di Pietro & Francisco Tini, fratelli (In Venetia, Appresso gli heredi di Giovan María Bonelli).

and in improving maize varieties made possible the development of complex societies characterized by hierarchy, urban settlements, long-distance trade, ceremonialism, and warfare. In some regions these developments affected the average overworked, poorly nourished woman negatively. These stresses, however, were nonfatal and populations grew, at least in part as the result of decisions made by women.

The Hardin Village site of Fort Ancient shows how increased commitment to maize may have led to an unbalanced diet that affected women. Skeletal evidence demonstrates that osteoporosis and cribra orbitalia were most frequent in children under the age of six and in women in their thirties. This is a sign of iron deficiency anemia, the result of weaning children onto iron-poor gruel. In adult women it is caused by insufficient nutrients. Women who got their calories from carbohydrates, and who consumed less protein than men, showed growing rates of dental caries and infections. At the Averbuch site in Tennessee, tuberculosis and anemia resulted in elevated mortality among young adults of both sexes. Life expectancy for females at birth was only about fifteen years, and about seventeen for males. The early loss of important working and reproducing segments of the population would have compromised the defense, agricultural productivity, and reproduction of the group (Buikstra et al. 1986).

An interesting aspect of women's health in ancient Georgia is that females show a growing incidence of periosteal reactions in the bone, indicative of major, but nonfatal, infections (Larsen 1984; Larsen and Ruff 1991). Earlier in prehistory such lesions had a roughly equal occurrence in females and males and were observed on various parts of the body. Here, however, the lesions were concentrated on the lower limbs of adult women. In horticultural activities the lower legs are prone to injury. In a situation where women were doing most of the farming, and especially if they were fertilizing the fields with night soil, they would have been exposed to a greater variety of pathogens than people whose exposure to human feces was more limited.

Another growing aspect of ill health that increased women's discomfort and lessened their capacity for labor was osteoarthritis. In much of the southeastern United States the incidence of this wear-related disease increased among women, but not among men, again suggesting an increase in the time women spent in laborious chores.

The intensification of maize agriculture in late prehistory had considerable effects on women's lives. In the eastern United States women increased their investment of labor in cultivation, food preparation, and food transport. In contrast, the roles of men changed less from the Archaic to the late prehistoric, and male skeletons record less variation from period to period, although the bow and arrow replaced the spear thrower in Mississippian times, causing increased arthritis in men's left elbows (Powell 1988).

Farmers of the North American Southwest

Southwestern North America was an arid land of unreliable rainfall. The Archaic adaptation in this area was diversified gathering and hunting, with manipulation of wild plant populations through burning, pruning, and other interventions normally associated with cultivation. Peoples of the Southwest and northern Mexico added domesticated species to their subsistence programs in the second millennium B.C. as they adopted what is called "casual agriculture": mixing foraging and horticulture in a low-effort manner in order to subsist while maintaining their traditional seasonal movements and other ecological and social relationships (Minnis 1984, 1985).

In the ethnographic literature of the Southwest, women are associated with agriculture and it is very likely they were involved in the initial decision to undertake cultivation. Factors that motivated their efforts might have included competition between local populations for wild food or a decrease in wild food resources due to environmental causes. Alternatively, early people may not have experienced great want but may have seen an opportunity to control the timing of food collection and to increase yields, predictability, and storability. Surely ancient kinswomen discussed the relative merits of foraging for wild species and experimenting with the domesticated species already used by Mesoamericans to the south. Some women from families with many potential workers may have favored the investment of labor in planting, tending, harvesting, and storing because it meant more security and flexibility for their families. As some individuals or families tried out the new technology for personal reasons, their modest successes were observed by kin who repeated the experiment if they recognized a good return for labor invested, or appreciated the value of an additional storable surplus.

The first experiments probably gave minor advantages to families who continued traditional activities as well. In the wake of this earliest cultivation, male family members may have been willing to alter their seasonal movements because of the potential of storable surpluses to underwrite trade, feasts, and ceremonial activities. The new cultivation efforts may have appeared desirable to older people who were stressed by changing camps, and they may have been attractive to women who sought to produce more palatable food or seeds that could be stored against the season of scarcity that was so hard on small children. Cultivation did not result in decreasing workloads.

In the first millennium B.C., the casual cultivation of crops of Mesoamerican origin, like maize, squash, and beans, fit into the production system because people already manipulated wild plant resources and were already familiar with cooking and eating wild grasses, legumes, and wild native squashes. Ethnographic evidence shows that small-scale plant cultivation does not alter patterns of mobility among foragers. Gardens may have been planted in the spring and tended for a while and then left until harvest time, as among the historic Western Apache. Men could have been drawn into agriculture because of the need for labor at the time of field preparation and planting and again at harvest time.

Women and men surely negotiated the investment of labor, the timing of work, and the amount of labor required. We imagine that the need for labor at planting time corresponded well to a period when wild resources would not demand much effort, that harvest times were flexible, and that families may have assigned the task of guarding the fields to less mobile individuals.

In the first centuries A.D., people living in stable, autonomous pit house villages adopted pottery-making and more food-processing chores. It is almost certain that the spectacular pottery of the ancient Southwest was made by women. Crown and Wills (1995) argue that women were motivated to undertake ceramics when, with greater dependence on cultigens, the scheduling demands of foraging, horticulture, and food processing increased. One way women cope with workload conflicts is early weaning. Worldwide, women who contribute to subsistence by cultivating plants introduce solid foods to their infants early. Grinding cultivated seeds and boiling these in water in ceramic vessels facilitates weaning. Giving an infant gruel for lunch allows a woman greater mobility and relieves the stress of producing milk. Because ovulation resumes when nursing lessens, early weaning has the unintended consequence of shortening the average birth interval and spurring demographic growth.

Women's activities, technologies, and choices have far-reaching cultural consequences. For example, ceramic production itself created new opportunities: pottery not only serves for mundane purposes but is often a vehicle of religious and social expression that can figure in gender negotiations.

Crown and Wills (1995) also hypothesize that as women began making pottery in the Southwest a new race of maize, more productive and more suitable for grinding, was adopted, further encouraging cooking innovations. Dry mature corn stores well and makes nutritious stews and soups. The use of large pots for cooking maize may reflect changes in the way food was distributed in the extended family group: it may have favored a more equitable distribution of meat, giving women and children access to stews containing a variety of ingredients. Boiling animal bones as a soup base may have made more fats available to the entire family.

The transition to greater maize dependency was delayed in the Mogollon Highlands, where people continued to be relatively mobile foragers and horticulturalists until after A.D. 650, the date of the adoption of a new, highly productive race of corn. In Diehl's (1996) interpretation, Mogollon people consumed increasing amounts of this maize even though it required more time to process and probably created scheduling conflicts. Because of time constraints for women, new grinding technology was adopted in the form of the Mexican trough metate with a two-handed mano. These arti-facts demanded greater energy expenditure and caused more fatigue for women, who could not shift the position of their arms and bodies to reduce muscle stress. Nevertheless, they were more efficient grinding tools than those used previously and scholars argue that women adopted the mano and metate in order to save time while maintaining nutritional yields (Merbs and Vestergaard 1985). Diehl (1996) argues that as a result of this technology, maize consumption increased in the Mogollon area, and this correlated with changing family organization, new kinds of settlements and land use, and increased trade.

Initially, food production and the new cuisine moderated seasonal scar-city in the food supply; gradually cultivation provided increased storable surpluses and better yields as well. The fact that maize became so highly integrated into the religions of later Southwestern peoples, with the devel-opment of Corn Mothers and other female spirits functioning as land givers and mediators of fertility, clearly shows that maize was critical in assuring community well-being.

After hundreds of years of mixed economy and casual horticulture, labor-intensive agriculture became the mainstay of many peoples in the Southwest. By A.D. 1000 women's contribution to subsistence had increased, populations had increased, and more cooking technologies had been devel-oped, such as griddles and stones for baking *piki* (flat) bread. Female skele-tons show kneeling facets on their bones caused by hours of grinding. They also show evidence of habitual hyperextension of the neck, due to the use of a tumpline across the forehead to support heavy burdens (Minnis 1985). Male bones show left arm degeneration at the elbow, probably related to bow and arrow use.

Despite the pronounced division of labor and the adoption of intensive agriculture, people continued to suffer from nutritional stress (Spielmann 1995). The analysis of human skeletons in the Southwest shows evidence of persistent malnutrition, although recent modeling has suggested that the disease load caused by crowding in nucleated settlements was as important a factor as actual protein-calorie malnutrition. Women, children, and the elderly, who spent more time at home and who had less access to meat, were at greater risk than males (Minnis 1985).

The extreme emphasis on corn (maize) in the Southwest in later prehistory had other implications for prehistoric women. Corn processing in this region was women's specialty, as shown by the modifications observed on female skeletons. Women and girls spent at least three hours a day grinding corn at special grinding bins, in sickness and health, throughout life (McGuire 1992). Spielmann (1995) argues that through time there were changes in the location of bins. Data show that in the early phases of intensive agriculture, groups of bins were located in interior household settings, whereas after A.D. 1300 single bins were moved to outdoor locations in plazas and on rooftops. This shift came at the same time that mealing bins disappeared from ritual locations in kivas. Male loom weaving was characteristic of the later kivas (known ethnographically), suggesting that men had appropriated the communal ritual space within kivas. Women may have responded by moving their work into more public areas in order to maintain visual and auditory contact with neighbors and access to news in the pueblo (Spielmann 1995:97).

In Arizona the Hohokam were intensive agriculturalists who developed an elaborate material culture, traded, and built irrigation systems and earthen ceremonial platforms. McGuire's (1992:148–149) analyses of early Hohokam burials at the village of La Ciudad show that there was considerable diversity and inequality in the grave lots. Households within the kin group varied in size and were probably ranked. If the burial offerings were made by the people gathered for the funeral ceremonies, one can understand why adult males were associated with more artifacts than adult women: the number of offerings may be indicative of the wider social contacts of men. Curiously, teenagers attracted the most offerings, perhaps reflecting the importance of young adult labor. McGuire identified household leaders as those individuals having hairpins, turquoise, and turtle shell in their cremations. These leaders were predominantly male, but one cremated individual with a hairpin was a female, suggesting the possibility that women might also have been household heads, as they sometimes are in ethnographic cases (154).

A study of 132 later burials from two Classic Period Hohokam village cemeteries showed that people were buried together with their kin in extended family or local lineage groups (Mitchell 1991). Most Hohokam people lived in villages organized and regulated by kinship, but the whole village was integrated into a hierarchical political system; thus the full range of ranks and statuses would be apparent only in studying all the constituent settlements and cemeteries. Evidently, among the people in the villages, there were also a few specialists and traders who participated in a variety of task groups and secular and nonsecular associations.

Some individual roles appear to be shown by grave goods. In Mitchell's (1991) study of mortuary offerings, burial associations were taken to indicate each person's functional role and social status, including power and wealth. Some individuals showed greater social position, in the sense that they may have had more duties and rights with respect to a wider number of people during their lives, and these are reflected in their burial furnishings. At the Grand Canal site, both adult men and women were buried in family plots. Subadults had fewer grave goods on the whole and adults were commonly associated with sex-specific items. The adult females were accompanied by an average of 4.8 vessels; subadults had an average of 4.1; while males had an average of 3.4. Only women were buried with more than 10 vessels each, and female burials were more likely to contain jars (42 percent compared to 26 percent for males). There was no significant difference in the occurrence of ornaments between adult females and males (46 percent of the males versus 36 percent of the females), but males had a greater number of ornaments, including marine shell and stone pendants, and subadults at Grand Canal were more likely to have ornaments than adults. It is regrettable that poor preservation has prevented an evaluation of the quantity and quality of textiles associated with women. In this case, relatively egalitarian gender relations are implied: neither the large number of vessels associated with women nor the greater number of ornaments associated with men can be construed as evidence of ranked statuses in this family context.

At the Casa Buena site, 70 percent of adult male tombs contained ornaments, compared to only 47 percent of the female burials, and several categories of ornaments, shell artifacts, stone pendants, and bone hairpins were associated almost exclusively with adult males; males also got more of what the excavators decided were "ritual artifacts." Males were commonly associated with arrow points, axes, and abraders, while spindle whorls and food-processing tools such as manos and pestles were associated with adult women (Mitchell 1991:115). These items may be ritually significant; spindles appear in the costumes of Mesoamerican deities, and grinding stones were often used in ceremonial contexts and elevated as "art-tools" (M. Graham 1992:165–206).

In these communities of food-producing people, women and men were identified with their separate work. The funerary rituals reconstructed at these two villages appear egalitarian, but the contents of the tombs suggest both gender complementarity and significant social differentiation and inequality. At Hohokam sites studied by Mitchell (1991:122–123), privileged individuals were buried in special areas, sometimes near platforms; at other sites highly ranked individuals were observed in only a few family plots, suggesting that economic and social wealth was concentrated in some kin groups and not others. A few unusual burial assemblages probably correspond to village headmen who had prominent social positions in ritual and secular contexts within and beyond the village. Most of the burials containing exotic items, including polychrome pottery, were those of males. This indicates that at least some of the best products of women's work were circulated to men for use in public ceremonies. Overall, Hohokam burial patterns show that although the standard of living was high for almost everyone, an individual's experience in society would have varied depending on the rank of her family.

At Grasshopper Pueblo, an autonomous Mogollon village occupied from A.D. 1275 to 1400, women and men had different experiences in society as stress increased. These people apparently tried various strategies to maintain their standard of living and health, all of which failed. According to Ezzo (1993), men ate mainly meat and maize in the early phase of the settlement of Grasshopper, while women consumed more wild plants. Men's access to meat and maize has been interpreted as a marker of high status, and this observation is supported by evidence that the men who died early in the history of the settlement were afforded more elaborate grave goods than women.

As time passed, male diet changed little, but female diet shifted dramatically to maize. Everyone ate fewer wild foods. A study of kin groups within the village showed that families consumed agricultural products and wild plants in different proportions, so that women's activities would have varied from household to household. Skeletal analysis revealed that later in time everyone in the village experienced reduced meat intake, probably reflecting environmental degradation and overhunting.

Ezzo's (1993) information from Grasshopper indicates a pattern of high infant and child mortality, a high load of pathology in both teeth and post-cranial bones, high rates of deficiency diseases, and low life expectancy with increasing stress through time (Berry 1985:59). Although some archaeologists suggest that males enjoyed preferred status at Grasshopper, the data show a life expectancy of about thirty-eight years for both females and males. One intriguing fact about Grasshopper is that female skeletons are disproportionately represented in the remains. Where were the men buried? It is possible that women maintained their domiciles in the pueblo, while men spent a considerable portion of the year away from Grasshopper, returning during the ceremonial round (57). This is a known pattern in the Southwest and may have been a strategy that reduced male demands on limited carbohydrate foods stored in pueblos. Male absence also meant that women and children did not benefit as much from hunted food, although females probably had direct access to rodent meat.

Because Grasshopper was an autonomous village, problem solving was probably undertaken at the local level, and frequently by households. Among the responses to stress were a reduction in household size, a decrease in expenditure in burial furniture, and a progressive loss of differences between the burials of males and females. Household autonomy might have given women a degree of flexibility and might explain why some kin groups did more foraging for wild species than others. One persistent question is whether poor female health was due to women's lack of power in a system biased against them or to other circumstances. Scholars believe that poor health was due to stress caused by crowding, to the rapid transmission of infectious diseases, and to resource depletion and protein-calorie malnutrition, all combining to reduce the life span of the people of Grasshopper Pueblo (Berry 1985:62).

At Grasshopper these combined strategies adopted by women and men to confront the obvious problems failed: environmental conditions became intolerable and throughout the region settlements were abandoned as some families sought new places to farm while others reverted to older foraging patterns.

Early Farmers in Coastal Ecuador

The development of food production took a different path in coastal Ecuador, where the Las Vegas preceramic horticulturalists were succeeded by the Early Formative Valdivia people (4000–1500 B.C.). The Valdivians lived in permanent villages; they were among the earliest ceramics makers and built some of the earliest ceremonial structures in the New World (Lathrap et al. 1977; Raymond 2003). They allocated more labor to cultivation and to fishing than the preceramic people. Valdivia women may have tended gardens along the floodplains of small rivers, hauled water and wood, collected shellfish, fished with their families, stored and processed foods, and produced cotton textiles and ceramics for daily and ceremonial use. In coastal villages, men may have fished and produced equipment like cotton nets, while using surplus production to create alliances and participate in exchange. Men living in up-valley villages hunted and may have collected forest products, cooperated in agricultural activities, maintained exchange networks, and manufactured artifacts of wood, stone, and shell for ceremonial use. Women and men participated in religious activities. Over time, population growth suggests the success of this way of life, and the size and number of villages grew in coastal Ecuador. The development of ceramics suggests that community cooperation and integration were fostered by ceremonial eating and drinking as people constructed larger and more complex social and economic networks.

Archaeologists envision a degree of specialization by household or by village. Every family grew its own food and harvested wild resources, but some villages may have specialized in fishing, exchanging their catch for agricultural products, raw materials, or craft items. Other villages may have invested additional labor in producing squash, beans, root crops, peppers, fruits, maize, and cotton or salt for exchange (Pearsall 1988, 2003; Chandler-Ezell et al. 2006). There is evidence that some households may have produced pottery, shell ornaments, and textiles in excess of domestic needs (Zeidler 1984).

In later Valdivia times, some people lived in dispersed settlements, but they practiced rituals that took place at village centers on platforms designed for communal ceremonies (and perhaps elite activities), showing that people were actively involved in a complex web of responsibilities and privileges that developed along with differentiated economic systems and intensified production (Staller 2001).

The site of Real Alto has two ceremonial structures on earthen platforms (Lathrap et al. 1977; Marcos 1988). One, the Fiesta House, gets its name from the broken vessels found there, perhaps the remains of celebrations involving beer drinking. The other, the Charnel House, is characterized by unusual burials and ceramic figurines representing females.

The Charnel House contained burials from Valdivia Phase 3 (2800–2600 B.C.). A female about thirty-five years old was buried beneath the portal in a tomb lined with grinding stones. Nearby were found the remains of two adult males and six subadults, probably members of her family (Zeidler 1984, 2000). The woman's unusual offerings indicate that she was a special person whose role involved grinding, cooking, or brewing. Real Alto shows that some adults and children merited burial in a special central structure, while others were buried in and around their houses (Zeidler 2000; Raymond 2003).

Village life and the development of dependence on horticulture had important health consequences for the Valdivians. One hundred and one skeletons from Real Alto show that life expectancy at birth was twenty-four years, lower than that in the Las Vegas Preceramic Period, but higher than that calculated for later peoples (Ubelaker 2003). The Valdivia life expectancy at the age of fifteen (after childhood risk was passed) was the lowest of all Ecuadorian populations that have been studied: the mean age at death for males was 38.7 years, for women 32.3 years. Compared to earlier people from the same region, Valdivia skeletons showed higher incidences of infection and trauma, including cases of interpersonal violence, along with high frequencies of dental hypoplasia, caries, and abscesses. Females lost more teeth than males but had no severe anemia.

Valdivia skeletal remains show the expected effects of incipient food production, increased sedentism, greater population density, and changing diet (Ubelaker 2003). The interpersonal violence among the Valdivians may have resulted from intergroup conflict over territory or intracommunity or domestic violence. The data do not suggest that men and women had very different life experiences of the kind often attributed to discrimination or stratification, or that warfare had escalated to the point of compromising female access to community resources. Valdivia populations were expanding, but the skeletons do not show the high incidence of diseases and growth disruptions characteristic of later, more intensively agricultural populations living in nucleated settlements.

Archaeological evidence from Las Vegas and Valdivia sites supports a hypothesis of change including an evolution of gender roles. Women and men domesticated themselves as they became task-oriented, disciplined farmers and fishers who manufactured ever-increasing numbers and types of structures and artifacts. The size of Valdivia houses increased through time at Real Alto (Zeidler 1984), indicating that larger cooperative units were coalescing. In order to work in these groups, people developed new kinds of social relations.

Food Production, Society, and History

Native American agricultural systems evolved in a variety of ways, and women were frequently the farmers at center stage. The archaeology of gender alerts us to the variability in ancient evidence. Food producers have lived in many kinds of settlements and communities, with mutable definitions of families and their activities. Women may have controlled the products of their labor in some cases, but not in others. Food producers have experienced an ever-changing division of labor with concomitant changes in the definitions of the roles of girls, boys, women, and men of all ages; they have had variable concepts of religion and of leadership.

For better or worse, humans construct social order and structure. Gender roles represent one response to the problem of order that has been highly successful. What is interesting is that the roles assigned to any particular gender vary from case to case and do not correlate with the biological sex of individuals in any fixed way.

Plants, gathering, horticulture, food processing, and storage are frequently interpreted as areas of female expertise. These cultural specializations are routinely gendered female not because of any biological imperative; they are selected for in many cultures because under conditions of simple technology, women, who are responsible for childbearing and nurturing, prefer to reduce their mobility in order to alleviate their workload and lower the risk to young children. By performing activities such as gathering, hand cultivation, food processing, and domestic crafts, women increase the predictability of the food supply for themselves and their children.

The early American farmers and their husbands were successful in that their communities grew and people lived in increasingly larger, sedentary settlements where they became progressively more productive cultivators. They solved some of the problems associated with foraging, such as seasonal shortfalls. From another perspective, they progressively destabilized their hunting and gathering systems, forcing additional changes designed to compensate for economic and demographic stress. In late prehistory endemic warfare was probably a consequence of competition among burgeoning agricultural populations governed by ambitious leaders.

Paleopathologists show us the downside of the transition to agriculture. Food production helped alleviate some seasonal shortages, but many early agricultural peoples still suffered severe and chronic stress as well as higher mortality rates caused by changing diet combined with the heavy impact of pathogens associated with sedentary lifestyles (Bridges 1991). This did not impede population growth, which gives us the impression that the ancient people adapted successfully. The expansion of agricultural populations, both in size and in geographic spread, was only sometimes associated with an improved standard of living for individuals. Moreover, inadvertent population growth and other factors destabilized some of the early agricultural systems, leading to new social and economic arrangements.

CHAPTER FIVE

Women in Households

History and archaeology traditionally have focused on the public lives of elites and the art and architecture associated with them. Because of this bias, the family lives of both our elite and our non-elite ancestors have been ignored. Moreover, archaeologists have given little attention to ancient kinship because of their personal experiences in post-industrial society, where a major school of anthropology held, erroneously, that kinship is no longer a salient factor in social life. Family life and kin relations are as recoverable in the archaeological record as any other abstract social dimension. Because the patterns and processes of history are generated by the activities of all members of a society in the course of their daily lives, many archaeologists today seek to give those individuals faces by exploring family contexts.

Family is important to all people at some stages of their life cycles, and throughout human history the household has been the basic unit of both interpersonal interaction and productive labor. The household is a group of people that shares a residence or domestic context that becomes the focus of parental, sibling, and other kin ties; the site of the procreation and social-ization of children; and the center of production and consumption. Women and men participate as members of households. In less complex societies, the household is often the dominant social unit; in very simple societies it is the sole focus of cultural activities (Netting 1987).

There is no necessary identity between family and household. Households are usually composed of people tied to each other by bonds of kinship and marriage, but a large extended family may be organized in several households, or a single household may embrace members of several different families and nonkin. These units are important to study because the lives of women and men are shaped by the kinds of families and households in which they participate. Within families and households, different cultural ideologies may be enacted: some peoples emphasize harmony or complementarity; others institutionalize conflict and its mediation. Within families and households, women and men may take divergent or similar roles, and they may be characterized by radically different or convergent statuses. Societies create different definitions of motherly and wifely roles.

Historically, Native American groups displayed a variety of kinship types and patterns, and it seems likely that in ancient America the same was true. Kinship and marriage patterns thus varied across space and time. We know that polygyny was practiced in some groups, whereas others were monogamous. Polyandry is also known in the Americas, especially in its fraternal forms. Some households were autonomous; others were integrated into polities such as chiefdoms and states in which some households lost exclusive control over labor, personnel, and products.

Flexibility is one of the key features of both family and household organizations. These social units are responsive to change because they are small, and through the agreement of just a few people the organization can alter its structure and function and evolve to meet the needs of its members and changing circumstances. Part of the function of families and households, in both stratified and unstratified systems, has been to engage in relations with other households, forming larger communities or networks of economic, ritual, or defensive interactions. In some settings the important links are forged by marriages, so that gender relations are crucial in the social relations of the primary building blocks of society. Men may be the links between matrilineal and uxorilocal families; or, more commonly, women may serve as links between patrilineal groups. Both women and men can gain political and economic advantage for themselves and their kin by marrying particular individuals and linking their families.

Households in ancient America ran the gamut of known domestic arrangements. Some were the sole locus of decision making and the fundamental unit of production and reproduction in society. In these units women were active participants at the center of the household, where people negotiated all important decisions and processes of production, biological reproduction, and the creation and communication of social and religious ideologies. Religious life, economic life, and political life were one fabric with many intertwined threads. Although labor may have been divided, both women and men were close to the functioning of all systems and would have been expected to participate in them all. In more complex societies, chiefdoms, and early states, families and households were subordinated in complex systems. Political structures such as the state can have profound effects on all domestic relations, including gender relations.

Reconstructing Family and Marriage Patterns

Archaeologists easily identify some of the activities performed by members of ancient households, but it is more difficult to reconstruct past social forms. Sometimes family relations are inferred using art and epigraphy, or by extrapolating from the ethnographic and historic record, or by arguing from archaeological data using general ethnographic analogies. In addition, burial data, including DNA studies and multivariate analyses of skeletal populations excavated in residential contexts, can help in determining who was related to whom. For example, the ancient people of Hawikku, an ancestral Zuni village in New Mexico (A.D. 1300), buried their dead in at least ten discrete cemeteries surrounding their village. Howell and Kintigh (1996) studied the human remains and other mortuary data belonging mainly to the latest prehistoric phase before significant European contact. They were able to find evidence that each cemetery was used by a distinct biological group of kin. In this case, the distribution of bodies in space was interpreted as a manifestation of kinship; this was supported by biological evidence. By focusing on aspects of dental morphology that reflect genetic affinity, the researchers concluded that kin (individuals who shared traits indicating their close biological relationship) were buried together in formal, spatially discrete mortuary facilities. This burial pattern reinforces the view that family life dominated the experience of individuals. The people who were buried together probably viewed themselves as members of the corporate family: their principal responsibilities were toward other members of this kin group, and they derived benefits as well as disadvantages from membership. Surely they worked together and played together, and through time, some families were able to achieve greater access to power and control of goods.

In archaeology, the skill and creativity of archaeologists are the main factors that determine what will be learned; new approaches are always possible. For example, a study of house pits in British Columbia by Hayden and his colleagues (1996) illustrates how the careful analysis of archaeological materials resulted in the identification of what the researchers claim to be the "world's longest-lived corporate group" (i.e., a family). At the Keatley Creek site, each of several house pits had a distinctive pattern of chert and chalcedony, raw materials for the manufacture of stone tools; this pattern remained consistent in each house for over 1,000 years. The archaeological inference was that the occupants of each house foraged in an exclusive territory that belonged to the members of the household. These kin groups apparently maintained both their residence and family economic rights for an extremely lengthy period.

The Archaeological Study of Households

The archaeological study of households and families, pioneered by Flannery and Winter (1976) in Mexico, has been based on the excavation of the places where people actually lived: rock shelters, open campsites, and the confines of buildings. Ethnoarchaeologists believe that the entire space utilized by a household, called the household cluster, must be investigated because many important activities take place outside the actual dwelling, in and around outbuildings such as storage facilities, menstrual huts, sweat lodges, pits, household gardens, and even tombs or graves. The household cluster is an important indication of the structure of the family and its activities. Because men as well as women make contributions to reproduction and production, archaeological remains of household contexts must necessarily reveal the presence of both women and men.

Early Ecuadorian Life

One area that has yielded useful archaeological evidence concerning ancient family life is the Ecuadorian coast. Between 3000 and 2000 B.C., agriculturalists of the Valdivia culture lived in hamlets located adjacent to patches of river bottom or along the tropical seacoast near the mouths of rivers (Damp 1979; Lathrap et al. 1977; Raymond 2003).

Much is known about Valdivia economy from the analysis of ancient tools and plant, animal, and human remains, but the organization of family labor is open to speculation. Accounts by the early Spanish explorers in the region might lead us to imagine that women worked in the river-bottom fields, bringing back to the village manioc, maize, *achira* (the edible rhizome of the canna lily), cotton, and squash. In some seasons the women would have done most of the work themselves, planting, weeding, and calling on men for labor seasonally to help cut down the forest to make new gardens. Historically, women also prepared food, storing it in pits that they dug with the help of the rest of the family. People also kept small kitchen gardens near the house to grow herbs and fruits. Women may have had their favorite places in the mangrove swamp where they fished and collected shellfish with their children. Young and old people walked away from the village in small groups to look for firewood, to collect fruits and nuts, and to draw water from pits dug along the river. In their houses, women would be found stirring pots over the fire or grinding seeds near the house doors. Some people might be seen manufacturing artifacts of shell, bone, or fiber, others spinning or pyroengraving gourds. In addition, in some communities pottery was manufactured, perhaps by women, with the collaboration of their families.

In this scenario men spent time fishing in the estuaries and the bay or worked in groups on the beach or in lean-tos alongside the houses, making craft items and repairing hunting and fishing equipment. When not otherwise engaged, men might work with others in building a new house or repairing an old one (although building shelters is commonly women's work in this area), or in securing raw materials for crafts and construction from the hills. In the dry season some groups of men set off to hunt and trap in the forested hills. Larger groups composed of a whole extended family or several related nuclear families may have made forays to more distant locales to collect salt, to harvest shellfish for dying cotton thread purple, and to mine good-quality chert for making stone tools, or red ocher for painting.

At many sites the remains of residential structures and middens form large circular or horseshoe-shaped mounds around an open area (Damp 1979, 1984; Zeidler 1984). At Real Alto seven houses were identified by tracing patterns of wall trenches in the sterile clay below the refuse layers (Marcos 1988). The trenches show that Early Valdivia houses were small circular huts about three to five meters in diameter (Damp 1984). These structures would not have held many people and may have been used mainly for sleeping and for sheltering a small family and their belongings. Most activities would have taken place outdoors.

Around the edges of the houses were concentrations of shell and other refuse, including charred beans and cottonseeds, wood charcoal, fish and deer bones, broken pottery, and tools. Inside, the dirt floors were kept relatively clean by sweeping. Each house had an interior pit and a grinding stone. In one house several figurines were found.

A household cluster uncovered at Loma Alta offers a glimpse of family activities (Damp 1979, 1984). The excavator recognized an area that may have been used for sleeping because a space about the size of two adults was free of any debris and characterized by a distinctive soil feature, perhaps the remains of a mat that decayed on the ground. Burials found under the house posts and outside the door are probably the remains of family members.

Investigations at Real Alto and Loma Alta suggest that the basic building block of the Early Valdivia community was the nuclear family. Rituals involving stone and clay figurines may have been performed in the domestic setting. Similarly, the disposal of the dead was a family activity: the deceased were put to rest where they had worked and played in life. In the earliest Valdivia villages there is no evidence of differentiation in size or function of houses, leading us to believe that there was little difference from household to household.

These villages probably contained 150–200 people at any one time. The individual nuclear families living in their little round houses may have been independent economic units, but one imagines a robust exchange of labor, food, and tools among relatives on a daily basis. Related people in villages would maintain close connections with their siblings, parents, and other relatives throughout their entire lives.

The structure of Valdivia family relations is open to question; it is not known whether villages were endogamous or exogamous, or whether households were matrilineal and matrilocal or had some other form. Certainly, there must have been some mechanism for linking the Valdivia villages across southern Ecuador, as they exhibit both coordinated changes and regional variation in their ceramics through the centuries.

The Early Valdivia villages were not static entities. Within a few centuries, Real Alto grew considerably in size; ceremonial earthen platforms were constructed and the space between the former tiny hamlets was filled with new villages, showing population growth on a regional level (Zeidler 1984). House floors changed as well, growing from an average area of 14.4 square meters in Early Valdivia to 49.1 square meters in Middle Valdivia, suggesting that extended family households had replaced nuclear families. This innovation may have facilitated more complex productive activities. Perhaps the autonomous nuclear families found making a living more difficult as good agricultural land became scarce, so that young people stayed under their parents' umbrella at marriage. Alternatively, perhaps some families had an economic or social advantage that made affiliation with that family attractive to relatives. Perhaps factional competition between groups forced the creation of larger, more competitive units.

Anthropologists have observed that when land is abundant, the independent nuclear family is a viable unit of production. When land is scarce, pooling efforts and centralized control may offer competitive advantages. In extended family groups, the more numerous producers are often organized under household heads who function as managers. Such households may undertake larger projects involving more labor: agricultural intensification can result in increased production per unit of land, and fishing and craft productivity may be improved. Extended families can also support some persons in activities other than primary production, moving the group toward greater specialization and stimulating technological change. The price paid by family members may be a loss in personal autonomy.

Based on ethnoarchaeological studies of the modern Shuar people of southeastern Ecuador, Zeidler (1984) has interpreted the use of space in large Middle Valdivia houses. Traditional Shuar houses are occupied by extended families; the interior space is differentiated into female and male areas. The sexes maintain spatial separation as they go about their daily activities, giving both sexes considerable freedom of action. Zeidler has noted that Shuar men congregate at the front of the house and keep their belongings there. The other end of the house is where women spend most of their time when not gardening or foraging. Here they tend their children, gossip, and cook for their families; here married couples and their young children sleep. There are also multipurpose areas used by all adults. The area where corn beer is stored is used by all the women of the household, as is the maize-grinding area. Men all use a given spot for blowgun manufacture and everyone uses the areas where machetes are habitually sharpened and where beer is consumed.

Zeidler compared Shuar domestic space to archaeological evidence from the floors of two Middle Valdivia houses, trying to see whether artifact distribution showed similar patterning. In one Valdivia house he found fragments of anthropomorphic figurines concentrated around a burned area where foods were prepared. He identified this and a similar area by the door of this house as female spaces. Because chipped stone debris was found all over the place, he concluded that everyone used stone tools. Because stone tools and evidence of shell ornament making were found around the periphery, he identified these spots as male craft areas. The remains of fancy ceramic vessels along the right wall are identified with a food and drink consumption area used by men and guests (based on the Shuar analogy).

This kind of ethnoarchaeological study focuses attention on the fact that females and males in indigenous South America often lead parallel lives, but it is doubtful that the modern Shuar are completely appropriate models for interpreting the ancient Valdivia people. We should be aware, as we engender activity areas, that our interpretations often rest on the restatement of our own cultural prejudices so that, for example, we see women cooking and grinding, even though cooking in many contemporary lowland societies in South America is very informal and not necessarily sex linked (Bruhns 1991). Even if archaeological remains accurately reflect ancient activities in the house, they may not represent any clear distinction between the activities of females and males. Kent's (1984) ethnoarchaeological studies of Navajo hogans and their yards in the North American Southwest have shown clearly that in groups with relatively few belongings living in a single space, virtually all tools and spaces are multiuse and multigendered. For ritual reasons, the Navajo paterfamilias had his sheepskin bed on the east side of the hogans Kent studied; this was the only truly gendered use of space.

Middle Valdivia settlement patterns reflect the use of garden land along the rivers, although marine and forest resources were important to the ancient people as well. Pearsall's (1988) archaeobotanical studies at Real Alto have led her to suggest that the major agricultural tasks, such as planting, weeding, and harvesting, were carried out by women and their older daughters, while males took care of field clearing and irrigation as well as hunting and fishing. A division of subsistence tasks in this broadly diversified economy would have required scheduling, especially for agricultural activities. Based on the anthropological observation that scheduling problems in agricultural societies can be solved by an extended family household organization, and noting the evidence of larger houses and spatially distinct clusters of some sorts of activity debris in Middle Valdivia sites, Zeidler (2000) has suggested that Middle Valdivia people organized a larger coresident labor force that could undertake spatially diverse subsistence activities. Within the household some adults may have watched the children and cooked while others invested more time in cultivation or banded together to leave the village for net fishing or hunting. These sorts of activities can increase the productive capacity of the group with benefits to all, permitting the local community to be self-sufficient.

The kind of social organization of the Middle Valdivia community is speculative, but many ethnographic communities in the tropical forests of South America are characterized by localized lineages or even clans. At Real Alto the members of the household may have belonged to a particular clan, members of which all lived in the same area of the village. Women may play significant roles in decision making in clan and lineage organizations.

Neither burials nor art suggests that this social system was dominated by males. Zeidler (1984) interprets the change in household size and composition as indicative of a strategy of competition among households in which the differential accumulation of wealth led to the emergence of social ranking. Feasting in a special structure such as the Fiesta House at Real Alto could be understood as a communal activity that served to integrate local households, but feasting can also be a mechanism of competition in which some families attempt to gain prestige and dominance over others. Burial in the special Charnel House may be an indication of ranking, with special treatment in death being the prerogative of individuals of a highly ranked extended family or lineage. That rank was hereditary is indicated by the fact that infants were found in the same burial context as a middle-aged woman and other adults in the Charnel House. However, there is no evidence of conspicuous consumption by elites at Real Alto and no other convincing indications of social hierarchy in life or in death. There is, for example, no evidence of the exchange of luxury goods, no sumptuous burials, and little evidence of storage facilities. Only a few figurines, all female, show ritual practitioners on stools, a traditional sign of ritual power or authority. It is unclear whether there was ranking either within the community of Real Alto, or among the Middle Valdivia communities. We do not know whether Valdivia social organization was favorable to women, to men, or to both as they moved through their tasks within the extended household context.

Reconstructing family and household dynamics from the 5,000-year-old remains excavated in Valdivia sites is difficult because the Valdivia people have no closely related historical descendants whose culture can be used to suggest interpretations. Luckily, as shown in the following example, there are some rare archaeological cases in which the archaeologists may benefit from excellent preservation of household contexts and may use ethnographic analogy with confidence.

The Village of Joya de Cerén, El Salvador

The Maya village of Joya de Cerén was buried as the result of a volcanic eruption that occurred one summer's evening about A.D. 590 (Conyers 1996). Because of the extraordinary preservation of remains under an ash fall, many details of ancient life can be recovered (Sheets et al. 1990). More than eleven structures have been excavated, including part of a household cluster with a

Figure 5.1. Group 1 in the ruins of Joya de Cerén in El Salvador has preserved the remains of a separate kitchen structure, still common in this part of the world, with its three-stone hearth intact. To the side one can see the swales of the kitchen gardens and, in the distance, two small houses, their walls blown flat by the blast of the eruption. Photograph by Karen Olsen Bruhns.

sleeping building; a shaded working area in the patio; a separate kitchen; a larger, decorated building that may have had ritual use or may have been part of an elite residence group; a sweat bath; and some small buildings, probably part of other household groups. The buildings are very like those of traditional lowland Maya households of the present. Made of wattle and daub on low earthen platforms, they appear to form clusters of small, separate structures that served as sleeping quarters, storage facilities, and kitchens (fig 5.1).

At the Cerén site, plants have been identified from the impressions left in solidified ash, and archaeologists have described an ancient household garden for the first time. In these kitchen gardens ancient Maya women cultivated manioc as well as medicinal plants, and right near the house they had agave plants from whose leaves they extracted fiber for textiles. In the habitation area the remains of three kinds of beans, maize, squash, chilies, avocados, and chocolate were found. *Ristras* (garlands or plaits) of chilies hung from the ceiling of a house, and the storage houses were full of beans and other seeds, as well as tools and supplies such as colored paints for religious use. The villagers also consumed considerable quantities of deer and dog meat. One victim of the eruption was a duck, tied to the stand of a metate! The remains show that the people of Cerén ate better than many of their descendants (Sheets 1992).

Metates in the kitchen area were mounted on *horquetas*, forked-branch stands very like those in use today, giving evidence that the women who did the grinding were not very tall. The big metates were used for processing maize and other foods, while miniature metates, apparently utilized for preparing cosmetics and paint, were found stored in ceramic vessels along with colored pigments contained in tiny vessels and seashells. Both the wall niches in the houses and the rafters were used to store tools, and apparently parents hid their sharp obsidian tools in the thatched roof where children could not find them.

Food was prepared in the kitchen but brought out and consumed in individual servings by people sitting on the benches in the houses or perhaps along the porch in the cool evening air. On the porch of one house, some man or woman flaked obsidian to make useful cutting edges. Another special craft area was identified as part of Household One, where someone was making ceramic vessels at the time of the eruption. Archaeologists were surprised to find how many vessels each family had in use at one time: one small household had seventy vessels, including locally made cooking and storage vessels and many imported painted vessels used for serving food and drink. The people of Cerén also had assorted gourds used, as they are today, for drinking and food preparation. Some of these were painted with designs like those on the pottery.

In an area that may have been used by the women of Household One for spinning and other domestic production, a crude miniature vessel and twenty sherds may indicate the play area of a child who was learning to count in the base twenty system used by all Mesoamericans.

Because life in these quarters was halted early in the evening, archaeologists have not discovered who slept where, but they did find evidence that the sleeping mats were rolled up and stored along the tops of the walls in the opening left for light and ventilation just below the roof.

The Cerén households indicate a social organization involving groups of nuclear families related by blood and marriage, demonstrating clear continuities with modern Mayan peoples. These ordinary families were probably monogamous, and like the later Maya they may have reckoned kinship bilaterally, although with a slight patrilineal bias. They may have practiced patrilocal or neolocal residence after marriage. One can imagine two women grinding side by side in the patio, one of them laughing as the children tease the captive duck destined for a special dinner. Another puts aside her spinning as the men come in from the field, leaning their digging sticks against the side of the house. An elder is sitting on the porch fixing a deer skull headdress that will be used in a ritual planned for after the harvest. A woman hands her adolescent son a painted bowl full of *atole*, which he is drinking as fast as he can, wiping out the gourd with his fingers in an attempt to satisfy his hunger. Then, without warning, the Laguna Caldera eruption begins, just as the sun is setting, and people flee, leaving their houses and their artifacts exactly where they were using them, to be covered with ash for 1,400 years.

This evidence, combined with ethnographic descriptions of modern Maya households, makes it easy to imagine women working and interacting in ancient domestic contexts. It is perhaps more difficult to create an image of women in the wider village context. Archaeologists working at Cerén have described a larger building with niches, columns, and a window. This building contained some artifacts unlike those found in other household contexts. Some scholars interpret it as the residence of the village curer and religious practitioner. Sheets (1992) believes that this person may have been a female, as is common today in El Salvador, where few villages lack a traditional female healer and fortune-teller. Presumably the sweat bath, used all over Mexico and Central America for purification before religious rites, was built and maintained by the villagers together, but as in the rest of Mesoamerica, a woman may have been in charge of the steam bath, used also for the treatment of physical and nervous ills and by the midwife in the care of young mothers.

Another building with larger rooms and benches has a wide doorjamb with the handles from broken storage jars set into the sides to hold a curtain or mat. Inside there are big vessels for beer, all of which suggest that this was a meeting house for the men of the village or a brewing house for the women. Simple graffiti on the back wall seem to be the result of children doodling in fresh clay plaster.

The Cerén villagers were part of a larger polity that probably had its capital at San Andrés, five kilometers to the west. Presumably the villagers paid tribute in the form of produce and were required to labor for the rulers, who reciprocated by sponsoring exciting multicommunity rituals and civic events. San Andrés, as the political and economic center of the region, may also have had markets where people could acquire elaborate painted ceramics, obsidian, jade from Guatemala, and seashells. The Cerén community, composed of various families, was probably autonomous for most practical purposes, although it formed part of a larger polity, described as a chiefdom. Many of the tropical and temperate forest peoples of the Americas formed chiefdoms: political organizations with a hereditary leader and ranked lineages. Chiefdoms may be characterized by more roles and statuses for women and men because of surpluses generated by the groups and collected by leaders. In situations such as Cerén, surplus was transferred to the regional capital, but the local village elders surely reserved some surplus to support community rituals and festivities. In the local context it is likely that women and men participated together in producing surplus and deciding how to expend it.

The houses of Cerén demonstrate that the nuclear family has been the basic unit of production and social interaction among Maya people for more than 1,000 years. The site also shows that engendering tools and activity areas can be done with confidence when archaeologists rely on historic and ethnographic material from related peoples. Archaeologists assert with considerable security that the women of Cerén engaged in grinding corn, cooking, and weaving because adult females among the later Maya do these activities. Digging sticks are male implements among the Maya. That the curer was female is a matter of speculation.

Families in Ancient Colombia

The late prehistoric Tairona were successful tropical horticulturalists living in a mountain environment of northern Colombia. They are famous for their lapidary art and gold working and exhibited their impressive architectural and engineering skills in drainage and irrigation works, terraced fields, roadways, plazas, and temples arrayed along the steep slopes of the Sierra Nevada de Santa Marta. Some historic data on the Tairona indicate that they had a complex stratified society with secular chieftains and war captains, a class of priests, and many types of artists and artisans.

Excavations at Buritaca-200 (Ciudad Perdida), described by Castaño Uribe (1987), have uncovered various kinds of domestic buildings, some of which required more labor investment than others. Some circular structures more than four meters in diameter have been interpreted as houses, based on analogy with the putative descendants of the Tairona, the modern Kogi Indians. Archaeologists have inferred that the ancient Tairona houses had conical thatched roofs, not unlike those of the Kogi. Excavation of these ancient houses often reveals, under the threshold, a pot containing a number of pebbles, which, according to Kogi custom, represent and magically protect the occupants (Reichel-Dolmatoff 1965:149). The floor plan of one of these ancient houses shows a probable women's area to the right of the entrance. Here, water jars, cooking pots, grinding stones, small axes and scrapers, and the fireplace are located. On the other, male, side are axes, hammer-stones, perforating tools, fishhooks, nondomestic ceramics, whistles and other ceremonial gear, and tools and debris from working gold and semiprecious stones. Male gear also included stools and bat wing pendants worn for dances. Such a distribution of goods gives archaeologists the impression that the houses were divided, with men working along one side and women cooking along the other. This interpretation rests, of course, on the stereotypical association of women with one set of remains and not the other.

However, an alternative interpretation of the way humans lived in these houses can be generated from Kogi ethnography and would indicate that the entire contents of a house belonged to either a woman or a man (Oyuela-Caycedo 1998). According to a study carried out before 1950, the Kogi reckoned descent through a gender classificatory system called *Dake* for females and *Tuxi* for males. Reichel-Dolmatoff (1965) understood this as an alliance system in which marriages could be either endogamous or exogamous, according to the needs of the people involved. In this system, a mother's land was inherited by her oldest daughter, and the father's land by the oldest son. Additional children sought to marry people who had land to bring to the union. After marriage, Kogi couples occupied their own houses located opposite each other, and meals were served and consumed in the space between the houses (Zuidema 1992:249). In this scenario the house with cooking remains might have belonged to a wife who, with her immature children, owned and used the items in both the right and left activity areas. These activities would have included manufacturing and using ceremonial items and nondomestic pottery. This social system may imply equality in gender relations.

Because of the unusual social patterns that people can work out for themselves, engendering the archaeological record can be risky business. In this instance, if we look at the Tairona's descendants, ceremonial pottery is made by male priests, and men also do all the weaving (as indeed they do in much of Andean South America).

The household clusters described by Castaño Uribe (1987) at Buritaca would seem to have been the loci of storage for food and manufactured items. Storage structures adjacent to houses contained enormous numbers of ceramic jars and stone tools. Craft activities such as goldsmithing, lapidary production, weaving, and woodworking may have taken place in buildings lacking fireplaces, found closely associated with domestic structures.

Burials are associated with these architectural groups, reinforcing the idea of the central importance of the family. Because bone was poorly preserved, there is no independent evidence for the sex of the interred, but researchers have interpreted some division in the offerings as indicative of two genders. Some burials have stone axes, celts, hoes, decorated staffs, and anthropomorphic figurines of semiprecious stone. The excavator thinks these are male, whereas the burials containing smaller axes, polishing stones, stone beads, and shale figurines are female. The interpretation that houses were divided along gender lines is not supported by burial evidence, since burials of both sorts are made under both sides of the house, in the patio areas, and in nearby refuse dumps. Apparently, the location of the burial and the kind and depth of the tomb are reflections of social rank more than gender.

The Tairona family was organized to carry out the fundamental economic activities of the society. Some families may have been more successful because of their size and access to labor. In this ranked society, people surely sought to arrange beneficial marriages that might enhance family fortunes. Polygyny among the higher-ranking families may have helped households grow and prosper. Despite the impressive architecture and sophisticated crafts of the Tairona, there is no evidence of specialized production apart from the family setting, nor is there evidence that a public arena existed apart from the sphere dominated by families.

Archaeological investigations in other areas of northern Colombia also illustrate the variability of family composition and organization. In the Río de la Miel region, the Colorado phase (ca. A.D. 100) people lived in dispersed settlements in defensible locations away from the big rivers (Castaño Uribe 1985). Families occupied oval *malocas* with floor areas of sixty to seventy square meters. Houses this size ethnographically are the residences of single extended families of no more than fifteen people. The dead were buried in urns in nucleated cemeteries near the villages. The burials showed little social differentiation. However, the next phase, Butantán, showed major changes in family structure. Villages now consisted of several huge *malocas* along the river's edge. These houses had three to four times the floor space of the earlier ones, indicating a growth in the size of the household unit. One of these large houses could hold eighty to one hundred people. Butantán people were much more involved in commerce and specialized crafts such as gold working than their ancestors had been. This more complex economic structure is reflected in the social structure. Aside from the fact that larger family groups were coresident, burial offerings expressed greater emphasis on rank.

Life in a Butantán village must have been much changed from earlier times. The tenor of life was altered by living in a larger settlement, by belonging to a household with many more people and more expressed ranking of individuals, by engaging in more frequent interactions with the outside world, and by enjoying increased possibilities for the acquisition of goods. The larger villages were apparently organized for defense as well as for production and trade. Leaders took a prominent part in production and distribution, and perhaps polygyny began among the more prominent families as a means of optimizing the production of goods for social events and gift giving as well as for trade. These changes meant busier and more active lives for everyone, but also increased stress caused by more people and the threats of neighbors.

Detailed information concerning the evolution of family structure in northern Colombia is lacking, but house size, burial patterns, and an altered artifact inventory all show that there were major innovations. Family organization did not alter randomly but was surely the result of behavioral changes adopted consciously by people in the course of their lives. At the microsocial level, girls and women surely promoted innovations they perceived as advantageous and resisted others. In an example of adaptive change, the ancestors of the late prehistoric Iroquois of the northeastern United States may have adopted matrilineal organization to increase their adaptability in a period of migration.

An Early Iroquois Migration

The Owasco people, who were the ancestors of the modern Iroquois nations, migrated out of central Pennsylvania and into what is now New York around

A.D. 900, displacing the Algonquian groups who were living there. The early Owasco people described by Snow (1994, 1995) were organized into bigger family groups than their Algonquian neighbors, and they had the economic advantage of a mixed economy, based in part on the cultivation of squash, beans, and maize. Because of the large size of the Owasco cooking pots, archaeologists have hypothesized that the dining units were large. An increase in the size of cooking pots is often accompanied by a growth in house size in the archaeological record, reflecting how prehistoric people organized to undertake warfare, trade, or large building projects. Owasco houses were large, although not quite as large as those of some of their descendants, who lived in multifamily dwellings known as longhouses.

Using the conventional wisdom of anthropological theory to understand the Owasco people, Snow (1995) has hypothesized that the Owasco adopted a matrilocal residence pattern that facilitated their aggressive expansion into the thinly populated northern regions. In this system, when a woman married, her husband joined her household and lived with her, her parents, and her sisters and their husbands. Matrilineal family organization has several advantages for migrating people. If their tribal organization is egalitarian, then the matrilineal segments can successfully occupy a new region without intergroup competition because hostility can be repressed and focused on an external enemy, such as the Algonquian hunters and gatherers. In this kind of organization, men from various families marrying into and taking up residence with their wives' families become brothers-in-law to men from various lineages, thus breaking up groups of potentially aggressive men related along the patriline (Snow 1994:32). It would be unlikely for these men to conspire against other Iroquois families because they themselves come from those families (including their own maternal family and the families where their brothers live with their own wives and children). In this way, feuding and internal warfare between Iroquois families and lineages might have been averted and aggression and violence focused outside of the community (Prezzano 1997).

The Iroquois, in the course of sporadic warfare, may have abducted, enslaved, and married females from the Algonquian populations they were displacing. This process would account for some of the unusual ceramic assemblages found mixed in pits in archaeological sites: the captive women continued to make and use their own styles of ceramics as they lived alongside women making Owasco pottery.

The late prehistoric and historic Iroquois longhouses were up to one

Figure 5.2. An artist's view of the interior of an Iroquois longhouse. Matrilineally related families occupied compartments along the walls, sharing hearths with relatives across the center aisle. Drawing by Richard McReynolds.

hundred meters long, and as many as five hundred people lived in typical villages (fig. 5.2). When Europeans arrived they observed six to ten nuclear families per longhouse, living in pairs, facing each other across a hearth. The nuclear families were formed around women who belonged to the same matrilineal clan segment. Women worked in family units in fields cleared by clan brothers living nearby. The men did the heaviest cutting and clearing, but the women did the rest of the horticultural work: planting, hoeing, and harvesting, along with collecting roots, sap for maple syrup, greens, nuts, berries, and small animals. Much of this was communal work supervised by clan matrons.

The longhouses were expandable at the ends, where storage areas were rather lightly built. Men married outside their lineage, but usually within the village or a neighboring village. Men were also frequently absent from home, especially as intertribal warfare increased in later prehistory. Both the structure of the family and the absence of men gave women autonomy: the villages were the domain of women, while men were said to own the forest. Social life was characterized by separate spheres for women and men, by reciprocal obligations between the sexes, and by gender roles that were nonhierarchical (Richards 1957; Schlegel 1972).

In Iroquois society, daughters may have been preferred over sons since a daughter helped increase the size and power of the household. Snow (1994:72–73) has suggested that women exercised control over family size through the use of herbal medicines and selective abortion. Abortion medicines were common in the Iroquois pharmacopoeia.

Gender behavior can be inferred through the analysis of Iroquois pottery, traditionally manufactured by women. Archaeologists observe that Iroquois pottery was made and discarded locally, whereas pipes, made and used by men, were spread widely over Iroquois territory. In this case, historical data tell us that men traveled widely to exchange gifts, to trade, and to engage in diplomacy and warfare. They required the contribution of resources controlled by women to undertake these activities (Snow 1994:39).

Historic studies and more recent ethnographic accounts of the Iroquois show that women participated widely in religious activity, including the performance of sacred dances in seasonal ceremonies. In each village, women formed societies for the purpose of maintaining these traditional ceremonies. They also formed mutual aid societies to cultivate private, nonclan plots (Snow 1994:69). Iroquois mythology illustrates the division of labor by gender: women were always farmers and men hunters and warriors. When the famous Iroquois League was formed, female delegates from the dominant clan segments in each of the constituent nations named the league chiefs (*sachems*). The women also replaced the *sachems* and removed them from office when necessary. In later history, when large belts of wampum became important ritual symbols, matrons spoke through belts to the war chiefs, demonstrating women's access to symbols of authority. These female elders were not, however, matriarchs (Snow 1994:65, 91–92). Both female and male authority were clearly defined in this kin-organized society. Women's roles as food producers were in part a basis for their authority, but it was the extension of the kinship system into political life that benefited Iroquois women. In contrast, in Europe the patriarchal structure of family life did not work to the advantage of women when it was extended into the public sphere.

Grasshopper Pueblo Families

The study of Grasshopper Pueblo in New Mexico has resulted in an increased understanding of ancient households and community organization. Burial information from Grasshopper, occupied by Mogollon Tradition peoples between A.D. 1300 and 1400, shows that gender greatly affected individual experience in that community. Grasshopper consisted of three major room blocks and several outlying groups of houses. Reid and Whittlesey (1982) studied room functions, as determined by artifacts left on the floor when the pueblo was abandoned, and identified separate households. While all households participated in the same range of activities, each carried out activities in different proportions and in different spatial contexts. Variation among the household units and change through time demonstrate that there was no fixed female or male experience in this society: a woman's experience at Grasshopper would have been different from a man's, but any individual born into a large, well-established household would have had a very different daily life and life trajectory from that of a same-sex person born into a smaller household.

Some family groups occupied multiroom houses in the main room blocks. Here, several women probably worked in a main room and used additional storage and manufacturing rooms. In single-room houses, presumably a smaller group of women or a single woman labored in one space that combined habitation, storage, and manufacturing functions. Studying the room blocks occupied by discrete kin groups in the center of the pueblo, researchers found that female equipment dominated in some contexts, male items in others, and that markers of women and men were mixed in some plazas and room blocks.

Different cranial modifications in the skeletal population indicate that several ethnic groups may have lived at Grasshopper. Although the residents of the site were divided into groups by kin ties, wealth, and perhaps ethnicity, they also interacted across these lines. An average of three households shared a ceremonial room, while six households seem to have combined to share a kiva. The great kiva of Grasshopper may have served the community as a whole. Kiva ceremonial life perhaps involved the members of associations not based on kinship, such as those found among the later Pueblo Indians. Reid and Whittlesey (1982) recognized several associative groups, identified by the emblems buried with deceased members, which apparently crosscut the community. A male might have belonged to one of three hypothetical groups that were mutually exclusive: at death some men were buried with either shell pendants or tinklers, or with bone hairpins. An adult male member of any one of these associations might also have belonged to a group whose symbol was a quiver of arrows.

In the interpretation of Reid and Whittlesey (1982), women too belonged to organizations that united people outside the immediate family and beyond the domestic context. Shell bracelets were worn in death by women as well as men, signaling a community association open to both sexes. Only women wore shell rings, ornaments that might identify an exclusively feminine organization.

Later in the history of Grasshopper Pueblo, household size decreased. More people lived in single-room houses. The size of cooking hearths also decreased through time, as did the size of cooking vessels. Large households may have become strategically untenable under the circumstances of the late fourteenth century. Such a change in household size implies alterations in customary workloads, roles, and gender relations. The greater frequency of single-room households later in time may not signal a beneficial change for women, since women suffered declining health as their diets changed in the later prehistory of this site.

Family Relations among the Ancestral Puebloans

A study of prehistoric funerary offerings in Arizona shows how careful observation and analysis can be used to test ideas about gender, family, and social patterns. Simon and Ravesloot (1995) observed patterns of vessel placement within Salado tombs of the western Ancestral Puebloan peoples (A.D. 1150–1250). By assessing the origin of the vessels, based on the composition of clays, they were able to construct hypotheses about the role of particular individuals within the community. Because different potters, coming from different families within the community, used different clay sources, the finding of vessels made from these different clays ought to point to interaction between the person who owned or was buried with the vessels and the people who made them. The vessels are evidence of individual social relationships in this extinct society. The researchers also think that burial goods may reflect the composition of the mourning group that contributed the gifts during the funeral and that the placement of vessels with respect to the body had social significance. For example, an eighteen-year-old woman in one tomb was accompanied by vessels that fall into six of the eight recognized compositional groups of ceramics known in the cemetery, indicating wide connectedness within her community.

The investigators found no simple correlation between gender and the abundance and variety of ceramic vessels. However, they did observe some relationships between the vessels and the status of individuals, probably a reflection of their wealth, access to resources, and the size of their social network. In the young woman's burial, the presence of many of these compositional clusters seems to show her relationship to other individuals buried in the cemetery. Some clusters, and the placement of vessels, suggest gifts from natal groups, while others may be gifts from affinal groups or groups with which she developed ceremonial ties. For example, multiple vessels from two clusters were located on either side of her head and shoulders. The researchers concluded that the placement of the vessels reflects her gender and age as well as her kin relationships and memberships in ceremonial societies. Older individuals commonly have vessels from compositional groups other than those associated with family membership, presumably reflecting wide relationships within the community. Studies such as these are exciting and promise the possibility of tracking a person's expanding responsibilities and relationships through life.

Family Life in Complex Societies

As some Native American societies developed state forms of government, family life changed. In states, individual families have less control over many aspects of their economic and social behavior. As some American states became more urban, elite control was heightened and both women and men often suffered. It has been argued that when there are more tasks and more gendered tasks; when there is a larger material culture, which also becomes gendered; and when female children are enculturated in a different manner than male children, women begin to lose status. In ancient American cities, family life was variable across time and space, just as it was in the rest of the world. In the Maya urban centers of the Classic Period, people lived in extended household units and occupied clusters of small one- or two-roomed structures. Presumably, kin lived contiguously. Excavations at Copán in Honduras have revealed large households of many families living close together (Hendon 1996, 1997). Evidently these were lineage settlements, where both rich and poor relations lived close by each other. However, different types of households are known from other areas of ancient America, and each would have affected the lives of women and men differently.

Apartment Life in Early Classic Mexico

Teotihuacán, located in a small valley some fifty kilometers northeast of Mexico City, was one of the largest cities in the world in its heyday. At its height, the city consisted of some twenty-nine square kilometers of densely packed buildings aligned along the Street of the Dead. It was an immensely influential metropolis whose art and architecture were emulated widely, and it had great economic and political impacts on its neighbors (Millon 1973; Cowgill 1997).

During the city's apogee, most of its citizens lived in apartment compounds. Within these buildings, individual residences were composed of groups of small rooms (Manzanilla 1996). Archaeologists have also identified in each compound at least one public area. Some of the best information on how ordinary Teotihuacanos lived comes from a compound called Tlajinga 33 (Widmer and Storey 1993). While the more elite stone and concrete apartment buildings of Teotihuacán had elaborate drainage systems, cement floors, and painted walls, Tlajinga 33 was built of adobe brick and had dirt and cobble paving. It had a series of irregularly interconnecting rooms and patios associated with one series of larger, more public rooms and patios, and a shrine. The excavators of Tlajinga have inferred that the smallest units, suites of two or three rooms with a small patio, were the residences of nuclear families. Areas of contiguous apartments are associated with larger courtyards, refuse heaps, and workshop debris. The burials of both children and adults who lived in the apartments were found under the rooms and patios. These people were neither wealthy nor influential. Rather, during a period of about five hundred years (beginning perhaps as early as A.D. 100), they engaged in craft activity, first lapidary and later ceramic manufacture, although they may have engaged in agricultural production as well (Storey 1985).

The best-preserved apartments in Tlajinga had a main room about 3.3 by 3.7 meters and a smaller room, both entered from a shallow roofed porch raised above a cobbled patio. These rooms are thought to have been used mainly for sleeping and storage. The Teotihuacanos had no effective artificial lighting and probably did most work and socializing outside. The common archaeological practice of counting nuclear families by the number of fireplaces cannot be followed here because the Teotihuacanos cooked on ceramic braziers that functioned as single-burner stoves. Because broken braziers were thrown out into the communal dump, there is no way to determine how many a single family had at one time.

The placement and size of workshops within Tlajinga suggest that ceramic production was organized at the multifamily or compound level. The workshops, drying rooms, and firing areas were located apart from the living quarters. People in other compounds in the same vicinity were also involved in pottery production, suggesting that ancient craft production was the specialty of a group of related families that were residentially localized. In contrast, the two lapidary workshops at Tlajinga were both associated with a small cluster of apartments, suggesting that only limited labor was invested in this activity. Perhaps these workshops reflect the specialization of a few individuals or just two nuclear families within the compound. Because both neighborhood and central city marketplaces have been identified at Teotihuacán, archaeologists think that the distribution of products was handled through markets.

Tlajinga 33 illustrates the physical and economic setting of family life at Teotihuacán. Based on this evidence, archaeologists can imagine some of the social dynamics of the ordinary inhabitants of the ancient city, and because of the custom of burying family members under the rooms and patios in which they once lived, it is possible to reconstruct some aspects of kinship organization. Spence's (1974) analysis of skeletal remains from several compounds resulted in the hypothesis that the Teotihuacanos reckoned kinship in the male line. The men buried in a given compound shared skeletal traits, indicating that they were more closely related to each other than to the women buried in the same compound. This suggests strongly that each compound was the home of a patrilineage, occupied by between sixty and two hundred relatives related in the male line. The total population of a compound would have varied because of economic factors and differing reproductive histories. The size of the apartments suggests that families were monogamous, a pattern seen among later peoples of central Mexico. We do not, however, know if groups of brothers and their families clustered together in one section of a compound.

The women who married into the patrilineages must have come from other apartments in the neighborhood. Yet Storey (1985) has pointed out that ancient cities did not reproduce their population and had to recruit from without. Strontium analysis supports this hypothesis (Storey 1985, 1986; Price et al. 2000). Probably the majority of marriages were between people of linked lineages within the same socioeconomic group, or between members of different segments of the same lineage, especially those who lived elsewhere in the Valley of Mexico.

Women in Ancient America

Evidence from Tlajinga and other nonelite compounds suggests that some women may have benefited from the high status of their families. This evidence comes from the larger, more accessible patios that contained shrines and the graves of apparent lineage heads and their families. The female burials seemed to have more offerings, especially if they were within or near the shrine itself. In this context, some tombs were found to contain women who were closely related to the males of the compound. These skeletons might be mothers of the men of the compound, or they might be the remains of women who died unmarried and were buried with their close kin. However, in these same contexts one finds burials of males who are evidently not related to the other males, suggesting that when nature failed to provide a male heir in those families with power and goods, a husband was married to one of the daughters of the patriline (Spence 1974; Sempowski and Spence 1994). This solution is seen in many patrilineal societies; in such cases the patrilineage is not broken, and the children of the union of the in-marrying male and the stay-at-home woman are members of the woman's patrilineage and inherit her position and goods. These daughters and wives might have had different experiences from those of other women in the compound. There is not enough skeletal evidence to indicate whether the women who brought husbands home were healthier or lived longer than the in-marrying wives of the compound.

Marriage arrangements may have meant that a young bride faced the problems of being an in-marrying woman, chief among which was the fact that she may not have enjoyed any prestige or authority until her own sons were adults. A young wife in Teotihuacán may have been trained and supervised by her mother-in-law, laying her open to abuse from her mother-in-law, but alternatively, parents may have chosen their sons' wives carefully, and the brides may have been valued for their potential contributions. The short life spans of the Teotihuacanos could have ameliorated a wife's treatment by her in-laws, making her suffering short in duration. If marriages were contracted within the neighborhood or quarter, a young woman might have had her own relatives close by to protect her.

A woman's daily life in these apartments would vary with her age and status. In the family residences of Tlajinga, women probably swept the house and patio, gathered trash to be carried out, and prepared daily meals. The analysis of domestic ceramics at Teotihuacán has shown a large number of griddles, evidence that tortillas were a basic foodstuff. This would have entailed the daily preparation of *nixtamal* (corn treated with lime) and the laborious grinding of the dough by women and girls. Women also shouldered domestic religious duties. The numbers of figurines and incense burners in household refuse suggest that domestic rituals were part of everyday spirituality. Women probably prepared food and paraphernalia for festivals, rituals, and other religious observances in the compound and beyond.

At Tlajinga, women integrated craft tasks with domestic chores and devised labor- or time-saving behaviors. Perhaps those women most involved in craft production reduced their food preparation time by acquiring ready-made tortillas. Tortilla production and sale traditionally was in the hands of poor women. Some women likely chose to prepare certain dishes, such as stews of beans and chilies, as part of a time-saving strategy. This behavior has been described among Aztec women whose labor was committed to weaving for tribute and who chose different foods and cooking techniques from those of women with other economic strategies (Brumfiel 1991, 1996b).

The construction and maintenance of clothing is extremely time consuming. Women may have made scheduling decisions similar to those of nineteenth-century North American women who, in order to free themselves to do the heavy and time-consuming task of washing on Monday, saved leftovers from the festive meals they prepared on Sunday to be consumed by the family on washday. In Teotihuacán, washing clothes must have meant carrying clothing to the river or transporting water to the compound; perhaps women hired help to get the washing done.

Spinning and weaving textiles for domestic consumption were certainly among the most labor-intensive and time-consuming tasks performed in homes, requiring the participation of girls, old women, and men. Archaeologists have not determined whether Teotihuacanos, like many other Mexicans of the past, had to pay taxes in cloth, but that too would have weighed on any woman's time, along with caring for children, including those who were chronically ill. Comforting an ailing child, trying to procure and prepare medicines, and suffering the emotional burden of watching a child sicken and die were part of a woman's burden.

Some open areas in the urban core have been called marketplaces, where women, men, or both might have gone to trade their wares or acquire items for family consumption. Fuel procurement was almost certainly in the hands of specialists who gathered wood from afar and brought it into the city for exchange. Ceramic workshops would have required quantities of wood and water that may have been delivered, as they are today, to the urban potters who maintain regular relationships with providers (Lackey 1982).

Evidence suggests that lower-class women experienced very difficult lives, and in the later years of the city, their condition seriously deteriorated. Investigations have shown that by the time the city was maximally nucleated, with virtually everyone living in compounds, there was a continuing health crisis that affected women and children acutely (Storey 1985, 1986, 1992). Infant mortality soared to 30–40 percent of all babies; the families of Tlajinga lost perhaps 50 percent of their new members by age fifteen. Deaths were especially frequent among three- to five-year-olds, doubtless due to weaning stress. The bones of survivors often show retarded femur growth at this time of life, evidence that stress affected the health of most children. A frightening aspect of neonate health was that fetuses showed no growth between the thirty-second and the thirty-sixth week of gestation. Skeletal remains demonstrate that infants had very low birth weights and were subject to the same problems that result in high neonatal mortality today. This situation seems to be due to serious malnutrition of the mothers. There was chronic poor nutrition among all the residents of Tlajinga, but some cultural practices associated with pregnancy likely affected expectant mothers.

Females who faced overwork, chronic undernourishment, and persistent infections would have experienced later menarche, earlier menopause, and longer lactation amenorrhea after the birth of a baby that survived. These women probably had low fertility rates due to undernourishment and physical stress, but an adult woman would have been under considerable pressure to produce children that could be reared to adulthood, even though pregnancy and lactation further impaired her health. Half of the inhabitants of Tlajinga were dead by age forty, and most of the rest died within the next fifteen years. Most young adults would have lost parents by the time they had begun their own families, depriving young wives of their support in child care. A young mother might also be expected to take up the work of her deceased mother-in-law, including raising her husband's younger siblings and other orphans from among his kin. Life was not easy for either men or women in Tlajinga, but physically burdened women had to cope with both contributing to family craft activity and taking responsibility for many other domestic jobs. In Teotihuacán, life was unenviable for most ordinary women.

On the other hand, women probably enjoyed the companionship of their husbands and children as they went about the daily activities of maintaining themselves and producing an economic surplus. The work was probably shared with a wider group of kin, including cooperating sisters-in-law, a few older women of the compound, and lively unmarried girls. When there are many hands and friendly conversation, life can be good for people living in a dynamic urban community.

In the majority of archaeological narratives about the past, emphasis falls on religion, warfare, and elite material culture, but most human life is concerned with household and family matters such as procuring food and shelter, making marriage alliances, paying tribute, and worrying about the baby. In household contexts, women and men live together and negotiate their participation in all spheres of activity and expertise that compose their way of life.

CHAPTER SIX

Women, Production, and Specialization

During most of human history, cultural systems have been characterized solely by domestic economies. All production was household production, and households were largely independent; the members of the group made decisions based primarily on shared values. Cheal (1987) has suggested that in this domestic mode of production, decision making has its foundation in a moral economy: in other words, individuals are motivated by a desire to produce socially preferred relationships. Thus, family members are not simply concerned with supplying their own material needs: they also seek to build and maintain cooperative working environments. In domestic contexts, both women and men may negotiate positive social status for themselves.

In many cases, gender is a key organizing principle of economic systems, and in times of change the ability of people to alter existing gender roles and relations is part of the flexibility of economic units of all sizes and degrees of complexity. Part of this flexibility stems from women, who have always had functions beyond basic nurturing. Prehistoric women, like modern ones, were often craft specialists and other kinds of professionals in addition to being mothers, wives, and kinswomen. Female labor has always been pivotal, even in male-dominated societies. States that systematically devalue females may simultaneously commit great effort to controlling female labor critical to their economic systems.

In prehistory, as some societies systematically added more task domains and statuses, women and men were assigned new, diversified roles. Anthropology shows that all domains—all specializations, crafts, and statuses—can be occupied by either females or males. In many ancient societies, the specialized knowledge of both women and men was critical and valued by the social group. In contrast, we live in a time in which critical knowledge is held by professionals, such as engineers and surgeons, whose ranks until recently have been dominated by men. While important functions continue to be performed by Doctor Mom and Mrs. Homemaker in domestic contexts, modern society is characterized by nondomestic contexts of production, where the most socially visible and valued activities are performed, but where women's contributions are still unequally valued.

There is considerable discussion about the origins and evolution of the division of labor by sex, and much attention focuses on how domestic economies are transformed as complex political economies evolve. This process involves the development of a social field beyond the household and results in a situation in which the division of labor is altered, gender norms are transformed, and the interests of individuals are compromised because the locus of power lies outside the family. The valued roles that women may hold in domestic contexts may have no analogues in the larger system, resulting in what to us is the familiar system of gender asymmetry.

As economic systems evolve, production of goods for consumption outside the household may result in craft specialization. Specialization by sex exists within almost all households, but in some societies households developed specializations in addition to the existing divisions of labor by sex, age, and personal preference. Labor was invested in production that allowed a household to be integrated into larger social, economic, and political networks. In late prehistoric complex societies, most households were organized to produce for both internal consumption and extrahousehold institutions and activities.

Formative Period Metalworking in Argentina

Households may be simultaneously characterized by both domestic and specialized labor. Work at the Yutopian site (600 B.C.–A.D. 600) in northwest Argentina shows that production of copper artifacts was an integral part of one household's activities (Gero and Scattolin 2002). The inhabitants made and circulated elaborate polychrome pottery and copper and gold ornaments. In the home and workshop of this extended family, archaeologists recovered the remains of communal food preparation and storage. This house was distinguished from neighboring ones by a hearth of fire-hardened clay with four

Figure 6.1. Adela Borbor, here seen by her forge, is one of the last bronze casters of southwestern Ecuador. Formerly, both women and men learned bronze casting from their parents and families. Photograph by Karen Stothert.

stones embedded firmly in its center as if to support a receptacle. The fireplace was associated with burned bones and beans, a fragmentary tuyere (the ceramic mouthpiece of a cane blowpipe), bits of raw copper silicates, and some scoria. It is evident, then, that this hearth was used both for the preparation of meals and for metalworking.

Yutopian people had no market distribution and no higher political authority. Craft production for exchange may have served to integrate many dispersed family units into an exchange network. Archaeologists are unable to say which family members performed any of the multiple tasks involved in the production of metal artifacts. While the ethnographic literature shows us that metallurgy is often a male activity, among the rural bronze casters of coastal Ecuador, both women and men may perform any task regardless of sex (Stothert 1997; fig. 6.1).

Other archaeological investigations show us that production organized at the family level continued to be crucial even as state societies developed.

Metallurgy at Batán Grande, Peru

The Sicán culture of the Lambayeque Valley flourished in the late thirteenth century A.D. The Sicán people are best known as producers of elaborate copper, gold, and gold alloy artifacts that have been looted from royal tombs at large necropolises. Based on the study of residential and manufacturing sites in and around Batán Grande, Shimada and his colleagues (1983) have demonstrated that metalworking was carried out by family groups.

Excavations at the site of Cerro Huaringa revealed an industrial smelting center that produced ingots and blanks of arsenical bronze to be finished into tools and ornaments in other workshops. The site was located near sources of copper ore and supplies of fuel. The three sectors of the site were connected by a road and each had well-built masonry and adobe room blocks adjacent to the smelters. The room groups may have been built by corporate labor to state specifications and were apartment houses for working families. As in the case of the pottery workers of Tlajinga 33, the residents of the room blocks of Cerro Huaringa worked in areas next to but separate from their living areas. Each small workshop had a set of three or four linked furnaces and a set of rocker mills: a flat stone slab (*batán*) and a curved stone that was rocked back and forth across the surface of the batán, crushing its contents. In Cerro Huaringa the mills were an essential part of the metalworking process. Furnaces were preheated, charged with a mixture of lumps of charcoal, hematite, limonite, and copper ores. Draft to the fire was supplied by lung power: two or three workers used blow tubes to force air into the furnaces to reach temperatures necessary to fuse the metal. The end result was a block of thick slag containing small droplets of metal known as prills. The slag, once cooled, was taken to the nearby rocker mills to be crushed and the prills were removed by hand.

Shimada and his colleagues (1983) suggested that the smelters were worked by family groups. Men and adolescents would have supplied the lung power for smelting, while other members of the family prepared the ore for charging the furnace and extracted the prills. These jobs could have been carried out by the young and the elderly working together. That groups spent considerable time in the workshop is shown by the remains of food, presumably brought to the people involved in the grueling and noxious tasks of smelting.

When the Chimú extended political control over Batán Grande, family-based production of arsenical copper persisted. However, after the subsequent Inca conquest, smelting was separated from slag crushing and prill removal because Inca administrators instituted a new tribute system. People paid taxes in labor, which meant that family organization of metallurgy was replaced by a series of discrete tasks that could be assigned to unspecialized laborers recruited as part of the labor tax.

Ethnographic evidence suggests that Andean kin groups commonly had some craft specialization. In modern-day family-operated ceramic workshops, adult women and men labor together and the most skilled and experienced elders do critical tasks such as firing. Children help with simple jobs, do housework, care for younger siblings, and do the tasks that involve little physical force. It is tempting to project this kind of arrangement back to Cerro Huaringa.

One of the persistent questions in gender studies is what happens to women, men, and their labor as societies grow more complex, differentiated, specialized, and hierarchical. In the Sicán period, people far removed from the producers made decisions concerning household quarters and the disposition of much of the family production. We see from Cerro Huaringa that family-organized metal workshops were ultimately dismantled by the Inca state, which assigned tasks according to its own needs. Textile manufacture is another area in which we have evidence of several distinct types of labor (Costin 1998).

Mississippian Weaving

Prehistoric textile production, using a variety of wild and domestic plant and animal fibers, was important throughout America. In the Mississippian region, spinning yarn and producing textiles were female activities at the time the Spanish arrived. At prehistoric sites like Wycliffe in Kentucky, textile imprints have been identified in ancient pottery. Drooker (1992) hypothesizes that women in every household made textiles on a regular basis. Her investigations demonstrate that the majority of textiles could have been produced by part-time artisans. However, a few twined textiles found in association with elite burials at ceremonial centers like Spiro and Etowah exhibited a variety of decorative techniques that would have required extraordinarily skilled weavers. Because there is no archaeological evidence of full-time craft specialists working in segregated spaces, it is likely that wives of chiefs produced textiles for the use of their households, as was the case in the sixteenth century. Women's labor supported the important political and ceremonial activity of the elite group. A woman's skill was probably part of her individual identity and prestige. Some textiles functioned as clothing, but others may have served for exchange, an activity that created political ties among communities. The sixteenth-century chiefs stored quantities of textiles, feathers, and other valuables for elite exchange.

In many societies, owning textiles demonstrates that a person or family controls both resources (fiber) and skilled labor. The complex iconography of decorated textiles can express the identity or ethnic affiliation of their owner. Elites used fabrics to honor their ancestors and to dignify chiefs in both life and death. Textiles were manipulated by elites and warriors in connection with a falcon cult and by commoners in rituals associated with fertility. Many of the Wycliffe textiles figure representations of weapons, animals, mythic beings, human figures, and symbols related to the community and its territory. By making textiles individual, women (and perhaps men) participated in creating social discourse.

Mississippian textiles demonstrate how part-time household labor can produce extraordinary items, and it is widely recognized that some of the most beautiful products of ancient industry were made before the onset of political and economic centralization. In early Mississippian times, the production of prized fabrics was not controlled by highly ranked persons, nor was access to such fabrics restricted to them. Later Mississippian households lost their autonomy as hierarchy developed and elites took control of community production. Under these conditions, some of the products of household labor were transferred into the hands of Mississippian elites at chiefly centers. This may have affected the quality of textiles, as the weavers of subordinate groups lost the ability to consume the fruits of their own labor. Some craft goods were produced by artisans, including slaves, attached to temples or elite households. This facilitated the production of items for exchange and increased the quantity of artifacts that marked status. Where more complex systems evolved, more kinds of female producers, including enslaved ones, appeared in society.

Aztec Tribute

Although ancient states created new kinds of economic organization, household production often remained the norm. There were different modes of paying tribute in the Aztec and Inca Empires, but women working in domestic contexts continued to produce goods for the state.

Figure 6.2. This decorated *cuauhxicalli* (a vessel to hold human hearts from sacrifices) details the military conquests of Moctezuma I. He is shown capturing the queen of Colhuacán, who holds spears in one hand and a weaving batten in the other. This, and her lack of a blouse, emphasize her female gender while her pose and spears show that she was a warrior. The *cuauhxicalli* of Moctezuma 1, detail. Museo Nacional de Arqueología e Antropología, México. Photograph by Karen Olsen Bruhns.

Spinning and weaving are key elements of the gender identity of women in many cultures. On Moctezuma I's *cuauhxicalli* (a giant stone container for sacrificed human hearts), a sculptor depicted the defeat of the queen of Colhuacán (fig. 6.2). She is portrayed naked to the waist so there will be no mistaking her sex; she holds a weaving sword in one hand and a handful of darts in the other, signifying that she is both female and a warrior (Solís 1992). All women, from the most exalted to the poorest, spun and wove. Originally, women wove only for their families, but local rulers exacted tribute in cloth from each household—a tax on women (Burkhart 1997). When the Aztec of Tenochtitlán extended hegemony over smaller states, they too demanded tribute, which men paid by rendering goods they manufactured or by serving as warriors or laborers. Most women paid their tax in cloth woven from agave or other fibers produced by farming families themselves. Local rulers who acquired cotton from the warmer regions of Mexico would issue it to women to spin as their tribute obligation. Brumfiel (1991, 1996b) argues that as the political situation grew more complex, with more layers of tribute exaction, women became more heavily burdened, leading to changes in family structure: polygynous households among the Aztec could produce more cloth. Polygyny may or may not have affected women's status, although it is known to have led to an increase in disharmony within families. Female slavery also increased considerably. Chiefly households had always been polygynous and had slaves, but with the increasing tribute demands, even relatively humble households sought ways to increase their labor pool.

Aztec rulers were continually at war to obtain sacrificial victims to feed their hungry gods and to grab land, tribute, and slaves. City-states that would not surrender to Aztec demands were subdued and required to render tribute in the form of young women and men. Female slaves were put to work doing domestic chores, but above all, they were required to spin and weave, freeing the wives of the household for myriad other tasks. Younger female slaves were also concubines who bore new workers.

In time, the exaction of tribute in cloth became so great (especially in the early Colonial Period when Spanish officials extended the tribute obligations of the dead onto the few survivors) that spinning, perhaps the single most female-gendered task in ancient Mexico, was also undertaken by men. Behind walls, men would sit and spin with their relatives. Intensive cloth production continued to be lodged in the domestic context until the Spanish introduced textile mills in which males, not females, were forced to labor.

In Brumfiel's (1991) study of women's production in Aztec Mexico, the distribution of artifacts in sites around Tenochtitlán reveals how women in different areas devised divergent strategies to cope with sociopolitical conditions. Brumfiel studied the changing frequency of large and small spindle whorls and showed how female productive activity, resulting in the textiles that were crucial to the functioning of the Aztec state, increased dramatically in some communities but not in others. By combining this analysis of spindle whorls with a study of artifacts used in food processing, she generated the hypothesis that those women of the Valley of Mexico who had access to water transportation specialized in the production of food for exchange in urban markets, while women more distant from the markets produced tribute cloth for imperial authorities. Furthermore, women altered their food preparation customs in order to weave tribute textiles while also preparing portable food for their men, who paid their tribute by working away from home. To save time, they made stews and wove textiles to exchange for tortillas. Despite the stereotype of unchanging female domestic activity, Brumfiel concludes that Aztec women adapted variably, depending on local conditions, to changes in state political economy.

Political Change in Peru

The Inca conquest of the Wanka people of late Prehispanic Peru precipitated a change in social relations that affected women's productive activities (Hastorf 1990:262–290; 1991:137–153; 1993). In the Andes, many social interactions involve the ritual consumption of food and corn beer, and relationships between men and women are expressed in all aspects of food production, preparation, serving, and consumption.

Hastorf (1990:275–278; 1991:137–153) shows that in Wanka 2 (A.D. 1300–1460), when the household was an autonomous socioeconomic unit in a loosely knit polity, potatoes were the staple crop. Maize, used for beer, was processed in the patio, where women may have worked communally. Skeletal analysis shows that both men and women consumed maize and potatoes in equal proportions in this period, suggesting to Hastorf their equal participation in community rituals and political events. This may reflect both the Andean pattern of complementarity at the household level and the fact that both women and men owned resources and produced food. Traditional patterns of bilateral inheritance in the Andes often gave autonomy to women within their households because both males and females had access to the resources of the social groups of their parents.

In contrast, during Wanka 3 (A.D. 1460–1532), after the Inca had imposed their government, potatoes disappeared and maize was processed in increased quantities, reflecting Inca state interests. There was more restricted crop deposition in Wanka 3 patios, which led Hastorf (1990:278–282; 1991:137–153) to think that, compared to Wanka 2, there was increased state control over household activity, meaning more constraints on individuals, including women. Wanka families in general, and women in particular, lost social status, and there was an increased circumscription of female activities in the Inca phase. Hastorf says that the quantity of maize and its distribution suggest increased female processing labor, representing an escalation of women's labor to support sociopolitical activities involving men. Skeletons from Wanka 3 showed that both men and women were consuming more maize, but that half of the males were ingesting both meat and maize in greater quantities than women were. This may have been due to the government's creation of work parties in which male labor was conscripted and rewarded with food and drink. Women's reduced social position is reflected in their lack of participation in the state rituals outside the house: they did not partake in prestigious meals of meat and corn beer. This reflects the Inca state's reconstruction of gender and its effects on production and social life.

The Chosen Women of the Inca

The Inca government had an immense and ever-growing need for both cloth and people to serve the state. To satisfy these needs, imperial administrators instituted a system wherein women labored for the state and, in fact, lost their identity (Costin 1998). This institutionalization of female labor avoided the interruption of women's production by childbearing and child rearing. In some societies, delayed marriage, artificial birth control, and long birth intervals are used to minimize the impact of reproduction on women's productivity, but the Inca solution was to remove some women from participating in marriage and motherhood, a solution that has appeared at various times in history. European nunneries once served as repositories for chaste women who produced prayers, cloth, baked goods, and craft items for the male-dominated church. In some cases, nunneries offered opportunities to gifted women who sought literary or political careers.

The Inca of Peru (A.D. 1438–1520) had a similar institution, the *acllahuasi*, or House of the Chosen Women. The chronicler Bernabé Cobo ([1653] 1990:172–174) tells us that each major town and provincial capital had one of these houses, inhabited by women who remained chaste and who served the state and religion (fig. 6.3). Every year, a government official would inspect all the ten-year-old girls in each village in his charge, selecting those who were outstandingly pretty. These "Chosen Women" were then educated in guarded precincts in the provincial capital. The handsomest girls were set aside for sacrifice, assured of a life of leisure in the other world. Others learned spinning, weaving, cooking, brewing, and religious observances for about four years and were then reclassified. Some were reserved to become concubines of the ruler or to be given as wives to men the ruler wished to honor. The ones chosen to be *mamaconas* spent their lives in the acllahuasi, tending shrines and preparing textiles, beer, and foods required for celebrations (Idrovo 1995).

Apparently, Chosen Women came from various strata of society, noble as well as common; it seems that daughters of the nobility occupied more

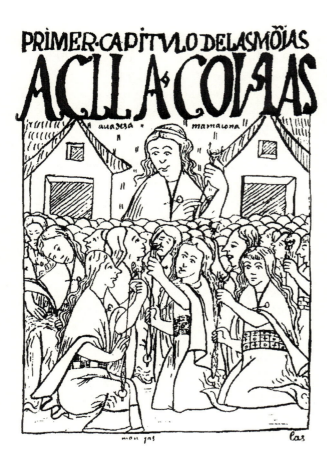

PRIMER·CAPITVLO DELASMŌJAS
ACLLA COUAS

auaxesa   mamacona

mou jns   cas

Figure 6.3. A sixteenth-century drawing memorializes the *acllas*, or Maidens of the Sun, who spin under the watchful eye of the head *mamacona*. Spinning and brewing for the Inca state were among the important economic duties of the acllas. Maidens of the Sun spinning, after Guaman Poma de Ayala ([1615] 1936, illustration # 298 [300]).

exalted positions within the acllahuasi. In each of these houses, a woman from an elite lineage served as the head *aclla* (Maiden of the Sun) and as the wife of the sun deity or of the *huaca* (shrine) that she served. In the main temple in Cuzco, the head mamacona was a sister of the ruling Inca. The head woman, like a medieval abbess, administered the acllahuasi and its work, both religious and secular.

The acllas and mamaconas were full-time professional workers, passing their lives in the confines of the acllahuasi and working for the state, which expended immense quantities of cloth and beer to support the government and to facilitate ceremonies and work parties. Women in the Cuzco acllahuasi wove clothing for the ruling family and created headdresses for the royal family and the nobility. The women also served the deity of their place with offerings of food, clothing, and beer. The Spanish chroniclers do not agree whether the acllas were confined perpetually to their convents, although they sometimes left to participate in public rituals. Draconian sanctions faced any Chosen Woman who became pregnant: the woman would be buried alive and her lover and his entire family, as well as the family's livestock, would be put to death as well (Garcilaso de la Vega [1609] 1961:130). The benefits that accrued to the Chosen Women were not insignificant. In this rigidly class-structured society, the acllahuasi was a means of social advancement for a pretty and intelligent girl. She might well find herself married to a man of higher class and more means than would have been available in her home village. She herself achieved higher status through education, and she was assured of respectful treatment in her new home if she was bestowed by the ruler upon a husband. The women who remained as mamaconas were rewarded for their labor with high positions in Inca society, which in some cases compensated their families for the loss of labor and reproductivity of their daughters. Earlier cultures in the Andes probably developed similar institutions that permanently added female workers to the labor force.

Gender and Work

Because of the necessary commitment of female time and energy to reproduction, a woman's involvement in satisfying the family's extradomestic needs is often limited during her young adult years. Today, as in the past, both families and states have frequently found it necessary to move men into what is normally defined as women's work. Men are weavers in many places. The Inca had male weaving overseers, who were themselves master weavers and who supervised tribute weaving and may well have overseen workshops where ordinary women, not Chosen Women, paid their tribute. Women throughout the Inca Empire wove for the government. Like Aztec women, they were often issued fiber and expected to weave a given amount in a given style. Generally, ordinary women wove plain textiles or cloth with simple warp patterns, both for their own family's use and for tribute. The find of a storeroom dating to the time of the Spanish invasions in the Acarí Valley suggests that women's taxes were paid with textiles woven to specific sizes, designs, and finishes, indicating that labor was highly organized and tasks were divided by skill (Costin 1998; Katterman and Riddell 1994). These pieces would then be delivered to a central authority who forwarded them to other women, who paid their tax by sewing together and finishing the borders of a fixed number of pieces.

It is also possible that sometimes women were gathered together to weave. An unusual structure at the site of Tarmatambo may reflect this practice (A. Galloway, n.d.). One building has many more doors and wider windows than is normal, a design meant to let light into the interior. Built into the walls are stone rings at various heights. The excavator has suggested that these correspond to the size of looms used to produce specific fabrics. Experiments indicate that wear marks on these rings resulted from affixing looms, supporting the hypothesis that this was a weaving workshop.

The Inca were not alone in starting to move supervisory tasks in weaving to males. It has been well documented that when domestic crafts are transformed into state-run industries, work and its supervision often pass into the hands of males, whose daily schedules are not interrupted with family care.

An illustration of this process is the evolution of the manufacture of ceramic figures at Teotihuacán, where excavators have uncovered a figurine workshop (Barbour 1976). The handmade figurines produced in the early Teotihuacán phases are overwhelmingly female. The smaller fingerprints that were left by their makers and fired into the clay bodies suggest that these figurines were modeled by women. In contrast, during the later phases of occupation at Teotihuacán, mold-made figurine types proliferated and the percentage of male figurines skyrocketed. The majority of late Teotihuacán mass-produced figurines represent males. The fingerprints on the insides of these molded figures indicate that manufacture had become a male activity. Thus at Teotihuacán, production was intensified and diversified as the manufacture of figurines moved out of the hands of women and relocated in the hands of men, who were presumably less encumbered with domestic tasks.

It is commonly argued that a woman's household responsibilities may prevent her from entering into intensive training, engaging in full-time skilled production, or undertaking technological challenges requiring commitments of extraordinary amounts of time and labor. How women's responsibilities are defined varies, of course, from culture to culture. Some women in the past, and today, through luck or because of their special motivation, did, and do, undertake skilled production and other specialized economic activities because of a personal preference, because they have fewer children than other women, or because they live longer and find the time to pursue extraordinary goals. A woman, like a man, finds it easier to cultivate her skills and talents when her society values her endeavors; when she has the support of her household, including junior wives, daughters, and servants; or when she can remove herself from the domestic sphere entirely.

Female Professionals

Domestic industry is one solution to the problem of organizing production and reproduction. However, under some conditions this mode of production is not sufficient for the needs of the community or polity, at which time specializations may emerge. In the socially complex states of late prehistoric America, both men and women entered professional life. Professions are defined as positions for which the person is highly trained in technical matters not known to the general public. The material culture of the prehistoric past is strong evidence for the existence of highly trained specialists, including astronomers, architects, metallurgists, and painters. It is usually assumed on androcentric grounds that these specialists were male. New insights coming from Conquest Period historical sources and from the writings of the ancient Maya and the pictorial manuscripts of the Mixtec all beg for the revision of earlier interpretations concerning the gender of specialists.

European historic literature generally fails to identify women as professionals in America, but a number of illustrated Colonial documents demonstrate that women occupied a variety of specialized roles among the late prehistoric Aztec. Apart from purely religious occupations, there were female merchants, members of the endogamous caste of long-distance traders. These ladies organized and administered expeditions and took the profit from them, although it is not known whether they physically accompanied their caravans to distant destinations.

Vending in the market was another common female role among the Aztec. Sahagún's famous book shows women selling foodstuffs, cloth, and other things produced by women (Baird 1993). Women were so important in the marketplace that there were special female administrators to oversee their dealings and to resolve disputes that might arise.

There were courtesans and prostitutes in both Mexico and the Andes. Inca sex workers were forced to live apart from other people and have no social contact with other women; their children were people without a family and position in Inca society and so were sent to the eastern Andes to work in the coca plantations (Garcilaso de la Vega ([1609] 1961:139). In the Conquest Period in Mexico, there were both female and male prostitutes in the major cities. Harlots wore colorful clothing and painted their faces. Although the Aztec were as family centered and as sexually prudish as the Inca, prostitutes do not seem to have been outcasts in Aztec society.

Modern understanding of prehistoric prostitution is frustrated by the historical sources, written largely by gynophobic clerics. Arvey (1988) has demonstrated how the *Florentine Codex* (1579), perhaps the major historic document describing the Aztec, owes its depictions of prostitutes to pejorative European art and law. However, there were different sorts of prostitutes. The *auianime* were trained courtesans and the companions of young unmarried warriors. Part of their public life was to dance with the warriors in various celebrations and rituals, wearing gorgeous clothing embroidered and painted with fantastic designs (Sahagún II, [1579] 1979, 2:364). The auianime were professional ladies who enjoyed a considerable degree of status in their own society. But Europeans assigned negative valuation to face paint, colored clothing, and bathing. When the Europeans disparaged prostitutes for these characteristics, they effectively tarred all native women, since these attributes of costume and hygiene were shared by prostitute and nonprostitute alike.

Curers and Midwives

Both the Aztec and the Inca had female curers, including trained midwives whose duties were both medical and religious. The Spanish remarked on the skill of Aztec midwives, although the European religious establishment tried to suppress native medical practitioners because medicine and curing were entwined with indigenous religious activities. Native curing involved medicines and mechanical manipulations along with incantations, prayers, and ritual acts. Female curers were prominent in the Conquest Period, if Colonial documents are to be believed, but gradually, their role was reduced by Christians (who defined their practices as witchcraft). Traditional curing systems in America survive, however, alongside modern Western medicine (Paul and Paul 1975; Ehrenreich and English 2010).

Ortiz de Montellano (1990) details Aztec medical practices and notes that the Aztec were considerably more advanced than their conquerors, especially in treating broken bones and injuries and in dealing with pregnancy and childbirth. Aztec midwives as well as other medical personnel were highly trained professionals.

Virtually all our knowledge concerning birthing practices and attitudes related to birth control and abortion in aboriginal America comes from art or from cultural behavior noted during the historic period. Regrettably, many accounts, such as that of Sahagún, were recorded only by Spanish religious men who heard the details of native culture described by upper-class Aztec men: thus much women's knowledge was lost. Similarly, knowledge of contraception and abortion, which was a concern for women in premodern

Europe, all but disappeared after centuries of religious repression and witch hunting (Riddle 1992), and after medical knowledge and practice became male preserves. In Peru, women who practiced medicine were denounced as witches or apostates and forced to abandon their practices on threat of terrible punishments (Silverblatt 1980, 1987).

Aztec medicine depended on various herbal remedies to bring on menstruation or speed labor. Some traditional remedies investigated in modern clinical settings have been shown to affect uterine contractions (Instituto Nacional Indigenista 1994, 3:1421). Among the Aztec, prenatal care began in the seventh month of pregnancy, when midwives began to visit expectant mothers. At this time, the midwife palpated the fetus to check its size and position, and the mother and midwife ritually purified themselves in a sweat bath. When the mother went into labor, the midwife helped her wash in the sweat bath and massaged her, performing an external version if the infant was in breech position. If labor lasted too long, the midwife would use one of several oxytocic remedies. The cleanliness considered essential for successful childbirth, and the skill of the midwives in dealing with poorly positioned infants, long labor, and bleeding, meant that most Aztec women were better off and safer in childbirth than their descendants were (Soustelle 1961:187–191; Ortiz de Montellano 1990; Sullivan 1966).

Nevertheless, the Aztec likened childbirth to the battlefield, and midwives made set speeches about delivering an infant successfully, or metaphorically taking a prisoner, which was the goal of Aztec war. Women were given miniature shields and spears to hold while in labor, and at the moment of birth the midwife uttered a war cry. Women who died in childbirth were, in official doctrine, welcomed to the same paradise as that of warriors killed in battle (Sullivan 1966; Soustelle 1961:190–191).

Depictions of childbirth in many art styles survive from Prehispanic times (Milbrath 1988). Mimbres painted bowls depict scenes of birth, and in some the midwife is represented as well (Hegmon and Trevathan 1996, 1997; LeBlanc 1997; Shaffer et al. 1997; Espenshade 1997). The Mixtec codices show infants attached by umbilical cords to their nude mothers, and several Moche vessels from Peru show women seated on stools or on the knees of a person who holds them from behind. In these vessels, the delivery is being overseen by a female curer, often shown as a supernatural Owl Woman. Owls remain important spiritual helpers in modern folk religion in northern Peru (Hocquenghem 1977b; Sharon and Donnan 1974).

Of the various sexual practices shown on ancient Moche pots, most would not result in conception (Larco Hoyle 1965; Kauffman Doig 1978; Gero 2004). These vessels probably illustrate specific myths or folk tales or may be evidence of ritual sex. Anal intercourse, fellatio, and masturbation might have constituted a contraceptive strategy, and Europeans noted their prevalence at the time of the conquest in Peru (J. Rowe 1948).

The one infallible method of birth control is abstinence. This strategy was certainly more effective in kin-based societies where goals and ideologies were shared communally. Among the Cheyenne of the Northern Plains, the belief that the spiritual power of the parents was diminished by sexual activity and that this power was needed to successfully grow a child resulted in decade-long periods of abstinence (Kehoe 1970). Taboos on parental intercourse while a mother is lactating are widespread, and religious fasting involving abstinence from specific foodstuffs and from sexual intercourse is also common in America. Today among the highland Maya of Mexico and Guatemala, a shaman is not considered good husband material because his position demands so much purificatory abstinence.

Ethnographic evidence from South America suggests that most abortion was mechanical and dangerous, a last resort when pregnancy would bring severe penalties on the woman. Inca midwives were said to be able to produce abortion, and modern Kallawaya herbalists have several methods for terminating a pregnancy, of which the best known is a dose of *chilca*, a shrub of the cold high altitudes (Bastien 1987). Infanticide was, and is, a more common way of dealing with an unwanted or deformed child. Abortion and infanticide are unidentifiable in the archaeological record.

Certainly, the herbal remedies utilized by ancient Americans for preventing conception and for causing abortion were relatively inefficient when judged by modern standards, but these remedies may have functioned to prevent or terminate some percentage of unwanted pregnancies in a population of women who were malnourished, carried a large parasite load, and engaged in heavy physical labor. Perhaps ancient professional herbalists and midwives were able to assist some women in making reproductive choices.

Scribes in Mesoamerica

The ancient peoples of Mesoamerica devised elaborate graphic notation systems to record genealogical, historic, and economic information, although true writing was invented only by the Maya and Zapotec. Writing, strictly defined, is a visible means of reproducing exact utterances, including both grammatical and phonetic elements. In contrast, the other Mesoamerican systems used stylized pictures plus a few more abstract notations signifying numbers, units of time, place names, movement in a given direction, warfare, and marriage—all designed to accompany memorized texts.

Until recently, archaeological opinion held that literacy was not widespread in the prehistoric period and that women, especially, did not know how to read, write, or memorize these Mesoamerican texts. This view is due to biases derived from the medieval European experience and overlooks the fact that in the ancient Mediterranean region, literacy was the norm, not the exception. The analysis of hieroglyphic writing on stone monuments from Maya sites demonstrates that monuments located in public places have more picture signs, while those found in more private contexts have more syllabic signs. This might indicate widespread literacy, although more sophisticated reading and writing fell in the province of elites, as was the case in ancient China.

Were Maya women literate? Like ladies of the Mixtec royal caste, Maya elite women were surely involved in matchmaking and power politics and therefore would have had as much need as the gentlemen to consult genealogical, historic, and tribute rolls—they were not stuck in a back room grinding corn. The same is true of the Aztec ladies, who had lands and households to administer. In fact, the relatively swift transition that nonelite Aztec people made to writing Nahuatl and Spanish in the Roman alphabet after the Conquest argues for a widespread literacy among quite ordinary people, including women (Lockhart 1992).

Scribes constituted a class of prominent professionals in ancient Mesoamerica. Book making must have been labor intensive, requiring a command of writing, graphic notation, draftsmanship, and painting. Recent studies have indicated that artists and other specialists were members of royal and noble lineages. Among the Maya there is increasing evidence from studies of architecture, carving, and mural painting that high-ranking artists signed their work or added self-portraits to their compositions. Some of these artists were women.

Women's participation in many aspects of elite culture is now well established, and, despite scholarly androcentrism, it is now recognized that numbers of Maya figurines show women as well as men associated with codices (painted, folding books). Years ago, Clarkson (1978) illustrated a female scribe represented on a looted vessel, but at that time scholars argued that the individual had to be male, despite the female dress. Later, people began to note Jaina style figurines of ladies with codices. Then, Closs's (1992:7–22) translation of a Maya glyph band painted on a bowl established with certainty that women could be scribes. The inscription first names a male as a *kahal*, a high-ranking government official; the second phrase names his mother "Noble Lady Scribe-Sky, Lady Jaguar Lord"; and the scribe finally names his father, also a scribe. Notable is that only the mother has noble titles. This inscription is unequivocal proof of a female scribe and further evidence that some noblewomen were trained as scribes much as their male relatives were. Women had inscribed possessions, including monuments and portable objects, so an equal literacy with men is not unlikely.

It has been suggested that another Maya noblewoman was a scribe, artist/ architect, and astronomer. This was Lady Xoc, one of the most prominent figures in the history of Yaxchilán in southern Mexico (fig. 1.3; Tate 1992; Herr 1987). Lady Xoc was apparently a sister or half-sister of Shield Jaguar I. Some have suggested that she was the wife of Bird Jaguar, although she was not the mother of his successor, nor did she succeed to the throne. Although her precise position in the royal hierarchy is unknown, it was evidently an elevated one because Lady Xoc appears on monuments with the ruler and with his successor, associated with bloodletting events and astronomical rituals. Her career spanned the reigns of two rulers, and she may have created a powerful role for herself within the government. Upon her death, Bird Jaguar appointed two younger women to high positions, and their ritual activity was commemorated in sculpture. Tate (1992) suggested that Lady Xoc was the artist who drew the text and figures on the famous Lintel 25: the inscription contains a glyph implying authorship, followed by her name. Extrapolating from inscriptions and from her prominence on the monuments of her time, Tate also suggests that Lady Xoc helped plan and execute Shield Jaguar's monuments. Were she not a female, in fact, archaeologists and epigraphers would probably look seriously at Lady Xoc as a prime minister within the governments of her close male kin.

The other direct evidence for female scribes in ancient Mesoamerica concerns an Aztec lady who was scribe for the emperor Huitzilihuitl (fig. 6.4), suggesting that elite daughters, like sons, were trained for special positions requiring skill. The system of parallel structures of administration and professions in Aztec culture makes the existence of female as well as male scribes probable. There were, after all, female medical practitioners, priests, and administrators, most of who would have been recruited from the

Figure 6.4. An Aztec female scribe, depicted in an early Colonial document, is glossed in Spanish as "The Painter." Redrawn by Thomas Weller from the Codex *Telleriano-Remensis* p 30r. Universitätbibliothek Rostock C T-R. Loubat, 1901.

nobility. Ladies, like their male counterparts, would have needed secretaries and bookkeepers. The schools attended by the children of the nobility may have trained women in writing, in learning the long narratives that recorded the history of individual polities, and in keeping track of incoming tribute. It is now well established that at least some high-ranking women among the Aztec were literate and that some functioned as scribes in elite contexts.

Production and Reproduction

The family is a dynamic economic unit because within it a few individual women and men may decide at any time to reallocate labor and materials, to economize, or to raise production by scheduling their time and increasing their labor investment. The behavior of these productive individuals is the basis of historical change. In each sociocultural system, activities are arranged in a distinctive fashion, and one of the dimensions of this variation is gender.

Women's roles in production and professional activity are inseparable from their efforts in reproduction. Humans, like other mammals, depend on females for the reproduction of the species, and human societies are designed to accommodate this role, usually assigning women tasks compatible with nurturing offspring. Nevertheless, it is universal among societies that women also substantially contribute to economic systems in many ways. History and ethnography demonstrate this variability, but archaeology is hampered by the problem of attribution: the identification of the sex of the ancient performers of productive activities continues to challenge archaeologists.

Archaeologists cannot afford to ignore gender as they reconstruct ancient production, because any study of historic and contemporary societies reveals that female-male relations are one of the crucial dynamics in the evolution of systems of production. Studies of economic change on the microsocial level demonstrate that it is initially individuals, and not whole households, who create and respond to economic opportunities. Because factors and forces affect wives and husbands differently, they will innovate distinct strategies. Economic and political changes may create opportunities that allow individuals to negotiate their roles in production and their control over the distribution of valued products. This may involve changes in the kinds of residential groups, task assignments, and gender ideologies. Gender relations have always been a dynamic aspect of change in production, distribution, and consumption—the constituent elements of economic systems. During World War II, women took men's positions in the workplace, and this experience, plus economic expansion after that war, opened the door for the greater participation of women in production outside the home, soon leading to their increased roles as consumers, and now to their acquisition of political power.

Historically, much of women's domestic production has been designed to satisfy the basic needs of the family, but the fruits of their labor also helped pay taxes and meet the escalating needs of elites and the state. Women's work produced valuable goods used to create social networks that supported the long-term well-being of their families; women labored to provide valuable gifts used in negotiating marriage alliances, and women provided the material accouterments and food that allowed their families to succeed in competitive political and ceremonial activities. Everywhere, women's productive work involved training and knowledge. Even if industry was domestic, women could be specialized in the sense that they produced for export rather than domestic consumption. Some ancient women were professionals.

Production has a creative dimension that is very important for individual women and women in groups: skilled women may produce ceremonial and ritual objects, as well as things labeled as utilitarian that nevertheless carry social messages. Ceramic vessels or textiles may express pride, membership, or sociopolitical resistance, and this is part of the negotiation process through which some women sought to maximize their power and influence in families and communities.

CHAPTER SEVEN

Women and Religion

An examination of gender in ancient society must assess the concepts of female and male expressed in cosmology and attempt to understand the roles of women and men in ceremonial practice. In Prehispanic America, religion permeated social behavior as people sought to communicate with the spiritual realms. Women were prominent in religious life. However, because of sociopolitical change and ultimately Conquest and the adoption of Christian cultural patterns, many Native Americans have been robbed of their traditional roles in religious ideology and ritual.

The roles taken by women in ancient religion, both in practice and in symbol, varied through time and space. In pre-Conquest societies, there were goddesses as well as gods, and both women and men served as curers, soothsayers, shamans, priests, sacrificers, sacrifices, divine ancestors, and innovators of and participants in domestic and community cults. Both women and men created ideologies and ritual practices that archaeologists attempt to reconstruct with the help of ethnographic models.

Shamans and Potters among the Canelos Quichua

The complexity and subtlety of gender relations and religious expression among contemporary South American peoples illustrate the problem of inferring past behavior. Many patterns are possible because the ritual roles of men and women are woven out of the raw materials of myths and tailored to serve ever-changing psychological and social functions.

In the artistic and ceremonial life of the Canelos Quichua people of

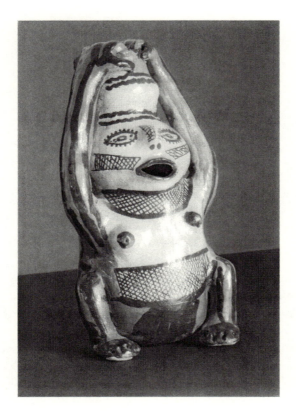

Figure 7.1. A ceramic effigy bottle, made by a
Canelos Quichua potter who lives near Puyo, Ecuador, probably represents Nungwi, a spirit associated
with gardening and pottery making. Collection of
Karen E. Stothert. Photograph by Neil Maurer.

eastern Ecuador, as described by the Whittens (1988), the apex of each
segment of the social system is a shaman. He achieves his position through
his knowledge of and experience in traditional and contemporary worlds.
Each powerful shaman has a sister and/or a wife who is a master potter, and
these knowledgeable women and men transmit the symbolism of tradition
and modernity to their offspring. These individuals are as familiar with their
counterparts' gender role as with their own and each may serve as an interpreter for the other. A powerful image-making woman "clarifies" a shaman's
visions while he is in trance, and a shaman himself, while chanting, may

bring to consciousness symbolism deeply embedded in his wife's or sister's ceramic art. What binds these distinct yet merged male and female domains is an ancient, enduring cosmology.

Among the Canelos Quichua people, female potters explore the actions of humans and spirits by using basic designs associated with the rain forest and the river: these represent life forces, living beings, mythic spirit beings, and spirit masters (fig. 7.1). For festivals, potters create vessels representing spiritual beings that remind everyone of their ancestral roots that extend through various layers of mythic time and space. Women making pottery link the past and present, the mysterious and the mundane. Canelos women paint their faces and adorn themselves to represent the mythic union of male and female figures, and men make music celebrating recently deceased family members, other ancestors, and ancient heroes.

Most Canelos Quichua adults are shamans or potters involved in complementary sacred activities: men transform the forest by clearing gardens and women restore it by planting domesticated plants; the male shaman and the female potter both manipulate souls and spirits, imparting these to vessels or spirit objects. Women transfer their knowledge to the new generation through the medium of ceramic manufacture, while men do the same through shamanic performance.

Archaeologists cannot expect to reconstruct ancient religious systems in such fine detail, but the Canelos Quichua case reminds us that women and men in the past built complex religious systems with important roles for all adults. It seems likely that both men and women were important in ancient religious activity, both had sacred knowledge, and both had the ability to perform rituals. Some ethnographic cases show how men can dominate in public ritual life, but others illustrate how women play prominent roles in religious life.

The Archaeology of Religion

Art, burial evidence, and ethnohistory all provide windows into ancient religious life. Painted, engraved, and sculpted representations of human beings should not necessarily be interpreted as naturalistic portraits or narrations of the daily lives of people in prehistory, as they often express religious concepts and offer us a view into ancient ideologies.

The images of women and men in ancient art were produced by the imaginations of their makers, who were intent on expressing ideas through symbols recognizable to other members of their communities. It is likely that artists were trying to promote, recall, encourage, or emphasize ideas about manhood and womanhood, leadership, elite status, and myth or to portray ancestors, cosmic forces, and relationships. Lacking the cultural gloss that could be supplied by ancient people, researchers can only make an analysis of art with the hope of discovering some details about society, ideology, and cosmology.

Ancient figurines, which are frequently gender marked, reveal the importance of sex and gender in the Native American worldview; the iconography is evidence of past gender. In literature, poetry, myths, legends, and stories, female and male actors do gender-appropriate activity.

Shamans

The numerous and diverse specialists charged with spiritual communication and the maintenance of well-being in Native American communities are commonly called shamans, a term found to be inappropriate for various reasons (Kehoe 2000). Nevertheless, in common parlance, a shaman is a religious leader, female or male, who acts as intermediary between human beings and the spirit realm, is a repository of esoteric knowledge, and may function as healer, diviner, agent of social control, or political leader. Shamanism is religious practice that may involve communication with spirits, souls of animals, inanimate objects, and the dead by mastering ecstatic experiences, acquiring spirit helpers, and using songs.

Late Preclassic ceramic sculptures from West Mexico depict female personages carrying out shamanic activities (Furst 1965): they prepare hallucinogenic peyote buttons, they hold cups containing psychotropic infusions, and they protect the backs of male shamans in trance as do Huichol women today (fig. 7.2).

Malagana Offerings

In 1992 a rich cemetery was discovered on the Hacienda Malagana near modern Palmira in the Cauca Valley of Colombia. Although the cemetery was immediately looted, rescue operations undertaken by Cardale and Herrera demonstrate that the Malagana people flourished in the midst of marshes and rich agricultural land, and the archaeological interpretation of ceramic models found in the tombs suggests that the ancient village may have consisted of rectangular houses on stilts (Cardale Schrimpff 2005).

Scientific excavations uncovered a series of offerings featuring women, perhaps shamans (fig. 7.3). Evidence was recovered from ritual pits dug to a

Figure 7.2. A West Mexican tomb figurine shows a male shaman calling up spirits while a woman protects him from harm, a practice that continues among contemporary Huichol shamans. Jalisco style figurine group. Height 49.5 cm. Cat. # M86.296.84. Photograph courtesy of the Los Angeles County Museum of Art.

depth of two to three meters. Each pit contained a set of sacrificed objects including anthropomorphic jars representing individualized young females, small four-legged tables, and bags or baskets (now decayed) holding rock crystal beads. One of these beads was placed inside each of the female jars. Some effigies were arranged in scenes featuring two women, a little table, and a small vessel that might have contained a potent liquid. Both rock crystals, commonly perceived as agents of energy and fertility, and hallucinogenic drinks were important in rituals in ancient Colombia.

Cardale Schrimpff and her colleagues imagine that the effigies of women commemorated a curing session or ritual, like those still held among the Kogi, during which people seek health for individuals, and fertility, energy, and equilibrium for the entire community and environment. While anthropomorphic vessels are common in the Malagana style, these effigies show a unique pose. The figures may represent patients or auxiliary spirits who help shamans cure; each figure could be a female shaman and healer whose power or immortal soul is represented by an interior crystal bead.

Today, few Native American women are shamans, due to half a millennium of indoctrination and ideological borrowing from Western religions, but in recent times some women, like María Sabina of the Alta Mixteca, who brought the sacred mushroom *teonanacatl* back to the notice of the Western world, have been recognized as shamans (Wasson 1974). Female shamans survive in South America among the Mapuche of Chile (Dillehay 1992, 1995), and in northern Peru, where Glass-Coffin (1998) has documented the important role of female curers in contemporary culture. Although Catholicism has succeeded in transforming female religious practitioners into "witches," in northern Peru and in Mexico there remains a strong tradition of female spiritual curers and diviners (Silverblatt 1980, 1987; Finerma 1989). Among the sixteenth-century Tupinamba, virtually all women were initiated as shamans and actively sought visions to foretell the future and to cure (Staden [1557] 1963).

Ancestors and Shrines

For people who believe in communication with the spirit world, death creates an opportunity to transform a deceased individual into a serviceable ancestor—a supernatural intercessor or guardian. Tombs and mummies in Andean culture often became shrines and loci of ritual communication. Cieza de León ([1553] 1984) remarked that in the early Colonial Period, Indians took more care decorating tombs than they did houses, because at death

Figure 7.3. One of several figurines representing young women found in an offering cache in the Malagana site, Colombia; each figurine contains a rock crystal. Photograph by Marianne Cardale de Schrimpff.

women and men were transformed into ancestors and worshipped by their descendants.

Mississippian Ancestors

Anthropomorphic sculptures and other objects bearing the iconography of the Southeastern Ceremonial Complex (SCC) are found near the summits of the great Mississippian earth monuments; other figurines have been recovered from elite graves or stone-slab tombs constructed for the figurines themselves. From A.D. 1000 to 1500, each of the increasingly complex societies of the Southeast was dominated by an elite group that manipulated SCC iconography.

In one center of Mississippian cultural development in Tennessee, only humans are depicted in free-standing figurines of stone, ceramic, and wood. While these figurines vary in style by region, they share features and express a common meaning. Kevin Smith (1991:123–138) argues that each is a portrait of an individual. These icons indicate an ideology that involved fixed roles for women and men. Males are shown seated cross-legged, but females, identified by breasts and genitals, are always shown kneeling with both legs

Figure 7.4. This pair of marble figures, representing Mississippian ancestors or guardians, was recovered in a high-status context at Etowah, Georgia. Here, as in many New World traditions, differences in clothing, hairstyle, and sitting posture distinguish the two sexes. Parks and Historic Sites Division, Georgia Department of Natural Resources, Atlanta. Photograph courtesy of Lewis Larson.

folded under the body (fig. 7.4). This male-female distinction was observed by early visitors to the Southeast.

In the Mississippian tradition, male figures were characterized by helmets or some sort of headgear, while females had long hair hanging down their backs. In the Southeast, historic Indian men decorated their heads, especially on ceremonial occasions. Female figurines were characterized by pack-like objects fixed to their backs. In the folklore of historic tribes of the eastern United States, the Earth Mother carried a sacred bundle on her back, containing ears of corn representing the first seeds given to humankind.

Mississippian figurine art evokes the association of women with maize, the birth and nurturing of children, and another important social role: the modification of a child's skull. Just as scarification, tattooing, or circumcision may shape the ethnic identity of individuals in the modern world, so in ancient Mississippian society mothers literally shaped the status of their children by modifying the form of their heads.

The figurines seem to reinforce the distinct roles of men and women in reproduction. In Kevin Smith's (1991) opinion, the smaller figurines can be interpreted as portraits of individuals memorialized in local household contexts. In contrast, the larger ones, over thirty centimeters tall and with a wider geographic distribution, were recovered at civic-ceremonial centers and are understood as paraphernalia for public agricultural rituals. These sculptures occur as female-male pairs and may represent ancestral mothers and fathers, evoked as guardians of sacred places and propitiated by elites for the welfare of the community. Chroniclers described both guardian sculptures in native temples and sculptured memorials in the likeness of the dead, and they told how native kings manipulated female and male idols in sowing-season ceremonies.

The figurines suggest that in Mississippian ideology, gender roles were highly differentiated, and that both females and males played significant parts in cosmology. In the early historic period, women's and men's roles were so differentiated that the two sexes were almost like different species (K. Smith 1991).

Other evidence shows that women were under considerable stress in late prehistory in some parts of North America and that public power in these societies rested in the hands of elite males (Eisenberg 1988; D. Wilson 1997). Nevertheless, funerary figurines show a fundamental ideology of complementarity: the ancestral couple consisted of a male and female, similar in size. While male posture associates them with power, female accouterments associate women with responsibility for agricultural fertility and human increase. Religious art was designed to reinforce the identification of women with these important concerns (Koehler 1997).

Goddesses and Priestesses

In South America, the oldest pantheon of supernatural beings is known from stone sculptures and relief carvings in a series of highland styles dating to the Initial Period and Early Horizon (1800 to 200 B.C.). This pantheon includes female supernaturals, some of whom still survive in the legends and folklore of Andean peoples. These beings often occur in female-male pairs, some of which may be ancestral to the late prehistoric male-sun and female-moon deities (Lyon 1978).

Later female supernaturals were associated with the moon, earth, and sea; sexuality, plants, and animals; trophy heads, sacrifice, and blood. On the north coast of Peru, the moon goddess was one of the most important deities, shown commonly as a stylized figure riding in a rayed "moon-boat"; she was also associated with children, *Spondylus* shells, and other marine symbols (Mackey 2002). She may be derived from a female supernatural in earlier Moche art, a woman wearing a feathered headdress, who sacrifices a prisoner in the Sacrifice Scene or rides in a supernatural reed boat, often in the company of a male god in another boat. Other female nonordinary beings were associated with birds, fish, and water creatures; one may have been the ruler of the piscine realm, called by recent peoples the Mistress of Fishes. One of these deities is known from the great site of Pachacamac, home of an oracle of the same name. Urpiwachac, the wife of Pachacamac, personified the Lurin River, which forms a lagoon on the northwest edge of the sacred site. The lagoon was the source of all fish. According to a story told at the time of the Spanish Conquest, Urpiwachac was away visiting the sea goddess when a local god attempted to visit her. He was annoyed by her absence and maliciously emptied all the fish out of the lagoon and into the sea. This sort of origin story describes one of many female deities associated with food sources and economic activities. Female supernaturals were not loving and nurturing mother goddesses but active, often bloodthirsty characters. Chavín females prominently displayed the *vagina dentata* (fig. 7.5); other female personages wore and carried severed human heads. In the historic period, a founding mother of the Inca waged bloody warfare, and the female oracle of Apurímac was bathed in the blood of sacrifices (Cobo [1653] 1990:108).

Figure 7.5. An image of the Staff Goddess of Chavín painted on a cotton textile, perhaps from the looted tomb at Karwa on the south coast of Peru. Her sex is indicated by the guilloches forming her breasts and by her fanged *vagina dentata*. She and her consort, the Staff God, were important deities of the later Early Horizon in Peru. Drawing courtesy of Dwight Wallace.

Female and male oracles were fixtures of ancient Andean religion. The Apurímac oracle was represented by a tree trunk with gold breasts. Dressed in the finest of women's clothing, with many golden *tupus* (decorative pins) adorned with tiny silver and gold bells, she lived in an elaborately painted building, surrounded by attendants in the form of smaller tree trunks similarly dressed. At the time of the Spanish invasion, Asarpay, a sister of the Inca, spoke for the oracle and foretold the conquest, instructing the Inca nobility to gather and warning them to use up all their stores and goods, so that there would be nothing for the conquerors. Later a Spaniard, who was granted the land around Apurímac, kidnapped Asarpay. She raised a tremendous ransom in gold and, being freed, threw herself into the river gorge to ensure that the location of the hidden oracle could not be tortured from her. Without historical documents, archaeologists would be hard pressed to appreciate the political and social importance of the oracle and her priestess.

In other parts of America, anthropomorphic representations may refer to female supernaturals, but scholars cannot always distinguish goddesses from other personages. Some images may represent deified ancestresses, as Marcus (1983) has shown is the case with female images on Oaxacan funerary urns. In contrast, goddesses were known to have been common among the Aztec: a pantheon of female deities was charged with a multitude of roles, governing everything from childbirth and drunkenness to the confession of sins.

Throughout the Americas, females are represented in prehistoric art, yet any approach that a priori identifies all these representations as goddesses is unwise. Goddess worship is the focus of new religious cults in modern times, but the reader is cautioned against projecting that faith onto prehistoric people without excellent archaeological data and alternative hypotheses.

While goddesses have not been prominent in standard interpretations of prehistoric America, current scholarship suggests that a female supernatural was the focus of a state cult at Teotihuacán, the center of one of the earliest and most powerful polities of Prehispanic Mexico.

The Great Goddess of Teotihuacán

When people first studied Teotihuacán art, they naively tried to pin Aztec deity names and functions onto the representations of supernaturals at least eight hundred years older than the Aztec. A common figure in the mural paintings that decorated many apartment compounds and temples is a male with prominent goggles around his eyes and a fanged mouth. On the basis of Aztec images, scholars identified these figures as Tlaloc, the Aztec rain god, or as priests or impersonators of the rain god; they emphasized these figures as the major supernatural of the ancient city, even though these figures are always subsidiary in murals (the major source for much Teotihuacán iconography).

In the 1990s scholars finally recognized feminine supernaturals in the art of Teotihuacán (fig. 7.6; Berlo 1992; Pasztory 1988; Cowgill 1992). Paintings of apparent goddesses are found both inside rooms and on porticoes in residential compounds. Some of these representations may evoke a single paramount deity, but they may also represent several different deities or even rulers of the great city. Attempts have been made to connect this female representation to Aztec or Southwestern culture heroines and deities, but she has no precise late prehistoric equivalent (Taube 1983).

The first identification of these figures as female was based on their clothing, especially the *quechquemitl*, a blouse that has been characteristic of central Mexican women's clothing throughout history. Once the equation between female clothing and female identity was made, other more variable characteristics associated with this female were identified. She is usually represented with a large headdress upon which plumes, bird or animal heads, and tassels are arranged; this headdress is sometimes dominated by butterfly icons, which are also military motifs. The goddess is often masked, and she wears jade ear spools and a nose ornament in the form of a bar with

Figure 7.6. An iconic figure (dubbed the "Great Goddess") appears in a Classic Period mural in the Tetitla Palace in the city of Teotihuacán. She wears a huge head-dress and ear spools, indicative of her exalted state, and a woman's blouse. From her hands flow water and precious jade artifacts. The mural shows a series of identical goddesses on the lower wall, but the designs on the upper wall have not survived. Photograph by Karen Olsen Bruhns.

fangs. When the nose bar is absent, her painted face exhibits a tooth-filled mouth and large oval eyes. The goddess can have prominent hands with red nails or claws. She is sometimes associated with decorated mirrors, perhaps indicating that one of her functions was prognostication. Other associations include streams of water filled with jade artifacts that gush from her hands or mouth, flowers, vines, decorated wings, birds, insects, water creatures, netted jaguars, and a red and yellow sawtooth design. Each of these items can stand for the goddess: sometimes the hands appear alone, or hands with water, or mirrors, or bands of eyes. These signifiers of the goddess relate to specific aspects of her character or duties.

A mural at Tepantitla shows her as a bust full of seeds with water and corn around her; humans offer her gifts while the so-called Storm God is shown in the border, a subordinate of the goddess (Furst 1974; Pasztory 1976; Berlo 1992). In the "Paradise of Tlaloc" mural, she is shown bestowing gifts, and in the "Temple of Agriculture" mural, she herself is a sacred mountain proffering gifts and receiving offerings. It now seems likely that the Storm Gods, or "Tlalocs," represent celebrants or priests in the service of this goddess (Pasztory 1988).

Of course, the paintings may not always represent the goddess herself. They may be images of her priestesses, idols, or humans who impersonated her during festivals. The ancient Teotihuacanos may have conceived of her as a series of supernatural beings or as one deity with various avatars. Recent critics have argued that there was no universal female nature deity for Teotihuacanos, and that the Great Goddess is a speculative fusion of "several different iconographic complexes" under one name (Cowgill 1997:129; see also Paulinyi 2006:1–15). However, these are many of the same people who argue that a series of subsidiary (male?) figures are more important than the main theme of a mural.

Nevertheless, the recognition of a "Great Goddess" represents an ambitious piece of gendered scholarship, drawing attention to an important dynamic in the religious (and political) ideology and iconography of Teotihuacán (Pasztory and Berrin 1993; Berlo 1992). Moreover, it is the first attempt to interpret Classic Period Mesoamerican religion on its own grounds, without imposing a model drawn from the culturally unaffiliated Aztec of nearly a thousand years later than the florescence of Teotihuacán. It would appear from contextual data that the "Great Goddess" was intimately connected with the local landscape and with the sacred geography of Teotihuacán, a place riddled with caves—entrances to the underworld and points for communication with ancestors. She was depicted at least once as the sacred mountain, the source of earthly waters, suggesting her association with local abundance and control of rain and aquifers, responsible for the fertility of land and the general well-being of the city. It is the highly localized character of the goddess that may explain why her representation is so rare elsewhere. Her power and gifts came from the local environment, not foreign ones. She may have been the prototype for divinities in the pantheons of later central Mexican peoples.

This goddess also had destructive capabilities, as indicated by representations of her with fangs, claws, and military paraphernalia. These may indicate that blood sacrifices were made to her. Many deities of Mesoamerica had both beneficent and destructive characteristics and had to be appeased with sacrifices of goods and living things.

Scholarly recognition of the Teotihuacán Goddess is an exciting result of long overdue work on the decipherment of Classic Period religion, and it comes from looking at the religious depictions of that city in terms of their own content, rather than trying to see them as illustrations of some later religion. It is now evident that the Goddess (or goddesses) of Teotihuacán is different from later female deities.

Scholars understand little about Teotihuacán religion as a whole, but it is plain that most rituals were conducted at the compound level. Depictions of the Great Goddess (in her various manifestations) are quite uncommon except in the city center, which must have been the center of this particular cult. Recently, this complex of images has been associated with rulership, another little-understood aspect of the sociopolitical culture of Teotihuacán (Cowgill 1997:151–156). The Teotihuacán Goddess (or goddesses) may have been worshipped by everyone or only by elite kin groups for the benefit of the whole city.

Did having a female paramount deity have any effect on the lives of Teo-tihuacán women? It may well have positively influenced elite women, who, if we can judge from historic peoples in the Valley of Mexico, might have func-tioned as officials and administrators of her cult and property. If the Goddess was made incarnate—a practice common among the later Aztec—she may have had a female high priestess or impersonator. Two monumental stone statues of women in elaborate clothing, but without the Goddess's signifiers, suggest that there were women powerful enough to have been portrayed in monumental stone sculptures in a culture where these were uncommon. It is doubtful that having a female paramount deity had much effect on nonelite women, whose life histories reflect poor nourishment and early death.

In societies with hierarchical religious institutions, the specialized reli-gious practitioners are called priests. Only recently in our societies have women begun to take on priestly roles, but in ancient America there were priestesses. As Aztec tribes migrated into the Valley of Mexico, priestesses and other women played roles in the yearly round of festivals, especially those dedicated to female deities (Graulich 1992; Brown 1983). A female baby might be dedicated to the temple by her mother, although the child stayed with her family until adolescence. Then she became a priestess. If she wished to marry, she was obliged to leave the priesthood, but her ritual

Figure 7.7. In this painted version of the "Sacrifice Scene," Figure C stands behind Figure B, ready to present a goblet of blood to Figure A. She wears long twisted tresses, and two four-pointed plumes decorate her headdress. Excavations at Sipán and San José de Moro have shown that this ceremony was reenacted by real people. Drawing by Donna McClelland, from Donnan (1978, fig. 4). Courtesy of Donald McClelland.

importance was signaled in an unusually solemn marriage ceremony. There were a great many different priestesses among the Aztec. In one of the most important celebrations, that of Ochpaniztli, priestesses held and sacrificed a female victim in the manner of male priests. In other contexts, women's professional participation was essential in ceremonies as well as in the everyday management of temples (Soustelle 1961:54–55).

Moche Priestesses in Peru

Study of ancient Moche art resulted in the discovery of the "Sacrifice Scene" (fig. 7.7; Donnan 1975). This seems to represent an ancient ritual involving an anthropomorphized hawk or owl (Figure B), who presents a goblet of human blood to a rayed male deity (Figure A). These figures are interpreted as warriors because of their distinctive costumes. A third figure is a female with long, braided tresses (Figure C), who proffers a goblet and sometimes a disk as well. Other common elements in the Sacrifice Scene include subordinate human warrior figures and prisoners whose throats are cut by a second female supernatural who fills a goblet with blood.

The woman (Figure C) is shown consistently in this scene, depicted in various media. She wears a calf-length dress with an elaborately patterned belt and tresses that terminate in snakes' heads, a common indication of supernatural status, along with the fangs in her mouth. She may wear a polka-dot mantle, and her headdress is highly characteristic: a long head cloth and a plain headband with two curved panaches.

Hocquenghem and Lyon (1980) identified this woman as a supernatural as early as 1980, but other investigators working on Moche iconography were not convinced, and she was identified repeatedly as male—despite her feminine tresses and dress. The problem was resolved when immensely rich tombs were discovered by looters in the Lambayeque Valley at a site called Sipán. Unusually, the looting was stopped and controlled excavation began (Alva 1988, 1990; Alva and Donnan 1993). The results changed many ideas concerning Moche political structure and religious ideology: the first two tombs excavated contained the bodies of people who were identified as having played the roles of Figures A and B in the Sacrifice Scene (Alva and Donnan 1993:2–16). These finds showed the tremendous wealth and power of these Moche lords and proved that living people had enacted the Sacrifice Scene.

In 1991 excavations began at San José de Moro in the Jequetepeque Valley, sixty-five kilometers south of Sipán, where another elaborate Moche tomb was discovered (Donnan and Castillo 1992, 1994). This time the body of an adult woman was found in a rectangular adobe chamber. Associated with the main burial were sacrificed llamas and humans, and ceramic vessels. The principal occupant of the tomb was interred wearing jewelry of lapis lazuli and other imported stones and accompanied by offerings of exotic *Spondylus* shells placed on her chest and hands. By her right elbow were a copper chalice and a cup with a hemispherical bowl and a tall, conical base. Associated with her coffin appeared a mask, two large plumes, arms and legs of gilded bronze, and a number of disks, all of copper-silver alloy. In one corner of the tomb was a second chalice, decorated with fine line painting showing anthropomorphized shields and clubs drinking blood from similar cups.

The implications of this tomb are considerable. Donnan and Castillo (1992, 1994) identified the woman as Figure C from the Sacrifice Scene. The plumes from the anthropomorphized coffin were identical to those shown on Figure C, and other funerary offerings, including the chalices, were similar to artifacts depicted in the mural representations of the Sacrifice Scene at Pañamarca, some 230 kilometers away. Like the male lords of Sipán, this lady must have participated in the Sacrifice Ceremony. She has been labeled

Figure 7.8. The burial of young Lady C at San José de Moro in northern Peru. Above her skull are two huge copper plumes like those she wore while performing the role of the priestess or deity impersonator in the Sacrifice Ceremony. A metal mask decorated one end of her anthropomorphic coffin, and gilded bronze arms and legs were found along the sides. Around her are a great many ceramic offerings, and it is hypothesized that she also went to the grave with many fine textiles, now decayed. Photograph by Christopher B. Donnan.

a priestess, not a ruler, in all publications. In contrast, the two male actors are only occasionally called "warrior-priests" but have frequently been featured in discussions of Moche rulership.

Continuing excavations at San José de Moro uncovered a second tomb containing a younger woman with offerings and a coffin similar to the first (fig. 7.8). The relationship of the two women buried at San José de Moro is not known. It is evident from these tombs that there were at least two women who, sometime in the sixth century A.D., played the part of Lady C of the Sacrifice Scene. Were these women reincarnates, that is, were they the deity herself? Or was the reenacting of an important myth part of the role of each elite Moche priestess? Was Lady C a ruler or member of a royal family? Certainly the offerings with neither Lady C are as lavish as those with the Sipán lords, although the tombs' now-decayed textiles hint at considerable wealth. These Moche ladies demonstrate that practices in which some elite persons reenacted deity roles were widespread in America.

A Divine Mixtec Ancestress

Historical materials describing the Aztec are replete with ceremonies in which a person reenacts the role of a deity. While Aztec impersonators were frequently sacrificed on the altar of the deity they served, this was not the case with all impersonators. In one case, politically powerful Mixtec women who ruled a place called Skull also impersonated deities in state activities (Pohl and Byland 1990). There were at least two women, both named Lady Nine Grass Death, who sequentially ruled this principality, and both led active lives in the eternal politicking and petty warfare that characterized the Mixtec states (fig. 7.9). Although Nine Grass Death has been consistently identified as a goddess, the situation is more complicated. Marcus (1983) has argued that Mixtec religion involved the veneration of ancestors and the propitiation of the forces of nature. Because Nine Grass Death was named for a day in the Mesoamerican calendar, it is likely that she was born on that day, making her a historical person who became an especially venerated ancestor. Her successors, always female, apparently took their ancestor's name upon assuming the throne. Royal representations in Native American art reinforce rulers' claims to divine ancestry by associating rulers with symbols of the supernatural and dressing them as divine beings.

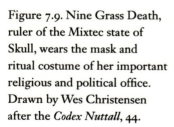

Figure 7.9. Nine Grass Death, ruler of the Mixtec state of Skull, wears the mask and ritual costume of her important religious and political office. Drawn by Wes Christensen after the *Codex Nuttall*, 44.

In the early 1930s, Mexican archaeologist Alfonso Caso excavated the Zapotec city of Monte Albán. He discovered a series of tombs that had apparently been reused by the later Mixtec (Caso 1969). In Tomb 7, Caso found extremely rich grave furniture including ceramic vessels; jewelry; objects of gold, silver, rock crystal, amber, turquoise, jade, obsidian, and pearls; mosaics of semiprecious stones; and carved bones, all associated with the nine people who were buried there. In the east chamber, four individuals, whose bones remained in articulated position, were associated with a mosaic-covered human skull distinguished by a knife in its nasal passage and a pile of red painted human mandibles perforated so that they could be worn as masks by the living (a practice shown in the codices). The west chamber contained five bodies: Skeleton A, the focus of the elaborate mortuary complex, was located at the far west end. This skeleton was seated, wrapped in textiles, and associated with the richest offerings in the tomb. Most of these were articles of personal adornment, such as rings, earrings, pectorals, and bead collars and headbands of obsidian, jade, gold, silver, shell, amber, crystal, and pearls. Jewelry among the Mixtec was not gender specific, except for pearl headbands, worn only by women.

Originally, Caso's physical anthropologist identified the remains as male. The assessment was complicated by the fact that the deceased suffered from Paget's Disease, a pathological condition that causes abnormal thickening of the bone. Curiously, the mandible was identified as female, forcing the argument that it did not belong to Skeleton A although it was found in an anatomically appropriate position. Recent reanalysis of both the physical remains and the associated offerings strongly suggests that Skeleton A was female (McCafferty and McCafferty 1994b, 2003).

Associated with Skeleton A were artifacts that reinforce the identification of this important person. In Mesoamerica, weaving, spinning, and plying were women's work, and female ancestresses and supernaturals commonly held weaving battens and had spindles or weaving picks stuck in their headdresses. With Skeleton A were four spindle whorls, a number of bone weaving tools, and a group of spinning bowls. During the Postclassic, throughout central Mexico, fine spinning was done with a spindle supported in a highly distinctive ceramic bowl. Skeleton A's spinning bowls were made of onyx and rock crystal, as were those of Aztec princesses. The most important offerings were thirty-four eagle and jaguar bones carved with designs related to genealogy, history, calendrics, and animals. These carved bones took the form of miniature battens.

The physical remains of Skeleton A and its associated artifacts suggest that the primary occupant of Tomb 7 was female. The lavish personal ornaments and artifacts associated with Skeleton A, the eight people apparently sacrificed as her companions in death, and the general richness of the offerings tell us that the deceased was a wealthy and important lady. In their reanalysis of Tomb 7, the McCaffertys (1994b, 2003) identified her with one of the important women shown with skeletonized features in the codices. The burial corresponds well with the important ancestress Nine Grass Death. This identification is plausible given that the ladies who bore that name were rulers of their own state, wielding considerable diplomatic and religious power. This calendrical and personal name was originally associated with a person who became deified or who had such power that her descendants abandoned their own names and took hers as a throne name. Nine Grass Death adopted a costume that included a skeletal mandible or entire skull mask and a black dress with bone designs. The lavish gifts made to her on state occasions, as illustrated in painted books, suggest that Nine Grass Death had the potential to build up considerable personal wealth that she, like the Moche ladies, took to the grave with her. The miniature battens may indicate another aspect of her ritual importance. It has been suggested that the marked miniature battens were used to tell fortunes. Divination, an important function of ancient Mesoamerican religious practitioners, often involved casting marked sticks, a custom that apparently came to America with the Paleoindians.

Both ancient books and the archaeological record in Oaxaca help scholars feel certain about Nine Grass Death's political status. It is clear that she ruled a kingdom, and that her influence and access to wealth were due in part to her supernatural status and to the ritual and diplomatic duties that she performed among the neighboring kingdoms. Perhaps the Moche ladies who impersonated Lady C had similar roles.

Figurines

Looters of archaeological sites in the Americas have provided the international art market and museums with a large corpus of ceramic figurines with no archaeological context. In many of these styles, images of female human beings are predominant. Because sex is often clearly marked, the corpus of images might be the basis for reconstructing change and variation in ideas about gender in prehistory.

Today, scholars are struggling to generate better interpretations of figurines and to deconstruct earlier, simplistic interpretations about fertility symbols and "Venus Figurines." It is clear that anthropomorphic figures had diverse functions and that they operated in various contexts. Archaeologists and art historians have speculated that they were used in marking life crises such as initiation into adulthood or transition to the next world at death; as receptacles for spirits in curing rituals and other shamanistic performances; as votive offerings; in rituals that recreated the cosmos or encouraged the increase of plants, animals, and humans; as idols in ancestor cults; as sacred icons or temple guardians; as substitutes for human beings in sacrifices; or as grave offerings. They may have functioned as focal objects, power objects, or teaching devices to intensify participants' experiences during rituals. Were they purely decorative? We have little idea of their meaning to the people who made them.

It is intriguing that female representations predominate numerically in many early styles, while in later styles both female and male bodies are represented. In early sociocultural contexts, female bodies were important metaphors embodying powerful and persistent religious ideas. The increased frequency of male figurines later in history indicates changes in symbolism and ideology that accompanied transformations in gender relations as some societies became more complex.

Pebble Imagery of the Lower Pecos

Native North Americans manipulated portable objects in rituals designed to mobilize power, promote hunting success, cure diseases, and restore health. Some objects were said to "come alive" as they were handled by shamans. Contemporary shamans use objects to represent ancestral spirits evoked to retrieve lost souls and restore a patient's health; some objects are also employed as part of vision quests, and still others serve to evoke guardian spirits or to channel evil.

Archaic people who inhabited caves along the Lower Pecos River in West Texas created painted and engraved pebbles, sometimes with painting over the engraving, which were repeatedly rubbed, ritually discarded, or wrapped and curated in preferred spots. The painted pebbles may have been part of rituals through which people attempted to regulate their relationships in the natural, supernatural, and social worlds (Mock 2011:115–132; Shafer 1986).

These pebble artifacts are water worn, and Mock (2011) argues that water is linked to female processes in the worldview of indigenous Americans:

water is the mythic home of ancestral spirits, game animals, and powerful and wise female deities. Thus the pebble is a natural metaphor, a form that may serve as an effective medium or repository of power in imitative magic.

Lower Pecos people selected anthropomorphic pebbles, some phallic in shape, and gave them features such as concentric circles or spiral patterns, which in recent times are life-producing symbols related to cosmic order, the point from which humans emerged from the earth, and to human reproduction, childbirth, and menstrual blood. Some late Archaic pebbles seem to depict female genitals; others show spiderwebs, evoking Spider Grandmother of the historic Southwest, a medicine woman with supernatural powers (Mock 2011).

The Lower Pecos pebbles express sex and gender themes in the ideology of these ancient peoples. They might have been made and used for feminine rituals, or we can imagine that these objects were sources of power for shamans. Male shamans especially need female power and the power of the earth that may be acquired from feminine deities. Male shamans themselves used female clothing and symbols as they labored to promote health and regeneration in communities.

Valdivia Figurines

In coastal Ecuador, the Early Valdivia people made America's oldest anthropomorphic figures: these were plain and engraved stone forms of indeterminate sex with a few stylized elements of face and hands (Blower 2001). Later, these small stone figurines were used alongside the earliest ceramic figurines in human form made in America. Shortly, the stone idols disappeared, and by Middle Valdivia times people produced and manipulated ceramic figurines with clear female characteristics, thus initiating a long tradition of image making in the New World.

Typical Valdivia figurines are painted red and depict nude females with elaborate coiffeurs (see cover photograph). The forms include immature and mature female bodies ranging from relatively realistic to abstract. There are pregnant figures, two-headed forms, figures with babies, representations with cut or partially shaved heads, figures with a variety of arm and hand positions, and both seated and standing figures. A few figurines show individuals with a protuberance on the lower abdomen that might depict the mons veneris of a prepubescent girl, stylized male genitalia, or perishable pubic covers.

Valdivia figurines come mainly from domestic trash deposits, although a few have been recovered in burials, and some giant ones have been found in ceremonial pits associated with public architecture. A number of figures, some male, were designed to be seated on tiny stools. This could mean that both female and male ancestors were venerated, or perhaps ceremonial seating was part of some initiation rites. In ethnographic cases, stools are associated with shamanic power, high status, and political authority. If lineage organization was important in Valdivia social and political life, then the figurines may mean that women of some lineages had access to authority and prestige in their communities.

Zeidler's (1984) study of the distribution of ninety-four Valdivia figurines in House Structure One at Real Alto demonstrates a clustering of figurine fragments around a burned area where food was prepared. He argues that Middle Valdivia households celebrated magical rites to encourage fecundity among women. One can speculate that this ideology developed to encourage population growth, which would have increased the labor available to farming families. At this time, there was a change in household composition as some extended families occupied larger houses and engaged in some specialized economic activities. The figurines might have functioned in ceremonies designed to ensure the welfare, reproductivity, and/or productivity of households and the community as a whole.

In another interpretation, by Di Capua (1994), Valdivia figurines are thought to represent various stages in the maturation of females. These were made and used by women in celebrations of transitions in their lives. Female initiation celebrations would be expected in Valdivia in times of economic expansion when the production of children was probably highly valued, when women controlled important agricultural resources, and when people may have been organized in matrifocal or matrilineal kin groups.

Valdivia figurines bring to mind some activities prominent in ethnographic female rites of passage. Some show depilation, which may refer to the widespread hair-cutting ritual that symbolizes a girl's death and her rebirth as a woman. Body paint on the figurines may symbolize the painting of an initiate's body or its scarification or tattooing, activities that are common in initiation rituals that prepare girls for womanhood. These rites frequently involve ceremonial headdresses or coiffeurs and activities that emphasize secondary sexual characteristics. Di Capua (1994) argues that figurines representing prepubescent girls show evidence of their social limnality: they have partially depilated heads, indicating that they are not fully adult; their arms are stumps or absent, making them unfit for women's work; and they have no breasts, showing their unreadiness for reproduction, although the pubic protuberance shows their potential to menstruate and conceive. Cult activity in ethnographic cases may involve vision quests and drugs. This is also suggested by Valdivia figurines, which seem to depict individuals in trance states. The features of the figurines suggest that girls' puberty ceremonies, like traditional ceremonies today, emphasized the importance of women in society.

Valdivia women living in large households might have created this cult, investing resources in the manufacture of paraphernalia and committing time to ceremonial activities focused on stages in the female life cycle. Groups of women may have invented their cult activities by creatively adapting traditional mythology, by commandeering old forms (pebbles and stone figurines) for new purposes, and by mobilizing new resources (ceramics) in developing meaningful ceremonies. Such rites of social intensification among women are intelligible if social and economic conditions favored new patterns of matrilineal descent and matrilocal residence.

Some shamans use figurines in healing rituals (Reichel-Dolmatoff 1961). Traditional Native American healing is a process that restores balance between humans and divines, between and among individuals, between humans and nature, and between men and women. Achieving balance and harmony may require that women and men act in concert, but a male healer might take on female characteristics or acquire a female helper in order to achieve balance. The preponderance of female figurines might support an argument that the shamanic healers were largely male, but this interpretation does not square well with other data, such as the figurines' distribution around cooking hearths.

López Reyes (1996) has suggested that giant Valdivia figurines depicting mature female bodies were icons representing one of the avatars of an ancestral creator goddess who was ritually sacrificed during Valdivia rituals. The broken figurines, along with the remains of decorated vessels, were found in a pit excavated into the clay floor of a ceremonial precinct at the Valdivia site of Río Chico. These figurines may have dramatized a mythic event in which participants commemorated an original sacrifice that brought the world into being.

The Transformation of Imagery in Coastal Ecuador
After Valdivia, the production and use of ceramic figurines continued for millennia, although the basic themes were transformed and elaborated by

later peoples. The earlier corpuses of figurines are dominated by female images, whereas the later ones are progressively more focused on male representations—indicating evolving ideology, ceremonialism, and gender roles (Stothert 2003).

The early solid Valdivia figures gave rise to a series of elite styles in which hollow figurines served as mortuary offerings. As societies developed increasing social stratification, one goal of the emerging elites was to create an ideology that buttressed and increased their prestige and power. Apparently, they celebrated their connections to ancestors, including prominent female progenitors, and emphasized myths about female divines. In the process of creating new elite culture, nascent leaders modified and developed the use of figurines outside the domestic context.

Cummins (1992) has noted that the emphasis on female images persisted into the later Chorrera period, even though a significant number of male images were made. The elite status of individuals is communicated emphatically. Chorrera artists introduced more markers of status and role on these figurines, consonant with their more complex social world. The social status of individuals was distinguished through visible markers including headdresses, costumes, body paint, tattoos, and ornaments for noses, ears, lips, necks, arms, and legs (fig. 7.10). Chorrera figurines portray both sexes with ornaments in equal portions, but some figures lack clear evidence of gender. In these androgynous images, male and female roles in worship, personal sacrifice, or shamanic practice were not emphatically differentiated. Unisex forms in this art could mean that elite roles were not as gender marked as they became late in American prehistory. During the ceremonies in which the figurines were employed, the *rank* of individuals may have been more important than their gender.

The widespread Chorrera tradition gave rise to a number of societies noted for their distinct ceramic styles. In Guangala, Bahía, Jama-Coaque, and La Tolita, gender themes are developed and some figurines show more diverse gestures, elaborate costumes, and dramatic postures than seen in Chorrera (Stothert and Cruz Cevallos 2007; Valdez 1992). These figurines reveal the evolution of ritual roles: women's roles had expanded, as shown by the association of female images with a wider variety of symbols, structures, and paraphernalia; but more dramatic development is seen in male figures, which demonstrate a great elaboration of costume, evidence of a proliferation of ritual activities and roles for men.

Women in Ancient America

Figure 7.10. A Chorrera ceramic figurine representing a high-status female with ear flares, face paint, a distinctive hairdo, and an incised and painted garment displaying a schematic vagina (inverted triangle with central slit) in the anatomically appropriate position. Cat. # GA-1-12-1289-79, Museo Antropológico, Banco Central del Ecuador, Guayaquil. Photograph courtesy of Tom Cummins.

Every aspect of sociocultural systems was subject to intensification in the post-Chorrera period: agriculture was more specialized and productive; settlements were larger; burial ceremonialism was elaborated; personal ornaments proliferated; and trade intensified. While more roles were available, women were not creating or filling as many of these as men. It is not known whether the individuals portrayed were humans, supernaturals, or figures acting out parts of myths; perhaps they were ancestors showing humans their assigned duties, or portraits of individuals, perhaps memorializing the recent dead shown in their characteristic roles. Nevertheless, both elite male and female roles in religious ritual were important enough to be portrayed frequently in clay. Female and male images occur in about equal numbers in these styles, but women and men are shown in distinct standardized poses, suggesting that gender roles were differentiated.

Both women and men participated in elaborate rituals and performances, but male figures show more dynamic poses, wear more elaborate costumes, and sometimes play musical instruments (Hickmann 1986, 1987).

Female personages adopt hieratic poses and wear elegant costumes. In the Jama-Coaque tradition, female images show the same hieratic pose seen in Chorrera, but with more elaborately detailed clothing and ornaments. While in Chorrera both men and women took this hieratic pose, in Jama-Coaque only women were portrayed in this way—as if they were keeping an older tradition alive, while the men were participating in newly elaborated rituals.

In the Chorrera style, female and male personages are often distinguished by their genitalia, while in the later Jama-Coaque style, gender is marked only with cultural signifiers like clothing and body ornaments (Cummins 2003). Similarly, Jama-Coaque women are not shown pregnant but only in their social role as mothers. While sex and age are important social dimensions in all societies, the Jama-Coaque artists do not appear to have been as interested in sex differences as they were in social roles: they call attention to the distinguishing details of costume characteristic of warriors, dancers, musicians, and other persons of rank.

In this period, gender roles as well as rank are spelled out in the figurines. Female persons display different objects than males do: females hold pineapples and some manufactured objects, including metal ornaments and textiles, which apparently signal social and political rank and ceremonial participation. People employed paraphernalia to signal their roles in the elaborate ceremonial life of the community. Elites invested heavily in celebrations designed to help them improve their religious and political positions. Female figures in the Jama-Coaque style are sometimes shown with roller stamps or clay seals, which were used to apply painted designs to the human body. Ritual body painting may have fallen into the province of women. Some female figurines wear pairs of seals suspended around their necks, which Cummins (2003) interprets as clan symbols, indicative of the powerful social roles of some women in Jama-Coaque kin groups.

In these regional ceramic styles, women are portrayed in many roles, but their poses are often static (either seated or standing), and their dress, while elaborate, never acquires the dramatic attributes of male costume. Women never wear fantastic masks, and only male figures are shown transforming from human to animal form. Female images are often associated with plants and containers, suggesting that women were celebrated for their valued roles as preparers of food and drink, including, perhaps, hallucinogenic brews. They may also have manufactured sacred paraphernalia, such as ritual vessels, and served as the custodians of significant symbols. Women's contributions in all these areas involve both actions performed in single-sex groups before the moment of the ceremony and ritual actions performed in public. The ancient viewer would not have seen these individuals as inactive, being aware that the food, drink, and paraphernalia were produced by female labor. Similarly today, during Maya rituals in Guatemala, fiestas in Amazonian communities, or holiday events in the United States, male roles are highly visible in public contexts, but if one looks into the entire celebration, one finds that many aspects of the ceremonies are orchestrated by women, whose contributions are central to the affair.

By showing females with objects, ancient artists created positive gender ideologies and identities, emphasizing ideal gender relationships, reinforcing desirable roles, and expressing the valuable public and nonpublic roles of women. These works of art help modern viewers imagine that women were taking an active role in shaping their own participation in ritual, society, and economics in ancient Ecuador.

In many of the regional art styles of the Andes, the concept of symbolic symmetry and social complementarity between female and male was expressed in prehistoric iconography. Human couples are often depicted in post-Chorrera art, reflecting the Andean belief that the universe is composed of complementary female and male halves, and that both male and female activities are necessary for the continuance of the world.

New Worship and New Roles

The Manteño people of southwestern Ecuador developed a more stratified sociopolitical system in the last centuries before European contact, and their material culture reflects elite activities, although nonelite families continued to use solid female figurines in domestic rituals. Manteño elites organized the production of quantities of goods and mobilized labor. They were known as great maritime traders, plying the seas from northern Peru to southern Colombia and beyond. Manteño artisans created hollow figurines in an elite style representing nude males, typically seated on stools, expressing their powerful ritual and political roles (Guinea 2004). The myriad activities of elite male priests and leaders represented in earlier times no longer appear in Manteño figurines.

The few ceramic representations of Manteño women include standing and kneeling females with simple clothing, few accouterments, passive postures, and limited gestures. Like the male personages, they are associated with no particular activity. Nevertheless these female and male images are evidence that the idea of gender complementarity was important in

Manteño ritual, but in the Manteño period the ceremonial expression of the complementary functions of females and males was no longer paramount. Elites may have replaced earlier rituals, which dealt with reciprocity between the sexes, families, and other social groups, with new rituals that emphasized hierarchy.

This case demonstrates how in some cultures gender roles are celebrated in art and how that celebration changed in the art of ancient Ecuador. We do not know what roles elite Manteño women played in late prehistory, or whether women's status was eroded as society became more hierarchical. Gender stratification commonly accompanies political stratification, although female chiefs were known at the time of European contact.

Religion and Social Life

If we consider alternative interpretations for figurines, it is possible to imagine scenarios in which females are framed in positive ways and in which real women are active. It would be absurd and androcentric to assume the biosocial passivity of women and to interpret each female representation and the remains in each tomb as evidence of victims of sacrifice, objects of divine sexual urges, or inactive wives and daughters of shamans, priests, and rulers. A balanced interpretation of America's past recognizes the wide range of religious and social activities performed by women and girls, and the significant portrayal in art of female goddesses, ancestors, and feminine concepts.

Figurines clearly show that women's and men's religious roles were differentiated and existed in societies with well-developed public religious spheres. Men's roles frequently predominate in some art styles, but this does not detract from the fact that women were active, authoritative, and spiritually powerful as a group. Indeed, in some native North American Plains groups, women traditionally led the Sun Dance and opened sacred bundles. Among some of these groups, women have been conceptualized as not only spiritually powerful but also innately powerful, which means that they do not need to quest for spiritual power as men do (Kehoe 1970).

Music, Dance, and Sex

In the ideology and practice of Native Americans, dance and music are important ritual activities performed in many contexts, although the participation of women and men differs widely across cultures. In some societies, dancers of both sexes ritually mimic the activity of animal spirits, seek contact with powerful supernaturals, or transform themselves through the process of dance. Among Native Americans, dance is widely thought to express the relationships of people to nature, to their creator, and to each other (Heth 1992). Costumed and painted people reenact mythic moments through their musical and dance performances, in which themes of death, fertility, and regeneration are expressed. Adult women can be seen dancing in ancient ceramic sculptures, both singly and as participants in community circle and line dances.

Dancing and music are shown in many ancient art styles. Donnan (1982) has described a variety of scenes painted on Moche ritual vessels in which males in full regalia hold hands and dance. Skeletonized women and children appear in another type of dance scene. Ancient Nazca ceramic sculptures from southern Peru depict women and men having a party with drinking and music, similar to the feasts described for the historic Inca (fig. 7.11).

Within the Andean sphere, women could be musicians, commonly drummers. From the Middle Horizon onward, women are shown playing small round drums that hang from the wrist, while men blow animal skull or conch trumpets, shake rattles, and play other instruments (A. Rowe 1979). Members of both sexes danced. In the Colonial Period, women became separated from their musical duties because of European missionary distaste for women having public roles in religion and participating in parties in which there was drink and sexual activity.

There is little association between women and music in Mesoamerican art. West Mexican tomb figurines show only men with musical instruments, although women are shown participating in dances and in poses that might indicate singing or chanting. In the Classic Maya Bonampak murals, only male musicians are depicted. However, six hundred years later, among the northern Maya of the Conquest Period, old women danced in the temple during New Year ceremonies. In religious festivals held outside temple precincts, music and dancing were an integral part of rituals, but men and women did not dance together (Landa [1566] 1978).

Recent scholarship emphasizes how gender is constructed socially through performance and how bodies are significant loci of the social struggle to shape gender behavior, involving parents, elders, and religious and civil authorities (Butler 1993; Joyce 2000, 2005). Joyce describes in detail how ancient Mesoamerican societies reinforced sexual statuses and behavior in domestic and public events. During calendar ceremonies, processions were performed in public spaces and included elaborate dances and "sexually charged performances by groups of men and women" that reinforced, by

Figure 7.11. A Nazca bottle from southern Peru depicts a party in which the participants are gathered around large jars of beer while a male drums. A stepped wall indicates that this party or ritual took place in a courtyard or other enclosure. The participants are both male and female (women have long tresses). Parties involving men, women, and beer were common in the Andes. This one may commemorate a raid or other military action, since three of the men have trophy heads hanging around their necks. Museo Nacional de Arqueología e Antropología, Lima. Photograph courtesy of Dorothy Menzel.

repetition, certain "bodily practices." Joyce argues that "gender and power are completely intertwined because the social control of the individual experience of the body is the most intimate level of discipline practiced by authorities" (2000:177). She finds evidence of gender performance in the burials and figurines of Tlatilco, a site of "public performances through which gender was incorporated in the bodies of young men and women." Evidence of Classic Maya dances is found in texts and images at sites like Yaxchilán; Joyce also notes that Maya pottery vessels "show mixed groups of men and women performing formal dance movements." Similar religious activities were observed by Bishop Diego de Landa in the Yucatán: there "women held bundles of cloth or dishes as they danced" (180).

In some ancient American art styles, sexual contact between females and males is represented. This so-called erotic or pornographic art may depict mythic scenes that were enacted by human impersonators or ritual actors who performed sex acts or carried them out symbolically. In many historic societies, there were rituals that employed human sex metaphorically to communicate powerful cultural meanings. In some ceremonies, coitus was performed as part of magical rituals designed to transfer power. In a study of the function of ceremonial sexual intercourse, Kehoe (1970:99–103) gives examples from North American ethnography of how spiritual power may be transmitted from man to man as first one, then the other, has intercourse with a particular woman. High-ranking, respectable, and chaste matrons and their husbands participated in the ritual and perceived their activity as spiritual. A woman, knowing herself to be the bearer and communicator of power, might value the opportunity to exercise spiritual and political authority by participating with men in rituals that expressed her status and brought prestige to herself and her family.

Native American fertility rituals may involve ritual intercourse, or the symbolic reenactment of mythical intercourse. Among the nineteenth-century Arapaho, an elder man and a woman would perform a coital ritual by transferring a symbolic root from his mouth to hers.

Ritual sex is often a strategy developed in matrilineal societies in order to reinforce the role of male "begetters" and balance the predominant role of mothers in reproduction. In performing ritual coitus, the roles of both become important. Religious interpretations of sex are likely to have been part of the negotiation of roles between men and women throughout prehistory. This negotiation resulted in the emphasis on female reproduction in some philosophical systems and an emphasis on male fertility in others.

Gender balance may be symbolized and negotiated in the ideology of a people, but in some ethnographic cases, in the Amazon region for instance, ritual sex became gang rape. Other intimidating demonstrations of male power are known: among the Blackfoot and other Plains groups, violent punishment of "errant" females was practiced.

Human Sacrifice

Aside from active roles as religious specialists or as believers, women could also be the victims, willing or unwilling, of their religious beliefs. Human sacrifice was widespread in the Americas. The scale as well as the ideological impetus varied with place and time, and with the type of society, but from the beginnings of settled life, human sacrifice was an established part of many religious traditions. Although salacious Western writers emphasize the sacrifice of trembling virgins, in truth, in most societies women were too valuable as producers and reproducers to be removed by sacrifice with any frequency. Although the sacrifice of virgin girls by throwing them into the Cenote of Sacrifice at Chichén Itzá has become iconic, actual analysis of the skeletons of victims found in the sinkhole shows that the sacrifices were mainly men and children—thirteen males, eight females, and twenty-one children (Hooton 1940). It is not surprising that children were sacrificed, since the cenotes functioned as shrines to the water spirits, and children were considered the most appropriate sacrifices to these deities. The fact that all the adults showed signs of having led hard lives suggests that they, as well as the children, were slaves, just as described by the chronicler Diego de Landa ([1566] 1978:48).

In ancient societies, human sacrifices were appropriate in the propitiation of deities and in some funerary contexts. Throughout the Americas, the sacrifice of female servants or lesser wives at the death of a ruler was relatively common. Cieza de León ([1553] 1984) writes that the Quimbaya of central Colombia would make women drunk before burying them alive in the tomb of the chief. In Panama, Gaspar de Espinosa ([1519] 1873:23–26) observed the burial of Chief Parita, wrapped in a bundle with all his jewelry, with one woman at his head and another at his feet. When the Spanish murdered Atahuallpa, some of the women attending him demanded the right to accompany their ruler. Such sacrifices were not always forced on women. Most archaeological and ethnohistoric cases involved small numbers of people. Among the historic Pawnee, one of the traditional ceremonies designed to revitalize the universe involved the commemoration of the sexual union of the Morning and Evening Stars (male and female), resulting in the creation of the First Girl, and later, all people. This ritual involved the sacrifice of a young female captive to the Evening Star. Earlier in history, young men had been sacrificed to the Morning Star (Grange 1979). From an archaeological site on the Smoky Hill River in Kansas, occupied around A.D. 1300, O'Brian (1990) described a burial mound with the remains of a number of individuals, including a twelve-year-old female. The mound has been interpreted as the site of a sacrifice to the Evening Star. Among recent Pawnee people, the ceremony involved firing a number of arrows into the victim's body, which was then exposed, head to the east, to be consumed by animals. In the pre-historic mound, archaeologists found arrow points scattered in the fill and recovered the gnawed, disarticulated bones of a young woman under the east side of the mound.

Human sacrifice was particularly common in Andean cultures. In the northern Andes, sacrifices as part of the dedication of houses may have begun in Valdivia times. Human sacrifice began to be widespread in the central Andes in the Late Preceramic. At Caral, a very early monumental complex on the coast of Peru, the body of a small boy was found interred as a dedicatory offering in the midst of the pyramids (Shady and Leyva 2003). By the Initial Period, human sacrifice was common and widespread. In one case, the skull of a woman surrounded by children's milk teeth was found in the Gallery of the Offerings at Chavín de Huántar, and abundant evidence of cut human bone was recovered from debris in the underground galleries of the same site. Chavín was the main cult center of the first religious movement to spread throughout Peru (Lumbreras 1989:206–216).

Human sacrifices continued to be made on an increasingly greater scale throughout the Prehispanic period, but during the time of the Inca Empire the number of sacrificial episodes escalated and new kinds of human offerings were made. Inca governors and priests regulated human sacrifice in their conquered territories. There were various means of sacrifice, like strangling the victims and then burying or cremating them; some hearts were removed so that blood could be offered separately from the body, which was burned; and throat cutting and offering the blood of victims repeats a pattern seen earlier among the Moche. Inca sacrificial victims were also buried alive or made drunk or insensible (with blows to the head) and then left to die of exposure on mountains. This was the case with the recently discovered frozen mummies from a number of peaks in southern Peru (Reinhard 2006).

Among the Inca and their predecessors, male sacrifices often involved bloodletting, whereas females were dispatched by non–blood-releasing means, with subsequent interment of the entire body in the earth. Most Inca sacrificial victims were children below the age of puberty. For example, the *capa cocha* ritual was a particularly elaborate form of sacrifice in which beautiful children were brought to Cuzco to be feted in a public ceremony; later they returned to their native provinces to be buried alive as dedicatory offerings or to propitiate female deities. There are historic accounts of capa cochas involving indoctrinated children like a beautiful child named Tanta Karwa, who was selected as a sacrifice by her father at her birth. At age ten she went to Cuzco for the state ceremony that consecrated all the capa cocha children. Upon her ceremonious return to her village she willingly entered the tomb where she was to die as an offering to an irrigation ditch. Her family gained prestige within the structure of the Inca Empire and her brother spent his life as the chief priest of the local cult, which kept alive her memory. Tanta Karwa was venerated as a minor deity at the time of the Spanish Conquest, when her tomb was opened and the offerings of precious metals were removed from her decayed body (Zuidema 1977–1978; Duviols 1976; Faux 2012; Hernández Príncipe [1622] 1923).

Children of both sexes were sacrificed like Tanta Karwa for various political and religious purposes. A few individuals seem to have been chosen by government officials or willingly offered by their parents.

In contrast, at the great shrine of Pachacamac, just south of Lima, Peru, there is evidence of sacrifices on a much larger scale that involved women (Uhle 1903). This shrine's apogee was in the sixth to eighth centuries, when a prestigious oracle held sway and Pachacamac became a large city prospering from the visits of pilgrims. By the time the Inca conquered the Central Coast, the shrine had fallen on hard times, but the Inca craftily embraced the oracle and assisted in its economic recovery. A huge temple dedicated to the Inca sun god and a House of the Chosen Women was built near the old Temple of the Oracle. A series of burials was excavated on the lower terrace of the Sun Temple. Uhle recovered forty-six well-preserved bodies but estimated that there had originally been at least twice as many. These burials were all adult women, mostly young, although one had long gray hair, and all had been strangled. The necks of some of the mummies were less than two inches in diameter, and the nuchal vertebrae of others had been dislocated. Some still showed how the strangulation had been done: a folded cloth, knotted in the middle, was passed around the neck and pulled tight. The large knot in front closed the larynx mechanically, quickening death (fig. 7.12).

Uhle (1903) speculated that these women were gathered from various highland locations because the plant food offerings associated with the burials were of highland origin. In contrast, ordinary burials at Pachacamac contained coastal cultigens. There was considerable variation in the shape of the women's heads, the result of cranial modification that varied by ethnic group. This suggests that the victims were assembled from various parts of the empire. Their clothing, some new and some well worn, was obviously their own. The associated pottery was both imperial Inca and coastal style,

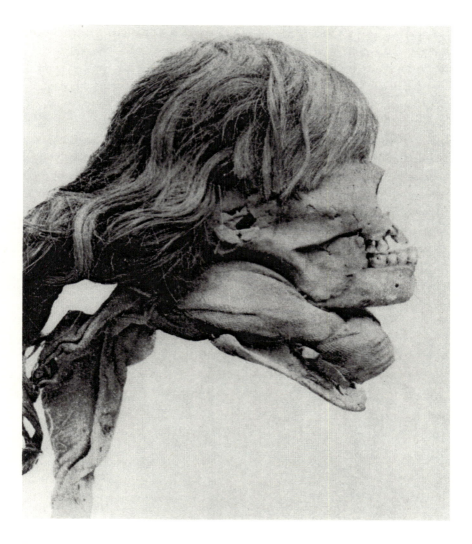

Figure 7.12. The head of one of the women sacrificed at Pachacamac. The strangling device, a knotted cloth, is still in place under her jawbone. From Max Uhle, Pachacamac, Plate #18, #13. Courtesy of the University of Pennsylvania Museum.

but the women were also buried with personal possessions such as sewing baskets and combs—some with hairs still in them. It is thought that they were brought to Pachacamac to serve the Sun, but there they were sacrificed. It is possible that the sacrifice was part of the rededication of the temple after its remodeling, but mass sacrifices were more common in response to natural disasters, such as an El Niño event or the death of a ruler.

Among the Inca and in other contemporary Andean states, the slaughter of women of reproductive age makes manifest an unusual ideology: women became commodities to be displayed rather than essential members of their community. Powerful religious beliefs, and perhaps religious and political fanaticism, account for these episodes of sacrifice, but one wonders if such a sacrifice would have been made had women held more power in the Inca state.

CHAPTER EIGHT

Women and Power

Modern people assume that hierarchy is normal and that super-ordination and subordination are natural or universal. Because the political domain has become preponderant in recent history and because considerable asymmetry in the power held by women and men has developed in many societies, women's roles in political history have been neglected or suppressed and male leaders have been the main focus of archaeological interpretation. However, it can be argued that neither the ranking of males and females nor male domination is universal or embedded in human nature. Neither sexual nor political hierarchy was invented until relatively late in human history, and even today such hierarchy is poorly developed or missing in small-scale, non-Western societies in which people are organized by kinship and cultivate egalitarian relations.

Some feminist scholars have argued that female subordination developed in tandem with private property and the state; others have suggested that gender equality and complementarity were prevalent in America until European colonization. A careful look at the archaeological and ethnohistoric record shows that in ancient America, as in the rest of the world, there existed many different ways of organizing social life: some women lived in egalitarian societies and others participated in hierarchical states. Research among Native American groups has shown that at the heart of many societies, in the family, there is often a pattern of balanced reciprocity, of collateral spheres in which "powerful" and "powerless" have no meaning and in which neither women nor men dominate the other. This is not to say that women and men did not quest for power over others, but in ancient America power was expressed in many ways and involved the interplay of politics, religion, economics, and gender.

There is no evidence of matriarchy in prehistoric American societies—or anywhere else in the world (Eller 2000). While it is unlikely that women in any ancient society systematically dominated their community politically, it is nevertheless clear that there were societies in which women held key leadership roles, and there were cases of matrilineal and matrifocal societies, such as the Hopi and the Iroquois, in which women exerted considerable influence within and beyond the family. Trocolli (1999:49–62) describes female leaders of Native American tribes that dominated their communities politically—just like male leaders.

In the past, as today, women and men may dominate in distinct realms of activity and they may develop expertise in different areas. In some Amazonian cases, men and women are separated, and each is autonomous and "powerful" but antagonistic to the other group. In the case of the prehistoric Inca, and in more recent Andean groups, men and women often formed parallel and distinct social groups and institutions. This arrangement confers upon both women and men leadership roles, power, and opportunities to shape their culture. Ethnographic evidence alerts us to the possibility that gender roles in the political arena were variable in the past, and that our interpretations should consider how both women and men gained and used power.

It has now become clear how difficult it is to reconstruct the power structures of past peoples. In the North American Southwest, scholars continue to argue whether the prehistoric Pueblo societies were egalitarian or hierarchical. McGuire and Saitta (1996) have suggested that this kind of oppositional thinking is unproductive and that a more nuanced interpretation is called for. Specifically, they argue that power should not be considered as something that is either present or absent; rather, it is always present in social life and involves the ability of individuals to alter events. They conclude that prehistoric peoples lived in communal societies that had both consensual and hierarchical social features. People were organized in kin groups that held resources and exploited them communally. There were inequalities among these kin groups, and hierarchy existed both within and between groups, but without monopolies on power and wealth, and without class stratification. The elites of the communal groups derived power from their own networks of social, material, and ideological relationships. In this view, power does not flow down a hierarchy but exists in many forms, and it is ambiguous and contradictory in societies where egalitarian and hierarchical features are mixed. This model is supported by the apparent stratification in burial data in many sites, including differential distribution of trade goods and ritual paraphernalia, indicating that some individuals had extraordinary roles.

In systems with checks and balances, power is expressed and exercised in complex ways, such that in the lived experience of people a variety of individuals might participate as conscious creators and negotiators of culture. This means that members of all sectors of society, including women, are expected to participate in the dialectical process of cultural change. If one is persuaded by this view of social power, it introduces the possibility that the power to shape events, influence history, and shape one's own life might have been lodged in women's hands as well as men's.

Burial symbolism often reiterates social differentiation of men and women, but evidence from the earliest periods of American prehistory demonstrates the existence of complementarity, real measures of symmetry and equality between the sexes. In later prehistory, asymmetry became more pronounced as men and some women took opportunities to acquire power in extradomestic arenas of activity. Lower-ranked women and men suffered negative consequences as progressive social differentiation left power and authority concentrated in the hands of elites and strangers. Women's domestic roles altered when families were integrated into hierarchical political economies. Division of labor and gender norms were transformed as economies grew: men gained power bases outside the family, and women's roles, valued in the family context, had no direct significance in the public sphere, where powerful people pursued interests that were sometimes inimical to women and families.

Many tombs in later prehistory were designed to signal the power and status of the deceased (Dillehay 1995). Men and women who were more successful in achieving high status from participation in warfare, trade, and religious practice were subsequently celebrated at death. Nevertheless, one suspects that the expression of the power of particular men in art, material culture, and funerary rituals outstripped the reality of their power. Conversely, one wonders if the lack of expression of women's power obscures the reality: that women had more power than archaeologists guess. The nagging question is whether women publicly deferred to men while privately contesting men's public control and cultivating their own power in domestic contexts.

In the Classic Period (A.D. 1150–1400) in southern Arizona, Hohokam society grew more complex and showed increasing social differentiation along lines of wealth. Studies of domestic production, architecture, ritual space, and burials have shown changing patterns of sexual stratification.

Crown and Fish (1996) suggest that there was increasing differentiation among women in Hohokam communities as some women were isolated in walled compounds, thus limiting their roles in the community while promoting female integration in the family work group. McGuire (1992) argues that labor invested in food processing and craft production increased during the Classic Period: the clay griddle appeared, and more elaborate ceramics, including high-polished wares, were manufactured. Numerous spindle whorls demonstrate that households increased their investment in processing fiber. As families abandoned pit houses, elite women living in these isolated corporate groups in walled compounds or in residences on earthen platforms probably enjoyed greater wealth but may have suffered loss of personal autonomy, although some senior women could have gained leadership roles. Grave goods indicate that female and male status was associated with different activities, represented by contrasting sets of offerings. The distribution of burials by sex and age in five Hohokam platform structures showed that adult females were not eligible for burial at all of these sites. Furthermore, females were underrepresented in box burials and lined-pit burials. In terms of grave goods, McGuire (1992) calculated grave lot value and concluded that although the remains of adult women were buried on some platforms and did occur in special burial contexts with highly valued goods, adult males and children were nevertheless buried in more valued locations with more valuable offerings.

In the Classic Period, however, children, young adults, and older females tended to have more elaborate burials. An elderly adult female was the only woman buried in an adobe-lined pit. Another older woman was interred atop the Las Colinas platform. She has been identified as a curing shaman: her pelvic area was covered with red hematite and a leather pouch containing a large quartz crystal and asbestos was under her head. Ethnographic analogy suggests that postmenopausal women might have participated with men in religious and political activities.

As family groups became more and more differentiated in the Classic Period, women's contributions in producing goods and children must have been the very foundation of family wealth and prestige. If women were confined behind walls, their influence in the public sphere might have declined even as their prestige as members of high-ranking families increased. However, if women were autonomous and in control of the domestic sphere, they would have had significant influence over men, who depended on their labor in the areas of production and reproduction. Their grave offerings increased compared to those of the pre–Classic Period, but their prestige was celebrated with symbols drawn from domestic life, not with imported personal ornaments or ritual paraphernalia. It appears, then, that the female prestige hierarchy was different from that of men. Crown and Fish (1996:803–817), who interpreted women's and men's statuses as complementary, quoted a modern Papago Indian woman: "But we have power. . . . Can any warrior make a child, no matter how brave and wonderful he is. . . . Don't you see that without us, there would be no men? Why should we envy men? We made men." If statements such as these are valid for the prehistoric past, then the complementary nature of grave goods may indeed reflect parallel statuses within the society.

Studies of Southwestern indigenous groups suggest that women and men may have had parallel leadership hierarchies, but these kinds of arrangements change easily and can be affected drastically by events such as warfare or conquest.

An archaeological study of 1,000 late prehistoric (A.D. 1350–1500) Puebloan burials at Hawikku, near the modern town of Zuni, New Mexico, demonstrated that members of ancient kin groups were buried in spatially discrete cemeteries. In this case, Howell and Kintigh (1996) identified the burials of community leaders as those with a greater number and diversity of burial goods or those that showed special body or other preparations. These offerings and preparations were taken to express the number of social roles that the individual performed in life. It was observed that individuals with such offerings were found with rare types of artifacts that might have been reserved for high-ranking people.

Eleven leaders' burials were found. Eight were of males. Most of the male paraphernalia, including bows and arrows, war clubs, and a single human scalp, suggests the importance of their roles in warfare, but the equipment in two burials demonstrates that male leaders were active in ritual performances as well. The three female leaders had three of the four most diverse burials in the sample. These women were associated with offerings of corn, squash, utilitarian vessels, decorated bowls, grinding equipment, baskets, shaped wood, paint-grinding stones, antler tools, gourds, decorated jars, feathers, human hair, and prayer sticks. Erected in one of the tombs was a unique painted shrine with hair. The grave goods show the association of women with domestic chores, food preparation, and ritual activities.

These important people of the community were not distributed randomly among the eleven kin-based cemeteries at the site. Eight leaders were buried in Cemetery 9 and three in Cemetery 1, suggesting that leadership was determined by ascription, and not by achievement. Members of only some kin groups earned leadership roles.

Howell (1995) has argued that after 1539, the encroachment of Spanish Colonial forces and the migration of hostile Apaches into the Zuni region resulted in the erosion of female authority. The reasons given are the increased need for military leadership, European political practices that favored male heads of household, and the imposition of European religion and gender ideologies. Understandably, at this time male leadership roles were associated with warfare. In contrast, evidence from the prehistoric period shows men assuming both military and ritual leadership roles. In the historic period, female leaders continued to be buried with items characteristic of matrilineal heads but not with emblems of their roles in ritual life.

Southwestern societies were characterized by prestige leaders rather than hereditary rulers. In some cases, archaeologists observe a pattern of inequality among individuals, suggesting that some wielded more power than others in their community. Nevertheless, even in more highly ranked societies, kinship would have been the dominant organizing principle. Because kinship is reckoned in many different ways, some systems were more favorable to women than others. Societies that had matrilineal inheritance and matrilocal residence may have allowed women more access to political power. In matrilineal groups, a line of related women usually forms the core of the social unit; lineage headmen are the sons and brothers of highly ranked women. After marriage, a woman continues to live in her mother's house and the young woman's husband becomes part of her household, although he continues to belong to his own mother's line and participates in activities with his own matrilineage. It is thought that matrilineal societies are less prone to internal warfare as a means of social and political advancement because matrilocal residence may diffuse the fraternal interest groups that are characteristic of patrilineal societies.

Women often prefer matrilocal residence so that work can be organized by groups of cooperating, related women. When external warfare is practiced, these women may take on additional productive functions and often assume leadership in community affairs, gaining higher status because of their increased contribution to economic activities that sustain the group while men are waging war.

The late prehistoric chiefdoms of the Circum-Caribbean region, including the southeastern portion of the United States, exhibited a matrilineal and matrilocal pattern. Several chronicles of the sixteenth century record the names of chiefs, some of whom were women. Because access to positions of leadership in societies organized by kinship is determined in part by membership in high-ranking lineages, both sexes may enjoy such access. One instance of this is shown in accounts of the historic Taino people of Hispaniola.

Among the Taino chiefdoms at the time of Columbus, the system of kinship and politics was complex: people figured relationships through both their mothers and fathers, and individuals and families competed for social status, wealth, and political power, manipulating inheritance and succession in order to gain advantage (S. Wilson 1990).

The Taino were characterized by matrilineal descent and inheritance: matrilocal residence was common and female leadership of political units was frequent. The Taino created very flexible situations in which political status could be transmitted in disparate ways. While men were usually the political leaders, women played key roles in politics (Sued Badillo 1985).

Making astute marriages was important to the success of political leaders: a key mechanism of change in Taino sociopolitical structure was the negotiation of exogamous marriages, which meant that high-ranking individuals, female and male, crossed the boundaries between chiefdoms. Because high-ranking people married only each other, they formed a circumscribed, powerful elite. Particular individuals could consolidate their leadership over several polities because caciques might succeed both their fathers and their mothers' brothers. A talented individual, capable of acquiring status through religious activities, warfare, trade, or politics, might also manipulate the rules of inheritance to build a power base.

Another route to power was the practice of polygyny. A highly ranked male cacique not only displayed his status by acquiring multiple wives but also gained advantage by making polygynous marriages that permitted him to appropriate the products of subordinate polities and acquire higher status by marrying a woman from an important Taino matriline—a person who transmitted social and political power along the female line.

Leaders also built political power through warfare, feasting, and reciprocal and competitive gift exchange. In many cases, women produced the prestige goods that dazzled the guests, signaling the host's power and status.

The case of Queen Anacaona shows how an elite woman held and manipulated power. When the Spanish invaded Hispaniola, they had a high-level meeting with thirty-two chiefs in the house of a woman called Anacaona, the sister of a cacique and the wife of the leader of a neighboring chiefdom. She owned several houses and controlled prestige goods, including wooden seats made by women, cotton textiles, and huge balls of cotton thread, stored in one of her houses. She also owned a royal canoe. When her brother died, she had him buried with his most beautiful wives and concubines. She was widely respected, even by the Spaniards. They burned eighty caciques alive but chose to hang Anacaona. One hopes she appreciated the tribute.

Throughout the Circum-Caribbean area in the latest prehistoric period, female leaders like Anacaona were common (S. Wilson 1990:22; Sued Badillo 1985). The early Spanish sources mention these ladies, but the conquerors often refused to deal with them and tried to have them replaced by men. Still, in 1514, in a census done in Santo Domingo, there were 37 females among 409 native rulers listed. Some of these ladies still had considerable numbers of people in their power.

The Caribbean plain of northern Colombia is an area of seasonally flooded swamps and immense resources. The societies that flourished from the third century onward exploited this region by intensive agriculture and fish cultivation, and communities developed a major industry in gold ornaments, for local use and for exchange. These peoples, called Sinú after the major river system, built their habitations on artificial earthen platforms that supported linear villages. On the platforms, they erected funerary tumuli where people were buried with offerings. The Sinú tradition was one in which women had tremendous social and political importance (Saénz Samper 1993). This is indicated by Spanish accounts and is traceable in the archaeological record.

At Spanish contact, this region was ruled by three closely related chiefs. The second most important of the three was the Lady of Finzenú, observed by Padre Simón, who wrote that she lived in royal state and never put her feet on bare ground but was carried in her hammock and supported by serving women who let her walk on them if she had to move about on her own (Saénz Samper 1993:79–81). Padre Simón also comments that the idols in Sinú temples, many portraying females, were richly covered in precious metal.

Little is known about the Lady of Finzenú, but by studying burials in the region, Saénz Samper has provided evidence of the importance of women. In tumuli containing females, she found multiple burials, often with a wealth of gold, including the mammiform pectorals (for which the region is known), female figurines, and other offerings. In contrast, male burials are simpler: gold ornaments are limited to lunate earrings, while multiple burials and abundant offerings are missing. Ceramic male effigies are scarce; of over a hundred human figurines studied by Saénz Samper, only four were male. Most figurines represent full-figure females in commanding postures, proudly displaying their ornaments, which are identical to those found in rich female burials. Many figures are seated on benches—a sign of high political and social status throughout the Andes. The association of women and gold, a substance restricted to the highest elite, suggests that the Lady of Finzenú was one of many important women in ancient Colombia.

Female rulers appeared in the early complex chiefdoms or primitive states in Mesoamerica. Our first view of them comes from the Preclassic Period Olmec of the Gulf Coast, a people who have the best claim to being Mexico's first civilization. Olmec sites were adorned with monumental stone sculpture that celebrated their rulers. Follensbee's (2000) pioneering study of sex and gender in Olmec art now permits an understanding of powerful women in Olmec political life. Working from clearly gendered figurines, Follensbee identified gendered garments, ornaments, and standardized ways of depicting female and male bodies. We now see women as rulers, important ancestors, and participants in politics, religious events, and warfare. Previously, one monument representing an elite female was reluctantly identified at the site of La Venta: Stela 1 depicts a woman standing in the open mouth of an earth monster, a pose commonly associated with Mesoamerican rulers (fig. 8.1). Follensbee suggests that the same ruler is shown on Colossal Head 1, while Colossal Head 4 also has female attributes. She is able to show that there are women depicted on the political monuments of virtually every known Olmec site and that three of the giant head sculptures from San Lorenzo are also females, almost certainly rulers. Several large stone sculptures, previously identified as male, are in fact wearing female ornaments and clothing. In Mexico's earliest complex society, women clearly had important leadership roles (Bruhns 1999).

Chalcatzingo, an Olmec-related site in highland Puebla, preserves abundant evidence of female rulers (Grove 1984). Monument 21 is a stone relief sculpture portraying a woman wearing a skirt. Because she is shown in profile, her breasts are clearly visible. Jewelry, sandals, and an elaborately patterned cloth worn over her head are other indicators of high status. This woman stands on a stylized earth monster mask and touches or presents a large deerskin bundle, elaborately tied with bands and knots. It has been

Figure 8.1. Stela 1 from the Olmec site of La Venta shows a female ruler standing, like other Mesoamerican rulers, in the open mouth of an earth monster. Museo Parque La Venta, Villahermosa, Tabasco, Mexico. Photograph by Karen Olsen Bruhns.

suggested that this bundle represents the marital exchange of the woman (Cyphers Guillén 1984). A more parsimonious interpretation is that this monument celebrates an event in the reign of the female ruler of Chalcatzingo. This woman, like many others in Olmec sculpture, is likely to have been a ruler because nonregnant personages are rare in Mesoamerican political art. A second monument at Chalcatzingo represents a female ruler, or perhaps the same one. In Monument 1 she is depicted seated in the mouth of an earth monster cave, holding an elaborate ceremonial bar of the sort associated with rulers; she is surrounded by clouds, rain, and vegetation. Although generally referred to as "El Rey" ("The King"), this figure would be better titled "The Queen": she is wearing women's clothing.

In the elite domestic refuse at Chalcatzingo, there are numerous small clay figurines of naked females with fancy headdresses and ornaments (Cyphers Guillén 1993, 1994). The figurines seem to represent various stages in the female life cycle. Curiously, the excavators originally identified most of the figurines as portraits of important males (Grove and Gillespie 1984), even though over 90 percent of the bodies were female. Such discrepancies in interpretation occur because figurines usually break at the neck, permitting the analyst to interpret the corpus of heads apart from that of the bodies.

It is possible that between 700 and 500 B.C., groups of kinswomen celebrated life-crisis rituals in areas where food was processed. These rituals may have enhanced the social integration of the group and propagated an ideology that facilitated the accomplishment of women's work. However, female-directed ceremonial activity may also have functioned to allow elite individuals to extend their social relations and to engage in reciprocal and competitive exchanges that were avenues to the development of power and influence in the community. Certainly highly ranked women, as well as men, were concerned with sociopolitics at Chalcatzingo.

Marcus (1998) has proposed a similar use of figurines in Preclassic Oaxaca. She sees the figurines as being made and manipulated by women in domestic rituals to consult recently dead ancestors. This interpretation is convincing because Marcus can tie it to both ethnohistoric and ethnographic data from later Oaxacan peoples, who are known to have venerated their ancestors and consulted ancestral remains in acts of divination. This interpretation of figurines is far stronger than the speculative interpretation of artifacts made in prehistoric societies without related written records.

During the subsequent Classic Period, evidence of female rulers is abundant. Some of the best data come from the Maya, because of their realistic art style and because they wrote their own history, which can now be read in part (Ardren 2002; Bruhns 1988; Freidel and Schele 1993; E. Graham 1991; Gillespie and Joyce 1997; Herr 1987; Hewitt 1999; Molloy and Rathje 1974).

Female rulers were first documented at Palenque in southern Mexico, where the royal line was descended from a mythical female ancestor, "Lady Beastie." Among the historic rulers of the site are three queens, two of whom were definitely queens regnant. The first of these, Ix Yol Ik'nal, came to power in A.D. 583, ruling until A.D. 604. Little is known of her reign; her husband is never mentioned in inscriptions. She may have succeeded her father, the previous king, because he lacked a male heir: in patrilineal systems the children of the succeeding daughter belong to her patrilineage. Patrilineal systems are prepared to manage any eventuality: a son-in-law might hold power, especially if he were closely related to his royal wife. Their children would belong to the wife's patrilineage and succeed just as if she were male. The second possible queen regnant was Kanal Ikal, whose husband did not rule and was not named as an ancestor by later rulers.

Another queen regnant was Zak Kuk, the granddaughter of Kanal Ikal; she ruled for at least three years beginning in A.D. 612, succeeding her paternal uncle. Zak Kuk is recorded on a number of monuments, including the sarcophagus of her famous son Pacal, buried under the Temple of the Inscriptions. Pacal recorded the name of his father on his sarcophagus, but nothing further is known of this man, who did not rule (cf. S. Martin 2000). At Copán, Honduras, the first king of the Classic dynasty, Yax Kuk Mo'o, was a foreigner. The chemistry of his bones and teeth reveals that he came from the central Yucatán. He was buried in the elaborate Hunal Tomb; nearby is the far more elaborate Margarita Tomb, the burial of the Copán heiress he married. This woman, although not mentioned by name in Copán dynastic lists, was more revered than was her in-marrying husband (Buikstra et al. 2004).

At Palenque in 1994, archaeologists found the body of a middle-aged woman laid out in a plain stone sarcophagus in a pyramid adjoining the Temple of the Inscriptions (Anon. 1994). It was first surmised that this was Zak Kuk's tomb, from its elaboration and location. Later, DNA studies revealed that the woman was unrelated to Pacal and thus may have been his wife, Tzakby Ajaw, while Zak Kuk's burial is yet unknown (González Cruz 2011; Tiesler et al. 2004). Maya scholarship has been slow in celebrating its noblewomen and their deeds, but close scrutiny of the indigenous histories of other Mesoamerican groups reveals that there were female rulers even in the most aggressive and androcentric societies.

It is now clearer than ever that many Maya city-states had powerful queens. In 2012 the excavation of a royal tomb at the site of El Perú-Waka in Guatemala brought to light the "notable historical figure" known from written texts and images of a seventh-century queen: Lady K'abel, who bore the titles "Holy Snake Lord" and "Supreme Warrior." Her tomb is located in a temple where the Maya continued to make offerings for generations after her death (Owen 2012).

The Mexican state of Oaxaca has been inhabited by the Mixtec and Zapotec peoples since at least the second millennium B.C. These closely related peoples form a unique cultural grouping within Mesoamerica in terms of languages, religious and political ideologies, art, and architecture. The Mixtec dominated in western Oaxaca, where they occupied settlements grouped into several small states, each one ruled, in late prehistory, by a king or queen who inherited the throne from a parent who was also a ruler (Spores 1974; Jansen 1990).

Mixtec society was characterized by distinct social classes and highly structured social relations. Outside the family, class status was more important than kinship in governing social interactions. In the Mixtec kingdoms, descent was more important than sex in inheritance. To be a ruler, a person had to be the child of a ruler; nevertheless, members of the ruling families and their supporters struggled constantly for power, making political life convoluted and unstable (Hanmann 1997).

Royal marriage was a crucial part of politics. Members of the royal caste married only other royals, Mixtec or Zapotec. In these marriages, wife and husband retained their own lands, titles, and obligations, and both wife and husband named an heir to her or his titles and kingdoms. When parents chose an heir they tended to favor males over females, yet daughters often succeeded even when they had male siblings.

The earliest evidence we have of power politics in Oaxaca shows women as well as men occupying ruling positions. In the late centuries B.C., the rulers of Monte Albán, located on a ridge above the modern city of Oaxaca, were carving a large kingdom out of their neighbors' realms. Their conquests were celebrated on a series of carved stone slabs, the Danzantes, so called because of the dance-like positions of the figures on them. Each of these monuments represents a conquest and the sacrifice of the conquered ruler. Of the three hundred carved slabs at Monte Albán, at least two depict women (Scott 1978). Female figures also appear on later dynastic and funerary monuments from Monte Albán: royal women are shown in relief carvings and painted on the walls of tombs. A stone stela, found in the heart of the royal palace on the North Platform, celebrates Lady 12N as she passes the throne to her son (Winter 1997). Zapotec art gives evidence of royal women from the Preclassic and Classic Periods. The system of inheritance and use of power known from the painted books of the late Prehispanic Mixtec had deep roots in southern Mexico.

Mixtec books are a principal source of information about power: they appear to be the genealogies and dynastic histories of specific families. Mixtec ruling and noble families kept these written records of their ancestors to support their rights to position and wealth. One book, the Codex Selden, records in its first six pages the story of a famous ruler whose ascent to power, military victories, political prowess, and final capture and sacrifice by another Mixtec ruler led to her being revered as an important ancestress (Caso 1964).

Six Monkey Serpent Quequechmetl was the daughter of Lady Nine Wind Flint Quequechmetl, the queen of Belching Mountain. Lady Nine Wind is shown offering copal incense to a bundle (perhaps one of her ancestors) in front of the temple of Belching Mountain. This ritual, which her two predecessors also performed, marked her ascension to the throne. After this she formally married. Since her daughter also waited to marry until she had taken possession of her inheritance, this may have been politically important in signifying sole rulership of a state. Lady Nine Wind and her husband had a daughter and three sons. The sons lived to adulthood but were all killed, sacrificed after a losing battle.

Although Caso (1964) and others have suggested that Six Monkey was heiress by default, there is every reason to consider that she was the designated heir all along. She is the main protagonist in the text and she is depicted discussing her impending inheritance with an important religious figure. She did not take the throne for some time, although she was apparently formally recognized as heiress, because eight years after her brothers were sacrificed her father had to defend Belching Mountain against an attack by his wife's brother. This battle was part of a larger dynastic dispute in a neighboring kingdom. In the wake of this turmoil, Six Monkey was advised by an elderly priest to undertake a round of diplomatic fence mending. The text indicates that she first consulted with another religious potentate; the

Figure 8.2. Six Monkey takes Lord Six Serpent prisoner. She is shown armed as a warrior, with sword club and shield, grasping his forelock in the conventional pose indicating the taking of a prisoner in battle. Selden Codex. Drawn by Tom Weller.

interview took place in a cave, and as part of the discussion or ritual, Six Monkey visited the underworld (or the burial place of the ancestors). She and her fiancé also visited the ruler of Skull, Nine Grass Death, a female religious potentate, bringing her lavish presents. This was an important summit meeting recorded in a number of Mixtec books. In all, Six Monkey, not her husband, is clearly the protagonist. After this meeting, Six Monkey participated in a dance ritual and her official wedding took place.

The next year, Six Monkey made diplomatic visits to two neighboring lords. Not only was no agreement reached but these two lords insulted Six Monkey. Enraged, she went to seek advice from Nine Grass Death at Skull, arranging the participation of warriors from Skull and from another town in the impending conflict. She and her allies then proceeded to make war on the two lords. Six Monkey is shown in the Codex Selden leading the troops and making the captures herself. She is identified by name and is shown, in her woman's clothing, in the standard pose of winning the battle and taking prisoners, with spear and spear thrower at the ready, grasping the loser's forelock (fig. 8.2). Six Monkey burned the captured towns and sacrificed the insulting lords. In celebration of her great victory she received a new name, Six Monkey Warpath Quechquemitl, and ever after wore blouses with woven designs signifying battle.

The rest of Six Monkey's life was not as adventurous. She had a number of children and carried out the normal life of a ruler, presiding over diplomatic events and ceremonies, and caring for her lands and people. Her military career continued, and in the fullness of time, Six Monkey Warpath got into a war with Eight Deer Ocelot Claw of Tilantongo. This time she lost the battle and, like the far earlier rulers shown in the Danzante bas-reliefs, ended up sacrificed.

Six Monkey's career parallels that of other Mixtec rulers. Her story is told in detail because she was an important member of the ruling family of Belching Mountain, revered as an ancestress and as a person who did mighty deeds.

In hierarchical societies, power, economic and political, is seldom restricted to members of one sex. Despite the androcentric assumption that women are mere pawns, it is evident that highborn women often manage to achieve positions of power in both public and private spheres.

The Aztec of the Valley of Mexico are famous as an extremely militaristic, male-centered society. Their chief religious icon was a god of war. Histories of the kingdom of Tenochtitlán stress the succession of male rulers and the battles and victories of male warriors. Yet careful reading of historical texts, Aztec picture documents, and the archaeological record together permit a reconstruction of Aztec society that includes women (Bell 2003; Carrasco 1984; Gillespie 1989; Kellogg 1984, 1995, 1997; McCafferty and McCafferty 1988, 1991, 1999; Schroeder 1992).

The ancestors of the Aztec were hunter-gatherers who arrived in central Mexico from the desert north. They began their rise to power by negotiating marriage alliances between their chiefs and elite women of the civilized agricultural societies of the Valley of Mexico. The Aztec dynasty derived from the marriage of such a leader with a Colhua princess named Atototzli (Bell 2003; *Historia de los Mexicanos por sus Pinturas* 1988). Later, Moctezuma I was succeeded by a daughter, also named Atototzli: she herself may have served as *tlatoani* (speaker or emperor), as indicated by some Franciscan texts, although her husband, Tezozomoc, is more commonly mentioned as having become tlatoani through his marriage to Atototzli. Tezozomoc was her paternal great uncle's son and the son of a previous tlatoani himself. Atototzli's marriage to a member of the Tenochtitlán ruling lineage kept power within the family, and she played a key role in dynastic politics whether she ruled alone for a time or not. It is certain that she carried the right to the throne in her person because her three sons by Tezozomoc became tlatoanis in turn. Although some historians have questioned the reality of the two Atototzlis, they have not impugned the historical validity of their fathers, brothers, husbands, and male children.

Figure 8.3. The surrender of Cuauhtemoc to Cortés, recorded in this early Colonial painted manuscript, was attended by two important women of the Conquest Period: Doña Marina (*far left*) served as translator for Cortés, and Tecuichpo (*top, second from right*) observed from nearby. She is the only figure in the painting to be identified by a name glyph (the three elements painted in front of her face represent her name, "Lord's Daughter"). Drawing by Tom Weller after the *Lienzo de Tlaxcala*, Lámina 5–6. Diego Muñoz Camargo (1529–1599). Editorial Innovación, México, 1978.

There is no problem with the veracity of the story of the last Aztec queen. Tecuichpo, later known as Doña Isabel de Moctezuma, was the legitimate offspring of Moctezuma II (fig. 8.3). She survived the upheavals of the Conquest, was taken into custody by Cortés himself (with whom she had a child), and died in 1551 (Carrasco 1997; Chipman 2005). Her career illustrates how a resourceful royal lady manipulated the system both before and after the European takeover.

Tecuichpo seems to have been more important to both the Spanish and the Aztec than her brother, who also survived into the Colonial Period. She apparently married the last real ruler of Tenochtitlán, the ill-fated Cuauhtemoc, also a distant cousin to her and a good general. She thus validated Cuauhtemoc's right to lead at a time when the Aztec needed a ruler legitimate in the eyes of all the noble factions. Cuauhtemoc did not survive his acquaintance with the Spanish, and his widow proceeded to marry a series of Spaniards in an attempt to keep the family property. These husbands aided her in lawsuits. The Spanish courts agreed that the property belonged to her and not to her brother. Other noble and royal women also undertook litigation. These ladies were not passive pawns of their male relatives or of the conquering Spanish; they were reared in the full knowledge of their own superiority and they had experience in Aztec power politics. Shortly, however, in the Mexican Colonial Period, because of the prejudices of the European system, the ancient roles of women in politics and religion were lost. Given that contemporary feminist theory indicates that women lose status, personal autonomy, and access to power in complex societies, it is worth looking at the evidence for women's roles in an early culture of Peru in the second millennium B.C.

Studies of religious iconography in ancient Peru indicate the importance of female deities, often paired with male ones, from the Initial Period onward (Lyon 1978). It is less sure whether women figured among the political and religious leaders of the subsequent Early Horizon. From Kuntur Wasi in north highland Peru, there is only tantalizing evidence (Kato 1993). Among five extraordinary tombs in the Central Platform of this site was the burial of an elite woman over sixty years of age. The other tombs contained the skeletons of middle-aged or elderly males. The woman was buried seated with an application of cinnabar around her head. Her offerings were different from those of the males: a gold pendant; a gold necklace of twenty-five flat, bird-shaped plates; necklaces made up of hundreds of green stone, lapis lazuli, and *Spondylus* beads; and a pendant of turquoise—all exotic materials. She also had a small marble vase, a ceramic stirrup bottle, and two ceramic cups. These offerings are equal in value to those with two of the males buried in the same precinct. The location of the tomb and its richness suggest that this woman was of considerable importance, although her social role has not been reconstructed.

Later, in the same region, the ceramics of the Early Intermediate Period Recuay culture reveal a world in which there were important roles for women. Gero's (1992, 1999) studies of the iconography of elaborately modeled and painted Recuay mortuary ceramics demonstrate that representations of humans are strongly differentiated by gender. Only men wear ear spools, fancy headdresses, and loincloths. Women can be identified by their head cloths and dresses fastened with long pins with decorative heads, called *tupus*, which are still used by women who wear traditional garments.

Recuay ceramics depict individual women richly garbed, holding cups, or as small rigid figures surrounding a larger male figure (fig. 8.4). Other vessels show a handsomely attired female copulating with a similarly dressed male, which Gero (1999) has interpreted as a representation of ritual sex. Both kinds of vessels indicate that women of high rank had ritual roles in Recuay society, even if these vessels represent the visualization of myths or legends.

Other vessels show men and women participating in feasts. In many instances, the male personage in the central position is larger than both the female and male figures that surround him. This contrast in size is an indication of a difference in social rank. There were powerful men in Recuay society, but Gero has suggested that in real life, families threw feasts as part of a strategy for building and holding power, and that women were key participants in furthering the political ambitions of their families. She has interpreted archaeological remains from the elite residential site of Queyash Alto as evidence of feasts in which people consumed quantities of grilled llama meat and maize beer (Gero 1990). Presumably the event was prepared and presented by the family of a regional political leader for members of the community or some other constituency. The archaeological remains in this hilltop feasting site included quantities of Recuay-style serving pottery as well as brewing equipment, imported obsidian artifacts, flutes, panpipes, and figurines. Because items associated with the female gender (metal, mother-of-pearl ornaments, and weaving implements) were also present, Gero hypothesized that women collaborated with men to gain and maintain political and religious authority. Women apparently shared prestige and high status with male relatives, but they may have customarily deferred to men or

Figure 8.4. An anthropomorphic ceramic jar in the Recuay style shows a prominent female whose dress is pinned at the shoulders by large *tupus*. Museo Nacional de Arqueología y Antropología, Lima, # C.C. P 32 R. A. B. Photograph by Raphael X. Reichert.

may have been subordinate to them in public contexts. This does not obviate the possibility that Recuay women were powerful in their own realms, producing the food, beer, and craft items necessary for the success of their kin group in politics, ritual, and warfare.

A few years ago a group of royal tombs of the Moche culture (contemporary with the Recuay) were excavated at the site of Sipán (Alva and Donnan 1993). Excavators identified the remains of male actors who apparently had participated in the Sacrifice Ceremony documented in Moche art (see chapter 7). Female actors from the same ceremony were identified in two rich tombs excavated at San José de Moro. Some royal tombs seem to contain identifiable priests and priestesses, while other individuals, like the Old Lord of Sipán (167–217), are less specifically identified but qualify as royalty and rulers.

These rich burials contain members of the elite of the kingdom: not only royal men (the Warrior Priest, the Decapitator, and the Old Lord) but also royal women (heretofore identified as priestesses). With the discovery of another royal tomb in a monumental edifice at the site of Huaca El Brujo, which contained the well-preserved body of a royal woman, it seems more likely that the warlike Moche had both male and female leaders. The Lady of Cao (a woman in her late twenties, as determined by medical examinations) is not associated with the Sacrifice Ceremony, but her status, power, and gender are all emphasized by the contents of her tomb (A. Williams 2006:70–83): she was wrapped in textiles, one of them seventy meters long; covered with cinnabar; and protected by a magnificent mantle of broad, shining metal strips. Her accouterments consisted of weaving equipment, weapons, and jewelry, including fifteen necklaces of lapis lazuli, rock crystal, and silver and gold alloy; nose ornaments; a golden bowl that covered her face; and a crown. A teenage girl and three males were sacrificed to accompany her in the afterlife.

It is important to emphasize that two large (ceremonial) war clubs, which normally are not associated with women, and a large number of decorated spear throwers are prominent in the tomb. The Lady of Cao was elaborately tattooed and had braided tresses, as shown in artistic depictions of Moche women. The richness of her burial, the sacrifices, and the location of the tomb on top of El Brujo all led archaeologists to conclude that she was a ruler, perhaps even a warrior queen (A. Williams 2006). If so, she is the first Moche queen to be identified in northern Peru, and her existence compels us to include royal women as we envision Moche rulership.

The suggestion that the Lady of Cao was a warrior queen, or that queens, like kings, had ceremonial roles as warriors, can be confirmed only as more royal tombs are studied scientifically.

The most detailed information on women's place in Andean social and political structures comes from accounts written in the sixteenth century. Because of the immediate impact of the European Conquest, these histories are as difficult to interpret as archaeological remains. Pre-Inca societies in Peru may have been relatively egalitarian and gender balanced, according to some scholars, but long before the Inca, many ancient peoples were probably constrained by social hierarchies. Apparently, the role of women was compromised with the rise of the Inca state. Silverblatt (1978) argues that Inca hegemony meant increased suffering for women and men, and that the subordination of women—part of Inca state strategy—was exacerbated by the ideology and legal systems imposed by the Spanish government.

Among the Inca, and many of the peoples they conquered, groups of bilaterally related kindred were organized into communities called *ayllus*, which were ideally endogamous and controlled the land needed for their own support. Within the ayllu, women and men owned their own equipment and personal effects and had usufruct over specific portions of land. Inheritance of goods in a society in which tasks are highly gendered is from women to daughters or other female relatives, and from men to sons or other male relatives. Inca inheritance of position was mildly patrilineal: sons sometimes inherited their father's position in the social and political hierarchy. However, women could and did retain land in their natal ayllu, even if they married outside it. Men often joined their wives in working her land if they lacked access to resources in their own ayllu. A woman could ask brothers or other kin to work her land if she lived too far away to do so herself, or, if widowed, she could return to her own ayllu with her children.

Females had status in Andean life because of their control of land and other real property and because of their roles in production and religion. Women took full part in religious rituals, and many of the shrines were female or associated with females. Most ayllus or ethnic ancestors came in female-male pairs, and gender complementarity was often expressed in social and political activities.

The chronicles record the participation of elite women in the rituals of the second month, called Camay. All the kin groups of Cuzco contributed sets of red and white clothing for a burnt sacrifice. The participants also had new black clothing for the ritual, all of which was made by women. Later, they took a large multicolored rope from a building next to the Temple of the Sun and danced with it, women on one side of the rope and men on the other, moving around the square and executing figures as they danced in their special costumes (Cobo [1653] 1990:135–136).

Women retained some status under the Inca because they produced the goods necessary for rituals. In Inca culture, women spun and wove the textiles that were indispensable in social life and politics. Textiles were worn as markers of ethnicity and social position; they clothed the dead and were a focal part of funerary ceremonies and ancestor worship. Textiles were the most prized commodities given as gifts in weddings, alliances, treaties, and initiations. They were sacrificed in quantities to gods and shrines. Both ordinary and elite women spun and wove for their families and for tribute. Women also made maize beer, an indispensable element in virtually every religious ritual and in political activities at all social levels. Elite women, religious women (acllas), and peasant women alike brewed beer and thus made possible celebrations and the achievement of ritual intoxication in religious and political life. In Inca contexts, feeding one's kin, feeding others, and feeding the dead were critical political activities, symbolically charged and part of women's responsibility, identity, and status. The production, distribution, and consumption of food, beer, textiles, and other goods not only expressed the power relations in Inca-period communities but created those relationships that defined the Inca state. According to contemporary theory, the material dimension of sociocultural activities does not simply reflect power relations but actually facilitates the construction of social relations, and of polities, while reinforcing both authority and inequality.

Women's centrality in the production of textiles, beer, and food was certainly part of their identity in both humble and elite contexts. We imagine that elite women also wielded considerable power through their wealth and kinship ties. Topic (2002) has carefully garnered information from the chronicles about the activities of elite women; because of their mobility, she infers that they enjoyed a considerable degree of autonomy. She notes that before marriage, the sisters and daughters of both nobles and of local-level lords traveled regularly with the Inca army. They spent the evenings singing, dancing, and in other amusements with the soldiers. Other elite women had interesting public lives, traveling to visit relatives, to attend shrines and festivals, and to administer their own estates.

The most powerful woman in the Inca Empire was the *coya*, or principal wife of the ruling Inca, who was often his full sister. Since the Sapa Inca was supposed to be the divine son of the Sun god, only his full sisters could be as divine as himself, and, beginning with Topa Inca, the ruler married his full sister to get fully divine heirs. The sisters apparently had some choice in the matter: Huayna Capac's first coya, Cusi Rimay, died in childbirth, and his second sister decided to pursue a life as a mamacona, so the Inca married his three other full sisters. The political reason for royal sister-brother marriage was more mundane. Although the later Inca rulers attempted to name their heirs and identify them as corulers, there was no principle of primogeniture, so circumscribing the number of people who could be legitimate heirs helped ensure peaceful succession. This strategy for both preserving the divinity of the royal line and limiting the pool of heirs is seen in many other cultures.

Normally, the Inca had only one coya (except for Huayna Capac, who married a number of his sisters). If a coya produced no male heir, the Inca would marry additional sisters as co-coyas . The Inca's daughters were also married in order to cement alliances. When Pachacuti lay on his deathbed, he summoned all his unmarried daughters and bestowed them upon their brothers, Inca nobles in Cuzco, and upon provincial lords. Presumably he was acting on a plan: marrying the women to men who would support his chosen heir. The Inca himself took secondary wives in abundance, many of them relatives or acllas, others the daughters of local lords whose lands he had conquered (Espinosa Soriano 1976). These women were brought to Cuzco, but when they produced a son they often returned to their home communities to assume important positions in local government. Garcilaso de la Vega ([1609] 1945) mentions one of these women, a secondary wife of Topa Inca who was living in Chachapoyas at the time of a local rebellion against the Inca. Normally, the punishment for rebellion was death to all involved, but the leaders of the rebellion asked this woman to plead for clemency from the Inca. Accompanied by a large retinue of local women, she approached the Inca, asked his pardon, and received it.

Coyas, like other women, had responsibilities and public lives. The coya was in charge of the Cuzco acllahuasi and regularly made inspections. Coyas must have taken part in the great public ceremonies in Cuzco and at other royal residences. They were also on the road a lot, visiting their own estates and traveling with their husbands. Some scholars say that the coya was the ruler of the feminine half of the empire and served as regent for the Inca when he was absent from Cuzco. If so, coyas must have had councils of advisors as well as large retinues of servants to administer their property, including the property they shared with their husbands. However, the fact that Incas tended to leave brothers in control of the empire when they were on the road mitigates claims of female rule. The two recorded instances of a coya participating in military and diplomatic activities are both tales in which she asks favors of the Inca. Both stories involve Mama Occllo, a daughter of the Sun venerated by her husband and children, who traveled with her husband as he went about establishing and consolidating the empire.

In one situation, the Inca wanted to march his army through the Cañete Valley, ruled by the widow of the previous ruler. This lady demurred, knowing full well what would happen. Then Mama Occllo presented a plan, and she herself met with the ruler of Cañete and persuaded her to hold a celebration on rafts in the sea with all her people and her army. While they were so engaged, the Inca army occupied the valley. The Inca praised his wife's strategy and caused the generals and officers of Cañete to surrender to the coya herself.

This and other stories show the coya's influence and acumen, but not her power. Even a strong coya, such as Mama Occllo, who was well situated because of birth and marriage and who had the ear of her husband, may have had no established political powers. The dual organization by gender of the Inca Empire was not a political reality, despite the wishful thinking of feminist scholars.

We know, however, that coyas had religious authority and were held in great esteem by their kin. Huayna Capac so venerated his mother, Mama Occllo, that he dedicated an amazing room to her in his palace at Tomebamba, in southern Ecuador: it was decorated with *Spondylus* shells, gold, and rock crystals, and a golden statue of the Coya, containing the Inca's afterbirth, was set up in this room and worshipped as a deity, even though the woman was still alive (Cabello Valvoa [1576–1586] 1951:321–325 and 360–371).

When an Inca ruler died, elaborate state ceremonies were carried out. Some of the Inca's concubines and secondary wives volunteered to accompany the Inca in death, but this was not the fate of the coya. When she died, her body was treated in the same manner as that of the Inca, wrapped in rich textiles with her face covered over, then placed with her husband's body in the palace they had shared in life. The bodies of the Inca, the coya, and other important persons were not buried but were curated and exhibited on occasion. Most of the preserved corpses of the Incas and coyas were still extant at the time of the Spanish Conquest: they were kept in their palaces, moved to other houses and estates with the seasons, and cared for by their ayllu, which had become a *panaca*, a royal corporation charged with the care of the dead Inca and coya and their estates. Thus gender equality and complementarity were expressed in death (Guillén Guillén 1983).

The few glimpses we have of the coyas through Spanish documents indicate that they were strong women who played direct roles in government and ritual, inseparable in the Inca state. They also managed estates and vast retinues of servants; they traveled with their husbands and also alone, in their managerial capacity; and, as representatives of the state religion, they attended ceremonies throughout the empire (Topic 2002). One can imagine the strength of character of these women and the influence they had on imperial policy, whether or not they took a direct public role in governance.

There is no denying that in late prehistory many human groups chose strategies that, while proving beneficial for the survival of their societies, resulted in the loss of ideologies and social organizations that were more favorable to women. In recent times, many societies have developed hierarchical and centralized forms of organization, decision making concentrated in the hands of male political leaders, and pervasive ideologies of male dominance. These strategies have been of great competitive advantage in the creation of large states. These societies, while common today, have not always existed and probably will be modified as circumstances change. As Gilmore (1990) has explained, the ubiquitous phenomenon of male dominance is not predicated on male biology but is rather a practical cultural device that may have outlasted its usefulness. In the future, as sociocultural systems change, the most competitively advantaged and successful societies will be different from what we see in the world today. Although some people promote stronger male leadership and female subordination as solutions to problems in our society, other people are eager to adopt new technological, social, and ideological strategies that will result in future sociocultural systems that are more heterarchical and gender inclusive.

This feminist reinterpretation of the archaeological record promotes female participation in the social processes of change by showing that in human history women were not always excluded or subordinated. Women's authority in decision making and leadership was and still is very great in domestic and small community contexts, but in the later part of history, as some complex societies emerged, elite men acquired prominent roles in the political, economic, and religious institutions constituted at high levels of organization and promoted masculinist ideologies. Warfare may have been one of the causes of the worsening of women's conditions in later prehistory, although bellicose conditions offered some women opportunities to change their social status and acquire power and authority. Fortunately, since World War II women have achieved much greater prominence and important leadership roles in many communities, organizations, cities, and countries.

CHAPTER NINE

Women, War, and Conquest

omen, men, and groups gain power and prestige by exploiting their kin relations, by manipulating ideology, and by controlling resources, including natural, social, and supernatural resources. People also pursue power strategies involving physical coercion. Scholars view warfare as an important cause of cultural change. The origin of social and political hierarchy is often thought to lie in the violent extension of hegemony of one group over another. Viewed cross-culturally, women are supporters, perpetrators, and victims of warfare, and they sometimes take prominent roles in it (see, for example, Davis-Kimball 2002).

Warfare is often related to status seeking and serves as a male rite of passage. Going to war turns boys into men even in modern societies. In many societies, charismatic and hereditary rulers may show their fitness by prowess in warfare. Thus among the Aztec and Maya a new ruler was expected to instigate a raid for captives to sacrifice in celebration of his accession (Hassig 1988). When men are actively engaged in military activities, women may adopt a variety of participatory and supportive roles, and frequently their lives are affected profoundly.

Stories of Amazon battalions are part of Eurasian and African folklore and history that do not appear in Native American legends. Great war chiefs like Boadica or Joan of Arc are seldom as revered as national, folkloric, or religious heroines among Native Americans, but there is considerable evidence that women took part in bellicose activities. Archaeology and art history supply some examples, but most cases are historical.

The prehistoric evidence for warfare is stronger in those periods when larger tribal groups replaced bands of foragers. Some tribal peoples developed competitive social strategies in which every male was socialized as a warrior (Redmond 1994). Archaeologically, this pattern is reflected in burial assemblages and in the appearance of war gods in the iconography of ancient peoples. Sometimes archaeologists find that females are more numerous in excavated cemeteries, presumably because so many of the males of fighting age died away from home. In other cases, victorious warriors seem to have been buried in special mortuary facilities. A Mississippian elite cemetery at Moundville (A.D. 1200–1500) contained a very large number of males whose bones showed war injuries and who were accompanied by high-status goods (Powell 1988).

In historic chiefdoms, warfare was generally a pursuit of chiefs who managed several tiers of leadership and elaborate systems of insignia. In these hierarchical societies, the elite were in charge of prewar rituals designed to buttress the authority of the chief. Chiefly warfare could be organized on a large or small scale, but it was aimed at neighbors. This warfare often caused populations to concentrate in nucleated centers and to construct defensible communities and systems of fortifications. Hostilities provided a route for individuals to gain status and for a community to gain economic advantage.

In ancient America, warriors in tribal groups sought reasons to undertake raids as a principal means of acquiring high social status and magical power. A warring chief could increase and buttress his authority by displaying human trophies, and he might acquire power by consuming the flesh of dead enemies. In ancient art and in historical records, women also manipulated these symbols and feasted on human flesh (fig. 9.1). Moreover, chiefly warfare created the opportunity for warriors to accumulate and symbolize power through postwar rituals of death. Those tribal warriors with great reputations as killers might both deter retaliation by enemies and protect their communities by their spiritual power.

Although ancient peoples staged ritual battles and represented metaphorical warriors in art, even highly ritualized battles fought for prestige and supernatural power probably had more mundane functions. Even raiding that did not result in the extension of hegemony of one group over another could be part of a strategy of competition for land and hunting territory: it served to space the population and allowed some groups to gain access to labor and resources. Many labor-hungry tribal and chiefly groups gained

Figure 9.1. A sixteenth-century drawing shows a classic "cannibal feast," with Tupinamba women boiling a prisoner in a huge pot and, in the background, breaking open a skull for the brains. Hans Staden stands at the side, praying that he is not the next course in the banquet. After Staden ([1557] 1963).

workers and maintained a positive rate of population growth by kidnapping women and children. This was not a minor part in warfare among settled groups. The Aztec enslaved women and children from groups who refused to send tribute, and the practice of stealing women and children from neighboring groups has persisted until recent times in South America.

Manly Hearted Women of the Great Plains

In the culture of the Plains Indians in the eighteenth and nineteenth centuries, rank and status were not hereditary but had to be achieved through participation in aggressive activities. This cultural pattern developed when the early Spanish explorers and colonists of northern Mexico introduced horses and horseback riding into North America. The Native Americans of the Plains, who had been river-bottom farmers and foot hunters, quickly developed a nomadic hunting way of life in which prowess in the hunt and in war were the main means of gaining personal status and wealth. Archaeology demonstrates that war among Plains peoples was nothing new, but the horse, and later the rifle, resulted in the escalation of earlier patterns. Raiding for slaves and horses, even outright massacres, became common as groups vied for control of hunting lands and other resources.

The ideal woman in most Plains societies was a modest, hardworking, and chaste person. Nonetheless, female participation in warfare seems to have been quite common (fig. 9.2). Documents from the mid-1700s onward record the histories of women who joined war parties as warriors. Commonly, these women were motivated by desire for revenge against an enemy that had killed a husband or another male kinsman (Lewis 1941; Medicine 1983; Ewers 1994).

The most successful female warrior known to history was Woman Chief of the Crow. She was born a Gros Ventre and captured when she was about twelve, and both her biological father and her adopted Crow father encouraged her interest in manly pursuits and trained her in male skills. Woman Chief dressed as a woman throughout her life, but she pursued the role of a male, successfully hunting large game both on foot and on horseback and skillfully leading war parties. Her prowess as a warrior was recognized when, later in life, she took a place in the male council and became the third-ranking warrior in a band of 160 households. She had four wives whose labor, especially in processing hides for sale to the Whites, made her wealthy in the mid-1800s.

Beatrice Medicine, in her 1983 study of sex role alternatives among Plains women, noted that female warriors were described only briefly in many journals, chronicles, and ethnographies. Nevertheless, the warrior woman role was widespread in North America, being found in the Southwest, California, among the Northwest Coast groups, and in the Northeast as well. This is an interesting counterpoint to standard North American Indian studies, which

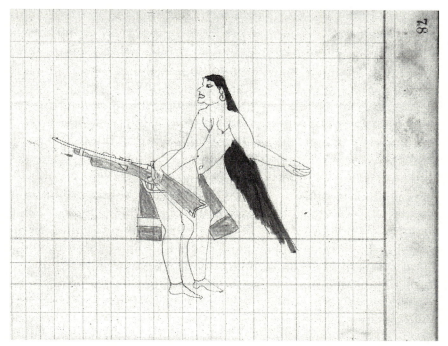

Figure 9.2. In this nineteenth-century indigenous drawing, a Cheyenne woman-warrior brandishes her rifle. Page 78 of ledger with drawings in colored pencil, watercolor, and ink by Yellow Nose (Hehúwesse) and others, before 1889. Cat. # 166,032; Neg. # 89-4691. Courtesy of the National Museum of Natural History, Smithsonian Institution.

stress the passivity of native women and which homogenize women's roles, emphasizing their victimization.

Although outside observers perceive the Plains Indian societies as male dominated, Medicine points out that in many groups Native American women traditionally could achieve prestige, power, and even wealth. One of the roles open to women was that called, among the Peigan, "manly hearted woman" (Lewis 1941). This was a woman who excelled in every important aspect of tribal life, including property acquisition and management, domestic life, and ceremonials. Medicine notes that manly hearted women often began their lives as favored children, as did Woman Chief, being indulged and given more affection and attention than other children, so that these girls developed very high self-esteem. Their fathers encouraged their daughters in dominant behavior and they led in games, played boys' sports, and took names of famous warriors for themselves. Unlike their sisters, they were also sexually aggressive and active from an early age, and this aggressive behavior and self-esteem led them to excel in female and male tasks alike. These were the women who sought wealth and prestige through military activities, gaining high status through their dominant behavior in all aspects of life. The role of the manly hearted woman was not, as is sometimes claimed, analogous to the role of the male berdache because no gender reversal was effected.

While manly hearted women and female warriors are described in both historic and ethnographic documents, they have not been identified archaeologically. Archaeologists, however, should be aware that a female skeleton associated with both male and female artifacts might be evidence that a woman played a variety of roles.

On the Great Plains and elsewhere, warfare provided a route for men, and a few women, to accumulate personal prestige, magical power, social influence, knowledge about the world outside the community, and wealth. Men also acquired women, including slaves and second and third wives, who presented the possibility of more offspring—another key to prosperity. Men, through wives and offspring, accumulated the labor and social ties necessary to host feasts, bestow gifts, and build alliances and reciprocal social obligations. Warfare commonly meant social mobility for men and sometimes for women as well.

Although wives joined their husbands in enjoying elite status, wealth, and special burial, the primary routes to power were made for men and not women. Among the earlier societies of ancient America, ideologies that stressed female and male complementarity surely functioned to counterbalance ideologies that associated male gender identity with warfare, but later in prehistory, Precolumbian art suggests that male-dominated ideologies of violence were most prominent in public discourse. Among the peoples who developed the first great American civilizations, elite ideologies featured male warrior deities, and the dominance of male leaders grew so that by the middle of the first millennium A.D., male warriors were being celebrated in artistic media all over America. The ideology associated with male military, political, and religious roles gained ascendancy late in prehistory, and metaphors involving creation, nurturance, motherhood, fertility, and sex were progressively deemphasized in public contexts.

Figure 9.3. The vanquished warrior queen portrayed in the murals of Cacaxtla in central Mexico. In one view (*left*) she is wounded by an arrow in her cheek; in the other (*right*) she is shown as a captive with bound hands. Courtesy of Sherisse and Geoffrey McCafferty.

The Warrior Queen of Cacaxtla

Mural paintings at Cacaxtla, a small Late Classic site in Puebla, show a bloody battle between a group of men in jaguar costumes and another group in bird costumes. The Jaguar army is winning. The murals clearly portray, in highly realistic style, the gore of battle, with spilling intestines and agony on the faces of the wounded, contrasting with the well-dressed arrogance of the leaders of the Jaguar men, who probably fought for the ruler of Cacaxtla. Among the warriors, in the heat of battle, stand two women wearing bird emblems, identifying them with the losing side (McCafferty and McCafferty 1994a). In addition to back ornaments in the form of wings, each lady wears a triangular *quechquemitl* and a short skirt. These garments are richly patterned and both ladies wear elaborate leg ornaments, sandals, and jewelry. These important women are the central personages in the murals in which they appear. The murals stand on either side of the central stair of the building. Although the women are represented as defeated, they dominate the scenes. The McCaffertys, who have done the only engendered study of these murals, suggest that the figures represent the same woman. This makes sense given the great similarity of costume and the fact that the first scene depicts the woman in the height of combat while the second shows her as a bound captive.

The first woman stands in the midst of the battle, grasping a spear embedded in her cheek. Blood drips from the wound and she is crying out in anguish while making the traditional hand-to-shoulder gesture of surrender and submission. The pose of the Jaguar warrior who stands in front of her, threatening with another spear, suggests that this must represent the moment of capture. Her feminine gender is emphasized by the exaggerated curve of waist and hip as well as by her female clothing.

The woman in the other mural is also threatened by a Jaguar lord, again with a spear in ready position. Her bare torso shows under the quechquemitl and her hands are held in front of her chest, crossed and tied at the wrist. Clearly she has been taken prisoner and most likely will be sacrificed. Who is this woman? Regrettably, the figures are identified by neither name nor place glyphs. One can surmise that she was the ruler of a neighboring state. This period of prehistory was characterized by increased warfare resulting from competition among local groups in the political vacuum left by the waning of Teotihuacán and the migration of northern barbarians into central Mexico.

In Koontz's (2009:75–76) critique of the McCaffertys' (1994a) interpretation of the murals, he suggests that these Bird army figures were really captive men who had been dressed up as women to humiliate them in public. It is unlikely that women's garments were ever employed to humiliate men and improbable that the public in Cacaxtla at that time understood transvestism as a political slur or deemed the female condition humiliating. Furthermore, Koontz interpreted the Cacaxtla murals as "a strategic public statement . . . meant to evoke certain associations in the audience," whereas Maya murals are known to record historic battles. This makes it more likely that the two figures are representations of one woman, the leader of the Bird army, distinguished by a central Mexican quechquemitl, a garment worn only by women since the Preclassic.

Other scholars reiterate the suggestion that female warriors are really transvestite performers, though such performers have not been identified with surety in the Precolumbian record. Modern transvestite dances, sometimes called *contradanzas*, are part of folk Catholic practices that unofficially arrived with missionary priests. Also, in the spirit of the *Iliad*, the Cacaxtla warrior women have been interpreted as female deities in scenes from myth. These suggestions are representative of the desperate manner in which some Mesoamerican specialists try to deny women active roles in prehistoric societies.

In reality, the clothing of the warrior in the murals identifies the woman as a wealthy member of the elite. The short skirt and quechquemitl mark her as being a Mexican, not a Maya lady. The central position of the female figure in the battle mural and other details are strong evidence that she was the leader of the Bird army in this war. It is worth mentioning that the great shrine of Xochitécatl, dominated by representations of elite women, is actually another sector of Cacaxtla (Serra Puche 2001).

Women have not yet been identified in battle scenes drawn by the ancient Maya, although sculptured representations and glyphic texts show that women did become sole rulers of polities, and new archaeological evidence shows that some bore titles such as "Supreme Warrior" (a title of Lady K'abel that would also suit some later heads of state such as Margaret Thatcher, Golda Meir, and Indira Gandhi). Maya rulers, male and female, are shown standing on prisoners and war palanquins (Freidel and Guenter 2003), but female rulers do not appear in scenes of capturing prisoners, as male do rulers. These ladies, like modern rulers, may have had a subordinate war chief or general, but the queens took credit for his victories whether or not they actually went onto the battlefield themselves.

Maya elite women did take part in the rituals associated with warfare. The famous murals of Bonampak show the ruler's female relatives letting blood, as part of the sacrifices of prisoners honoring the naming of the little heir, as well as participating in other aspects of the festivities (Miller 1986:149–151; 2001). Similarly, a number of lintels from Yaxchilán show royal ladies presenting the armor to warriors who are their husbands or other relatives, and stelae from a number of sites show royal ladies participating in the presentation of royal prisoners.

In the Late Postclassic in the northern Yucatán, warfare fell entirely outside of women's spheres—that is, if we can judge from de Landa's ([1566] 1978) description of the culture of the Yucatán city-states at the time of the European invasions. He says that each state was served by two war captains: one hereditary, one elected. During his three-year term, the elected war captain was forbidden to have anything to do with women, even his wife. He was kept in a state of ritual purity, fed only on fish and iguanas, and not permitted to be served by women or to mingle with ordinary people. Since warfare was a major means of elevating social and economic status among the Maya, this ideology—that women are polluting and that sexual behavior has a negative effect on success in warfare—would have made it difficult for women to achieve higher position through involvement in military activity.

Accounts of War in South America

One of the few lengthy accounts of indigenous warfare in South America (prior to the major calamities brought by the European invasion) was that of Hans Staden, a German mercenary in the pay of the Portuguese, who was captured by the Tupinamba Indians of coastal Brazil and held captive for some years in the sixteenth century (Staden [1557] 1963). He describes in great detail the care of prisoners of war by Tupinamba women. Living within a Tupinamba village until his escape, Staden was able to observe the work of women, including their crafts, their participation in ritual, and their roles as shamans. He was most personally concerned, however, with warfare and with the ceremonies of sacrifice of prisoners of war. Staden says that when prisoners were first brought home to the village the women and children beat them. Then they painted the captives and danced around them. After this each captive was kept in the village, where a woman took on the responsibility of caring for him and having sex with him, although any children would be treated as captives and eventually eaten. Prisoners were well treated and well fed while preparations for sacrifice went on. At the time of the final rituals, the women again painted and decorated the prisoner, singing over him and drinking with him. The women also led the prisoner out for sacrifice and gave him a pile of stones to throw at them while they ran around and threatened to eat him. Despite the major presence of women in the preparation of the sacrifice, a man clubbed the prisoner to death. Next the women took the body to be singed and scraped. After a man had cut it into quarters, women took the pieces, running and singing, to complete the butchering. Women and children were allotted the entrails and internal organs, which were cooked up and consumed communally (fig. 9.1). Many tropical forest people apparently held similar feasts in the early Colonial Period, although not all practiced cannibalism (Caillavet 1996).

In recent times, indigenous warfare has been observed among the Yanomami (Yanoami) Indians of northern Brazil and Venezuela. Anthropologists have described patterns of intense intervillage strife, mitigated by trading between allies defined as trading and feasting partners (Ferguson 1992, 1995). Yanomami men are raised to be extremely bellicose and violent toward other members of the society. The paramount reason for raiding, according to the participants, is to attain women, although there are probably several other functions. Anthropologists have observed that epochs of intense fighting interrupt the years of careful negotiations necessary for a man to arrange marriages for his brothers, sons, and himself. This interruption in marriage negotiations leaves villages with a shortage of labor, owing to the practice of a long bride service among the Yanomami.

The autobiography of Helena Valero, a woman captured by the Yanomami in the 1940s, offers a perspective on the lives of women under conditions of escalating tribal warfare, stimulated by conditions of disease and the introduction of machetes and shotguns by White traders (Biocca 1971). Like Yanomami women, Valero suffered from living in a village without her brothers to protect her; she endured the aggressive abuse of males, and she had to deal with competition among cowives for food and favor.

Valero describes the mixed reception given to captured women by Yanomami wives. On the one hand, the older women welcomed and protected captured women, who represented useful labor and wives for their sons and brothers. The younger women rightly feared loss of favor and tended to torment the prisoners, usually without hindrance from their husbands. Valero's firsthand account gives us a glimpse of how a war captive might acculturate into her new society, negotiating position and even happiness in this kind of situation. In Valero's narrative, women had inconspicuous roles in war. In other cultures, such as among the sixteenth-century Tupinamba, the ritual aspects of warfare must have served to integrate women into the largely male pursuit of battle and allow women access to the benefits and prestige gained from bellicose activities.

Warfare in the Ancient Andes

Female warriors do not appear in the representational art of the ancient Andes. The first great military-themed art work, the relief sculptures of Cerro Sechín in coastal Peru, shows only males, although it is difficult to identify dismembered body parts (Tello 1956). Although war and warriors are favorite themes in the modeled and painted ceramics of coastal Peruvian cultures as well as in painted textiles showing nude prisoners from the Late Intermediate Period, no female figures have been recognized among them.

The absence of females in this art and the magnificence of Andean fortresses, like Chanquillo and Sacsahuaman (today's Sacsayhuaman), present the idea that ancient Peruvian societies may have been dominated by male warriors. In an alternative view, the Topics (1997) have argued that the so-called fortifications and military monuments built in the Andean region since the Late Preceramic were ceremonial centers where ritual battles called *tinku* were staged by related communities or by segments of an ayllu. Both ancient people and contemporary indigenous Andean people celebrated battles, considered analogous to sexual intercourse, in order to ensure agricultural increase. Today, women join the men in ceremonial battles as part of a ritual cycle. Ritual warfare is compatible with an ideology of gender complementarity, a principle that might have been expressed socially in order to counterbalance hierarchical social organization and male dominance.

Moche painted ceramics sometimes show the aftermath of battle, and some vessels depict women taking part in the ritual manipulation of prisoners, severed limbs, and other trophies (cf. Hocquenghem 1977b, plate 44). This conforms to the historic data from the tropical lowlands, which suggest that women had roles in the rituals following battle. In Moche art, Lady C is often illustrated in the act of presenting a goblet of blood to a deity, but on some Moche vessels she, or another female supernatural figure, cuts the prisoner's throat and collects the blood herself while another female supernatural, with a feather crown, sacrifices the prisoner. On other vessels both human and bird women feed and touch prisoners about to be sacrificed. The excavation of massive human sacrifices by Bourget (1997) at the Huaca de la Luna has demonstrated that painted vessels accurately depict the prisoner sacrifices of the Moche. We can imagine that some Moche women, as well as men, participated in these sacrificial rituals, given that the Moche themselves showed women involved with the prisoners.

The discovery of the body of the Lady of Cao, an important female ruler buried with weapons, albeit elaborate ceremonial ones (A. Williams 2006:70–83), changes archaeologists' belief that women did not customarily participate in warfare in the later kingdoms of Peru, and that only in exceptional cases, and in some myths, were females involved in military action. Normally, we think that because women could not go to war, because they could not make multiple marriages (with several men), and because they were not eligible to receive gifts of labor, wives, land, and other benefits given to victorious rulers, they had limited ability to achieve status and gain authority. Now it is possible to think that some women might have participated in warfare and through that means increased their power and advanced themselves socially. The Lady of Cao, who was not only royal but whose power and authority was symbolized by the weapons in her tomb, may have taken advantage of her position in a very bellicose society.

In another case, Sarmiento de Gamboa ([1572] 1943) recorded a Colonial Period narrative in which an Inca woman named Chañan Kori Coca was the head of the Chococchono ayllu, now Santiago Parish in Cuzco. She led a troop of ayllu warriors against the Chancas, who were advancing on Cuzco.

There are no other details concerning her deeds, save an eighteenth-century European painting showing her with the iconography of Judith carrying the head of Holofernes: she stands on the decapitated body of a victim and simpers while she holds up a head.

Winners and Victims

The ubiquity of ancient armed conflict among later indigenous American cultures is evidence that it was positively evaluated and frequently adopted as a strategy. Apparently the people who waged war, presumably the winners, benefited. Bellicosity is known to supply the winners with labor (slaves, concubines, or wives), sacrificial victims, land, and access to other commodities, but it also acts as a catalyst for social change by facilitating the development of leadership and other new social and political institutions that may make systems more competitive in the future. Ancient women certainly supported warfare and enjoyed its fruits, as do some women today.

On the other hand, despite the advantages that accrue to the winners of war, prehistoric women may have been unable to participate in the important social processes initiated by male warriors, and furthermore, they were often the primary victims of war. Those few women who were war leaders or warriors suffered the same fate as their male compatriots: wounds, death, and sacrifice to the gods of the victors awaited women like Six Monkey and the ruler of the Bird army. Ordinary women were also affected by bellicosity.

More than two hundred excavated skeletons from Norris Farm in the Illinois River Valley indicate the scope of chronic warfare in that region around A.D. 1300. The remains of forty-three women and men showed embedded projectile point fragments, massive skull injuries, penetrating skull wounds caused by ground stone axes, defensive trauma on arms and hands, and mutilations such as scalping and decapitation. Of five women who survived attacks (they had healed injuries), three had been scalped. Milner and his colleagues (1991) reported that five tombs contained individuals of only one sex: three of these held groups of women who may have been surprised while working together away from the village. They suggest that raiding was common and that work parties were sometimes attacked at remote locations, shown by carnivore damage on some skeletons.

Norris Farm is not unique. A study of some 751 archaeological crania of adult females and males from the Middle Missouri Valley, dating from around A.D. 1600 to 1832, shows that women had about as much chance of being scalped as men. Scalping was, of course, the prime means of securing war trophies among the Plains tribes. It has been noted that the incidence of scalping increased with the introduction of steel knives to the Native Americans, but evidence of scalping and the massacre of whole settlements—female, male, aged, and children alike—extends far back into the prehistoric period in North America.

Although many prehistoric groups made trophies from human bodies, there is only a little archaeological data that can be given a gendered interpretation. In Early Horizon Peru there is abundant evidence of headhunting from the south coast: trophy heads appear in art imagery, and burials confirm that people buried some bodies lacking heads, and other bodies with additional heads (Conlee 2007). Caches of disarticulated skulls prepared as trophies have also been recovered. Trophy skulls were prepared by removing the brain and knocking a hole in the forehead so that a carrying strap could be inserted. Browne and his colleagues (1993) note that in the Nazca Valley, although male trophy heads are in the great majority, there are occasional female ones. Children's heads prepared as trophy displays have also been found among the Middle Horizon Huari (Tung and Knudson 2010).

Women in the northern Andes were likewise victims of the endemic warfare and slaving that characterized late Prehispanic cultures in that area. Caillavet (1996) has documented how the capture of women and children for food and sacrifice negatively impacted the northern Andean chiefdoms. Moreover, just as among the Tupinamba, women captured by the northern Colombian tribes were impregnated by their captors and their children were reared to the age of eleven or twelve and then dispatched for meat.

At certain times and places, mortality among noncombatant women and children was very high, especially when people tried to cross frontiers and encroach on another group's territory. There are abundant archaeological examples of changes in settlement patterns showing that in response to hostile conditions people sought defensible locations for their villages and constructed fortified sites. Burial and osteological data dramatically illustrate the impact of violent competition. At the Heerwald site in central Oklahoma (late 1300s), the remains of a young adult female, a fetus of approximately eight months' gestation, and another child were found in an abnormal burial: apparently they had been thrown into the grave. The woman had a stone projectile point embedded in her first lumbar vertebra and another point was found in her chest cavity. One rib had a deep cut, and another rib and the scapula were damaged from blows just before her death. Finally, the poor woman had been scalped. The child buried with her was incomplete, missing some long bones (Owsley 1994).

The archaeology and history of Plains cultures attest to the central place of warfare, from small-scale raiding to wholesale slaughter. To revenge himself, a warrior might kill either enemy men or women. At the Crow Creek site, where a massacre took place, 90 percent of five hundred individuals were scalped. In the historic period, large-scale slave raids and massacres became very common in the Plains. In the Southwest, massacres at Hopi and at Ancestral Puebloan sites, such as Mancos, demonstrate that women as well as men were killed and sometimes consumed (White 1992).

In Mesoamerica, excavations at Tikal and Uaxactún and the decipherment of their monuments have shown that on January 16, A.D. 378, Uaxactún was conquered by Maya forces from Tikal, led by the king Great Jaguar Paw and a close associate, Smoking Frog. The victors chose to exterminate the enemy army instead of taking prisoners for sacrifice or ransom, but the king of Uaxactún was captured, displayed as a prisoner, tortured, and eventually sacrificed. His principal wives, one of whom was pregnant, and two small children were buried alive: thrown into a tomb, sealed up, and left to die (Haviland 1997; S. Martin 2000).

In central Mexico, there is both archaeological and historical evidence concerning territorial wars in which massacres of the elite and enslavement of many commoners was the rule. The Aztec waged wars to secure tribute and gain territory. Negotiations between the Aztec and the beleaguered might allow the civilian population to avoid violence by increasing their tribute load, but any intransigence or betrayal might provoke the Aztec to slaughter women and children as well as noncombatant males. Many women, however, ended up as slaves, in part because the growing state had an enormous appetite for cloth and the rapidly expanding noble class required increased services. Much the same has been noted for the Mogollon region of the North American Southwest. Here, near Kayenta, some women were thrown into a grave without offerings; their bodies exhibit clear signs of systematic abuse: death finally came after they were beaten with a heavy digging stick. The remains of these women show that they performed much heavier work in life than did the women who received proper burial at the site. It is surmised that these burials are those of captured and enslaved women who were abused by both women and men.

The co-opting of women's labor and their recruitment into sexual servitude are widespread consequences of warfare known in modern times. Moreover, the displacement of women and families by wars takes a substantial toll on entire communities and their way of life. When the Inca armies moved into the southern Ecuadorian highlands to consolidate their conquest of the Cañari peoples, uprisings by the indigenous folk resulted in tremendous massacres. Spanish sources estimate that a few years later the sex ratio in the Cañari region was fifteen women to one man. The Inca state then implemented its *mitima* policy, in which whole villages of people were moved long distances to replace bellicose peoples. Some Cañari were, in fact, forced to move to Cuzco in southern Peru, a linear distance of over 1,500 kilometers, while large numbers of Inca and non-Inca people from Peru were moved into southern Ecuador, where they still live, speaking Quechua, the language of the Inca (Hirschkind 1995). Unlike refugees, *mitimas* had no hope of returning to their native land.

These are the more dramatic consequences of waging war. Prehistoric women, like modern women in wartime, surely felt the increased workload. Women often have to carry out basic production while men are engaged in battle. In this sense, female labor underwrites the process of arming, equipping, feeding, and deploying raiding parties and armies. Historic Iroquois women, by withholding the supplies of food that they controlled, could effectively veto men's plans to wage war. The feminine half of society is often called on to fill in for missing male kinsmen, and women continue to shoulder the burden when men are killed. They pick up the pieces after losing, and they also enjoy the benefits of winning.

The Impact of Conquest

The European Conquest of the Americas, which is widely recognized as having had tragic consequences for native peoples and cultures, was especially disastrous for Native American women. The conquerors successfully imposed upon American peoples European religions, land tenure, leadership, and gender roles, denying women many of the opportunities and rights that had been available to them in indigenous societies (cf. Kellogg 1997, 2005). The conquest destroyed some of the parallel institutions controlled by women, and women lost virtually all public and remunerative roles once available to them. For example, female administrators in the Aztec markets disappeared, feminine cults were suppressed, and in Peru, Spanish officials refused to deal with female rulers. Because of disapproval by the church, female musicians disappeared from public rituals.

Women in Ancient America

Women, in many ways more than men, bore the brunt of the initial European Conquest. Many were simply violated and left to die or passed on as slaves to the next man. We read uneasily the accounts of Pedro de Cieza de León ([1553] 1984), one of the major chroniclers of the Spanish Conquests of Andean South America, who discussed the women of different ethnic groups, ranking some more attractive and willing than others. Women were torn from their homes and forced to accompany soldiers, cook and clean for them, and serve as their sexual partners (Trexler 1995). Accounts of female conscripts who accompanied invading armies emphasize how these women had bleeding hands and died quickly from overwork because the Spanish misunderstood the amount of labor required to grind corn. When the epidemics introduced by Europeans began, women who were pregnant were most vulnerable, and those women who survived lost many children and other relatives (Black 1992). Despite the decimation of families and the loss of labor power, women were often forced by alien overlords to produce the same quantity of tribute goods as in aboriginal times (Brumfiel 1996b; Harvey 1986). Few detailed accounts of the sexual violation and abuse of ordinary indigenous women exist; still, it is easy to imagine their fate based on the better-documented experiences of high-caste women.

The Lady of Cofitachiqui

In the 1590s Garcilaso de la Vega ([1605] 1951) recorded interviews with survivors of the de Soto expedition in the southeastern United States. While in Florida, where de Soto and his men unwittingly started the first of the great epidemics that eventually felled the Mississippian kingdoms, the expedition was involved in pillage, vandalism, and rape on a large scale. When de Soto heard about the teenage female ruler of the Cofitachiqui kingdom, he demanded to see her. The Spanish had already robbed the charnel house where her relatives' bodies were stored, helping themselves to the metal, pearls, and other wealth accompanying the bodies. The Lady of Cofitachiqui appeared in great state, in a large canoe attended by eight noblewomen and pulled by another canoe that carried many paddlers and six noblemen. She tried to reason with the Spanish, telling them that the scourges of the past year had taken their toll on food stores. Although the lady offered them substantial supplies and valuables, the Spanish kidnapped her, but she escaped her captors boldly some days later with a chest of pearls. The Spanish never forced any of her subjects to disclose her whereabouts and she was never recaptured (Trocolli 1992, 2002).

The Maligned Doña Marina

In contrast, in Mexico Doña Marina was enslaved as a laborer and concubine both by her own people and then by the Spanish. Like the Lady of Cofitachiqui, her aboriginal name has not been recorded, even though she was one of the key players in the European conquest of Mexico. The Spanish baptized her Marina and the indigenous people who came in contact with her called her Doña Marina or Malintzin (her name with the Aztec honorific equivalent to *doña*, "lady"). A native of Veracruz, she had been sold to the Maya, but when the Europeans arrived she was stolen again as a worker and sex object. The Spaniard who acquired her observed her linguistic genius, and Cortés then took her as a concubine and interpreter. Marina traveled with the Spanish, serving Cortés in both capacities, eventually bearing him a son. When the baby was very young, Cortés passed Marina to a colleague who was going off to invade the Yucatán. In the course of this strenuous campaign, she became pregnant by her current master, bore a child, and died a month later from the consequences of childbirth. Although Doña Marina was a helpless slave, forced to service sexually each of her owners, tragically dead to her own people, and with no one to protect or help her, she has been excoriated in Mexican history. Later writers have labeled her "La Chingada," an obscene and vile term, in an attempt to transfer the guilt of the men who bought, sold, and used her to the lady herself. This is clear misogyny: a woman who is defiled need not be interpreted as villainous, and Doña Marina certainly cannot be blamed for the conquest of Mexico (Barriga 1994; Karttunen 1997).

The Lady of Cofitachiqui was a ruler and, presumably, had the help of her subjects in escaping. Marina had no place to go; she was a slave, and wherever she went she would have been in the same situation, with the added threat that slaves were usually sacrificed when they outlived their usefulness. Other women, if wealthy, were married off to Spaniards as prizes. In Mexico, Tecuichpo (chapter 8), who was raped and impregnated by Cortés, later creatively used her marital alliances to keep control of her family estates. Ordinary women were sometimes married, or more often forced to become concubines, if not simply abandoned with the results of their victimization.

Declining Status of Women in the Great Plains

When the first Europeans in North America observed indigenous women, they described miserable drudges, leading lives of unremitting toil. Weist (1983) has documented the origins and nature of the European understanding of indigenous women and argues that the European vision had both factual and ideological components. On the one hand, in order to perpetuate the myth that European control of indigenous peoples and their forced acculturation was beneficial, the conquerors developed an unfavorable concept of indigenous culture. Also, they excused their illegitimate attraction to Indian women by characterizing them as dirty and sexually promiscuous. These distorted visions were easily formed, since European observers had a poor understanding of the alien economies, social practices, and ideologies of native peoples. Nevertheless, they observed correctly that Indian women were overworked, as shown in the following example, but did not recognize that this was due in large part to the impact of European economic exploitation on native cultures.

By the nineteenth century in North America, European traders had created a demand for fur and hides that far outstripped the productive capabilities of traditional foraging households in the northern United States and Canada. Women's work increased tremendously as families reallocated labor to meet new demands. Women continued to perform the traditional tasks of child care, cooking, gathering wood, and fetching water while endeavoring to vastly increase the time they spent tanning hides. The Plains peoples increased the number of female workers by acquiring secondary wives, capturing slave women from other tribes, and punishing female adulterers with hide processing. As males were the source of hides and controlled the trade with the Whites, women lost more autonomy and spent more of their lives working. When Whites finally arrived in villages they observed that women were exploited. Because Indian men had greater access to wealth through trade, and to the prestige that accrued from warfare and ritual performance, power became ever more concentrated in male hands. In contrast, female Arikara traders maintained social and economic power as they traded directly with European men in the contact period (Hollimon 2005; Kehoe 2005).

During the historic period, as traditional societies broke down under foreign attack and forced missionization, some women's roles became even less enviable. Nevertheless, other women managed to turn the introduced ideologies of oppression and pollution to their own advantage, as described in a study by Patricia Galloway (1997). She suggests that women used menstrual buildings to create social, ritual, and economic bonds with other women that supported them in facing the demands of their lives. In some societies, women successfully resisted the genocidal and ethnocidal forces of the conquerors while developing ideologies and activities that made their lives meaningful.

Women in Inca and Colonial Peru

Silverblatt (1978, 1987) has argued that a loss of autonomy and status was suffered by women within the Inca Empire. As that polity extended its hegemony by military force and coercion, power became associated with men, and the state became the primary locus of decision making. Even though the household continued as the basic tax-paying unit, the Inca government, followed later by the Spanish government, decreed that only males could represent households; thus women lost their accustomed roles of self-representation as they were integrated into the hierarchical system. History records little about the regulation of Inca households, but the fact remains that the Inca bureaucracy was masculine, and, according to Silverblatt, conquered women were married to Inca men, including the Sapa Inca himself, framing the relationship between Cuzco and the conquered ethnic groups as marriage—but between a victorious and a defeated partner. Although polygyny became common among the Inca elite, women, even Inca noblewomen, could not themselves have multiple spouses. Elite women were commodified as gendered possessions, owned by men for whom they labored producing cloth and food. Even though these women were amply provided for, the products of their households may not have been theirs to dispose of as they wished.

After the horrors of the Conquest, women found themselves stripped of legal majority. In the Spanish view it was appropriate for females to be docile, chaste, and reclusive: they should not act for themselves, but they and their goods should be administered by related males or by guardians all of their lives. Silverblatt (1980, 1987) has argued that Spanish colonization was characterized by European misogyny that was prejudiced against women of all classes. Women lost their autonomy, access to land and other resources, and their dominant roles in female religious and political institutions. Only male community leaders were drawn into the Spanish colonial system, and religious persecution, called the "extirpation of idolatries," directly affected women in town and village. Guaman Poma de Ayala ([1615] 1936), writing in the sixteenth century, eloquently described the abuses of women by indigenous governmental and religious authorities.

Inca nobles and both female and male members of the aboriginal *curaca* class (local political elites) in the Inca state responded to the Spanish Conquest in various ways. While some resisted Spanish government, dying in native uprisings, others (represented in historical accounts and Colonial paintings) developed strategies of colluding, collaborating, and consorting with the Spaniards, thereby successfully entering the Spanish ruling class and maintaining some control over the native population, the source of wealth (Cummins 1991). Doña Beatriz, the last Inca's daughter, married a European, as did the woman who became the mother of the chronicler Garcilaso de la Vega: both males were far inferior to the women in rank.

In the early Colonial Period, some women were able to develop powerful positions as witches, based on the Spanish belief that women were characterized by "unbridled lust and diabolism." The healers and religious women whom the Spaniards labeled witches, idolatresses, and heretics became the foci of cultural resistance; they were sought by other members of their communities as magical curers, and recognized as defenders of Andean traditions against the European onslaught. Ironically, it was Spanish belief that created witches in the Andes, where there had been no such category before. Andean women and men continued, as they do in the present, to seek traditional curers and healers. Many Colonial curers were women who continued to carry out indigenous practices in the face of Christian religious and civil persecution. For example, in the region of Otuzco (where many men ran away from their families and communities to escape impossible labor obligations), some women fled to the high, cold puna, beyond the sphere of Spanish settlements, where they persisted in worshipping deities and ancestors at sacred natural places and tombs. Male leadership in local ritual became difficult under Spanish oversight, so women became the leaders of local cults. Male indigenous leaders encouraged women to take on this role, which the Spanish stigmatized as idolatry and witchcraft.

One leader who emerged in the seventeenth century was the priestess Catalina Guacayllano, respectfully known as La Doctora, a teacher and master of ancient ceremonies who defended aboriginal customs (Silverblatt 1987). She instructed disciples and directed people in the worship of community deities and ancestors. According to the description of her activities left by Spanish priests, she prayed, danced, and sacrificed guinea pigs, maize, coca leaves, and fat to the idols of the local deity that watched over local fields and irrigation canals. When the Catholic priest in charge of destroying native religion burned the idols of the cult, Catalina Guacayllano replaced them twofold and continued her leadership until she died and was buried in the traditional manner. Priests discovered her tomb and destroyed it, but the Spanish description of its trappings, including the special clothing that she wore when she made offerings, indicates her important religious and political position (199–202).

Although virginity was not traditionally valued by Andean peoples, the Colonial Period indigenous priestesses of the underground cults were virgins or widows who eschewed remarriage. These women resisted all contact with the Spanish system. By remaining celibate they separated themselves from contact with and exploitation by Spanish men. Their asexual behavior may have seemed virtuous from the Spanish perspective, but more importantly they were able to escape taxation because single women did not constitute a tribute category for Colonial censuses. Guaman Poma de Ayala ([1615] 1936) describes how such women lived with their children in the puna, working together to support themselves, afraid of the priests and civil authorities who would exile them from their native communities and compel them to labor in the weaving workshops and convents in which women accused of witchcraft and idolatry were confined. Living isolated in the inhospitable highlands, these women effectively vanished from the Spanish world.

The stories of La Doctora and women like her illustrate how women resisted domination and exercised a form of alternative power, serving as authorities and autonomous agents outside the reach of the early Colonial government. According to Silverblatt (1980), women temporarily reinvented the female component of Andean culture, some of which persisted into modern times. But by the seventeenth century, women routinely killed themselves and their children in the course of their resistance to the government. Some women also resorted to male infanticide, which Silverblatt interprets as the result of deep disillusionment due to the abuse they experienced at the hands of both indigenous and colonial male authorities.

Women engaged in religious and political struggle against the unjust Colonial system and participated in several military rebellions that indigenous groups mounted unsuccessfully against the Spanish. The wars of independence of the 1820s ended the Colonial Period but failed to deliver women into a just social system. Indigenous Andean women continued to suffer under the exploitation of national governments.

Culture Wars

Miraculously, all over America today indigenous peoples resist, contest, and refuse to disappear. They are winning some battles in the culture wars as they gain recognition of their right to exist and as they develop political and economic power (cf. Meisch 2002). In modern times the historic pattern of devaluation and exploitation by European religious and governmental institutions has not ended, and in some places indigenous peoples have come under increased pressure to acculturate through physical attacks of violent, Mestizo-led political forces and drug traffickers. Today throughout the American continents, men, women, and children are stressed by economic conditions, weakened by alcoholism and diseases of poverty, and threatened by guerrillas, soldiers, and mercenaries from various factions: indigenous peoples are killed and kidnapped and men and whole families flee to the cities, where economic forces and alien cultural practices devastate them.

In other instances women actively participate in political and guerrilla movements whose objectives are revolutionary change, either because they have no choice (a new twist on the capture of wives) or because they see no other way to change their lot in life. Ancient women and men confronted similar challenges and adopted similar strategies throughout history; in the process they produced the tremendous variety of cultural adaptations that characterize the prehistory of America. As American women struggle for better lives in modern societies, they can be encouraged by the history of their ancestors.

CHAPTER TEN

Women in Prehistory

A rchaeological narratives about America's past have been, at best, gender neutral or simply lacking in people. At worst they have been biased in favor of men's activities and have ignored the contributions of others. Happily, this has begun to change. We now recognize that history has more integrity when viewed as the result of the activities, relationships, and ideas of everyone, including females, lower-class people, children, the elderly, and individuals who fall into other gender or social categories. Microsocial, personal, and engendered interpretations are the basis of more satisfying analyses, leading to a better understanding of cultural change and cultural process. In this narrative we have derived views from contemporary political and social agendas and we have followed other scholars in rejecting androcentric interpretations of the past while endeavoring to avoid the trap of searching for, and finding, only politically correct interpretations.

The foregoing narrative may be no more truthful than any other interpretation of the American past, but it has the virtue of including women as actors. Engendered archaeological research is productive for a number of reasons. For instance, we have tested the hypothesis that women were significant players in the development of prehistoric cultures from the first peopling of the Americas until the emergence of ancient states, and we can demonstrate that women's experiences in the Americas varied dramatically across space and were subject to fundamental changes through time. When we take women and gender into account, we can show that women's lives are interesting and that women, as well as men, have influenced the course of history.

Imagining Alternatives

This narrative about Native American prehistory is designed to stimulate thinking about ourselves and our society. We have described and attempted to understand some aspects of prehistoric life, rejecting the androcentric bias that has been so common in archaeological research. We have discussed the risks of making engendered, as well as unengendered, interpretations of house floors, figurines, and stone tools, showing how gender is an arbitrary social script, frequently and variably rewritten throughout American prehistory. The research of numerous contemporary scholars opens the door for more responsible archaeological reconstructions and serves our present social purposes, not the least of which is to change the image of archaeology as a male-only science. Another purpose is to find women in the past, to appreciate their life experiences and historical contributions, and to understand how gender was an important factor in both life and history. This awareness can inspire contemporary people as we make decisions about our own lives and as we shape our evolving social institutions and make our own history.

There are precious few facts about the past, and ultimately, these are neither as useful nor as memorable as the narratives created from them. These narratives are highly interpretative cultural products. In the past, experts imagined men hunting; today we can confidently tell the story of ancient America with women in it.

In the twenty-first century many of us would like to live in a world in which women and men, as well as other segments of society, have equal access to work, wealth, power, status, and prestige. Part of the process of reaching our goals is the deconstruction of the past and the creation of new origin myths. In many cultures people look to the past for utopian social models. Some people look back and see an Old European society focused on a great goddess (Gimbutas 1991), while some archaeologists think that this modern myth is built on exaggerated interpretations of evidence (Conkey and Tringham 1995; Hayden 1986; Nelson 1987; Rice 1981; Russell 1991).

Many of the archaeologists cited in our narrative looked at history and found that both women and men were creative participants in ancient indigenous cultures. Working with the results of their research, we have tried to create a larger narrative that stresses the roles of real people in systems characterized by ideological, political, moral, and economic struggles. This narrative can help the reader explore both the nature of social life and the nature of female roles and has the potential to stimulate thought. Today, as archaeologists reconstruct prehistory, they are providing us with new ways to think about women and power (Sweely 1999), and Barstow (1978) imagines ancient women and men using power cooperatively: "power with," not "power over." One can easily imagine both sexes as powerful if, as in the ideology of the modern ecology movement, people use power for "competence, not for dominance." It is better to understand that women have shared political power, been involved in gender-balanced systems, dealt with technologies, controlled resources, created ideologies, and managed social relations. Because of our habitual ways of thinking about power, we have exalted the roles of men, but there is reason to think that women in the past wielded power as well. In ancient America, women as a group did not rule over men in any society, and many scholars believe that matriarchy is a myth that is not useful for us today (Eller 2000). Still, it is clear that women were leaders in Native American groups: women of high status wielded power in various contexts (Trocolli 1999, 2002), and elite Maya women ruled over the lower orders of society along with elite men (Joyce 2008). Perhaps more important is that women created important discourse, perhaps even dominant discourse, in some contexts; they certainly manipulated both ideas and material culture with competence, and, to paraphrase Barstow (1978), women certainly had the power to express themselves autonomously in some spheres of activity and thought.

Across both time and space in ancient America, female people had diverse social and cultural experiences. The variability that we perceive in both the archaeological and ethnohistoric records is the result of dynamic social processes that have frequently been obfuscated by our intellectual habits. We tend to think about women and men in categorical ways, naturalizing and universalizing the two concepts, creating aesthetically pleasing dualistic and polar images that prevent us from appreciating gender as a variable social script, changing with the conditions of the moment. There is a tendency to conceive of history as an uncomplicated evolution from simple to complex, a process in which the normalized "rise of the state" has predictable consequences for "Woman" and "Man." Our own research has led us to reject these formulas and views.

Gender—the process by which societies interpret the fact of biological differences and create social roles based on those differences—is a fundamental dynamic of history and social life. As such it is worthy of study. We need to understand gender because human beings have habitually used the fact of sexual difference to assign roles and statuses, to open and close opportunities for women and men, and to empower and constrain. The negotiation of gender relations can be thought of as script writing. The involved parties seek to gain advantage or to minimize disadvantage as they invent technologies, alter economies, change social relations, develop different politics, and generate ideology. These creative activities are what humans do as they solve the organizational problems entailed in social life.

The study of ancient gender relations pays attention to the way the story of the past is told and both shapes and reflects the way we think about ourselves. The images of ancient women that are commonly shown to young girls will shape their thoughts, plans, aspirations, and life experiences. Parents with the utopian goal of giving great self-confidence and wider opportunity to both female and male children will be supported by a vision of the past in which both women and men participate as creative agents of change in all areas of social, economic, and intellectual life. Archaeological interpretation can help achieve such a vision and erase the stereotype that women are impaired by their biology.

Ancient Native American solutions to the problems of living are relevant to all of us today. They are examples of ways of being human that move us and satisfy our curiosity. The story of America's past has the potential to instruct us about the patterns that characterized everyone's ancestors on all continents—and half of those ancestors, everywhere, were women.

An Archaeology of Gender

All knowledge about Native American prehistory is subject to change as scholars use innovative methodologies and theories to generate new evidence and to make plausible interpretations. Because gender is an important dynamic in social life and history, and because women's activities and gender relations need to be documented, it is important that archaeologists develop and exercise methods and theories useful in illuminating gender relations in the past.

Interpretations derived from ethnographic and historic analogues are the backbone of archaeology, but they are always ambiguous and often lead to risky assumptions. Categories of evidence such as architecture, art, tools, and food remains have been used to identify ancient gender patterns; far more useful hypotheses are those that are also backed by emerging scientific techniques. Some productive strategies for identifying female activities and life experiences include examining bone chemistry to study diet and geographical origins; studying pathologies and trauma; and analyzing muscular and joint stress, dental wear, and DNA, which can reveal biological sex as well as kin relations within a group.

Archaeologists are becoming more skillful in finding gender patterns in the prehistoric record by analyzing archaeological contexts. They increasingly recognize that women have always contributed to the material basis of life, the elaboration of religion and philosophy, and to the functioning of society, including the reproduction of humankind, which may still be the most costly contribution a woman can make to her society.

In the near future we hope readers will see more reconstructions of history that take into consideration the contributions of women as well as men. There will be more studies in which the sexual division of labor is treated as an important variable in understanding change, and we will cease to see women omitted from narratives concerning the great episodes of change in American prehistory. The social revolutions that resulted in the emergence of states and empires had important gender dimensions. Any treatment of the development of plant cultivation and food production systems in the New World needs to describe the participation of women because in ancient America women continued to have central roles in agriculture until European contact and beyond.

Today, people are promoting and benefiting from alternative stories about ourselves and our past. The goddess movement has inspired some women and men and given them an ideological alternative to patriarchal religious institutions. Popular fiction entertains us with active heroines in Paleolithic contexts where there were once just men with clubs (cf. Thomas 1987; Auel 1985). New archaeological narratives also serve the needs of young people in constructing images of themselves and their society, and many archaeologists today are more aware of our own cultural and masculinist biases.

People who want to see women as having been more powerful or man-like in the past may not be pleased. No examples of matriarchy are known, but many prehistoric societies were dominated by goddesses (female images predominate in the earliest religious expressions of both Europe and the Americas), and anthropological and archaeological research and theory has led some writers to think that in ancient America female personages were important deities, ancestors, rulers, priests, healers, shamans, and participants in ritual and sacrifice. We believe that social life was not very hierarchical in deep prehistory, where women and men sometimes held power together in systems characterized by complementarity. Community harmony did not necessarily reign in the past. More likely, women's and men's interests frequently came into conflict, but it is also evident that women and men struggled, negotiated, contested, resisted, and finagled, working out their roles, statuses, power, and authority as they went along. It is known from ethnography that women and men negotiate in myriad ways on a daily basis and that their struggles are affected by their rank and class. Cultural change happened as individuals and members of different interest groups engaged in social activities and experimented with new behaviors and ideas. Today it happens the same way.

Roads to Power

Feminists have always been concerned with the autonomy, self-determination, and power of women—all perceived as limited in recent contexts. Fortunately, it is no longer necessary to project onto ourselves only recent historic scenarios derived from Colonial America or from nineteenth- and twentieth-century industrial societies. New theory has made it possible to think about power in different ways. The view of power in ancient America developed in this narrative grows out of anthropology's understanding of the extraordinary variation possible among cultures.

In some societies, people take measures to avoid concentrating power and by custom they eschew hierarchy. In these societies individuals find that no avenues lead to power and authority, although they may earn the admiration of their relatives for their personal qualities. In other societies, people increase their productivity, manipulate kinship, and create opportunities for accumulating and wielding power. Some opportunities are designed for one sex and not the other. Trade, warfare, and religion are routes to power associated with men in recent European and Asian cultures, but these same routes offer opportunities to women in other societies in Africa and America. In some cases women have leadership roles within households, and in some societies they dominate in trade and religion. In ancient America, women's power was often related to their roles in marriage, kinship, economy, and religion, and that power was expressed and negotiated on the ideological level in ancient art.

Viewed cross-culturally, where men become powerful beyond the household and occupy the obvious positions of authority, women often find ways to exercise power in spheres where they can maintain a high degree of autonomy and control. For example, some women gain prestige and control by taking on religious roles, and in some communities men respect or are afraid of women because they believe that women are able to mobilize supernatural forces for good or evil. In some circumstances women can accumulate wealth by management of resources and labor, or they can create and promote ideologies through media such as decorated ceramics, baskets, or textiles. Women can exercise control and affect decision making by forming interest groups, like sodalities or sororities, or by managing political and social institutions in parallel with those operated by men. The archaeological record might reveal patterns of female power if archaeologists were clever enough to recognize and interpret the evidence.

In some complex societies, women's social behavior is controlled and elaborate ideologies have been developed to justify the abrogation of women's self-determination. Rapp (1987) has described contexts in which women are confined and otherwise required to conform to special standards of demeanor, expression, and movement; their sexuality is controlled and there are severe penalties to women for loss of their virginity; women's relatives determine their reproductive and marriage choices; and their productive labor is managed by others. Nevertheless, ethnographic studies also inform us that even in these circumstances women can be autonomous and exercise authority in certain spheres. When power is not flaunted it might be difficult to document in the archaeological record, but this does not mean it is not there.

Extreme cases of female restriction illustrate the tremendous variety of social arrangements possible in human culture. No pattern is biologically based or inexorable. The story of the many roles of Native American women, some of which have been documented in the archaeological and historical records, is relevant to us in the early twenty-first century as American women move back into leadership roles in religion and politics, where they have been underrepresented for a long time.

Glossary

Agency: Refers to the anthropological focus on the individuals who participate in processes that result in cultural change.

Agriculture: A system for producing food and other useful materials by cultivating domesticated plants and tending domesticated animals, usually involving intensified labor investment, land modification, irrigation, and animal traction or other nonhuman sources of power. Compare **Horticulture**.

Analogy: An inference based on the idea that if two or more things are similar to each other in some respects, they may be similar in other ways as well. Analogical reasoning is one form of interpretation in anthropology. See **Ethnographic Analogy**.

Androcentric: Focused on males and their activities and values, and favoring these above the activities and values of females and other genders.

Anthropomorphic: Having the form of a human being.

Anthropomorphize: To add human features to an artifact or artistic representation of non–human beings, such as supernaturals.

Archaeological culture: A unit of study identified by a recurring assemblage of diagnostic artifacts thought to correspond to an ancient social group, distinguished in time and space from other groups and having a distinct adaptive system. See **Culture**.

Archaeological record: The totality of the remains of past activity recovered in association with each other in their original position in the earth.

Archaeology of gender: The scientific and humanistic study of the past through its material remains that seeks to reconstruct aspects of ancient gender systems and identify the activities of women and men.

Archaic Period: The period following the Paleoindian Period, characterized by people who followed the foraging way of life. Some Archaic groups developed sedentary lifestyles and horticulture. Equivalent to the Old World Mesolithic.

Artifact: An object whose form is the result of human manufacture or modification.

Berdache: In some North American indigenous societies, a person who cross-dresses and adopts the work of the opposite sex. This is a recognized social status and can be considered a third, or fourth, gender. Today, gay and lesbian North American Indians often refer to themselves as "Two-Spirits," or berdaches.

Biface: A lithic artifact produced by reducing a core until it has a lenticular cross section caused by the removal of flakes that originate along the entire periphery and leave scars across both faces.

Cacique/Cacica: Hereditary chief or leader. See **Chiefdom**.

Camelid: Any of several species of New World animals that include domesticated llama and alpaca, and wild guanaco and vicuña.

Chiefdom: A kind of sociopolitical organization distinguished by a permanent, hereditary, central political authority that manages the activities of several kin-based communities.

Colonial Period: In the New World, the period before the establishment of modern nation states when indigenous peoples were dominated politically by Europeans.

Context: Spatial context refers to the relationship among archaeological remains in their original position in the ground. Temporal context refers to the location of evidence in time. Cultural context refers to the inferred social, cultural, and natural environments in which past people and things operated.

Coprolite: Preserved feces that can be analyzed in order to reconstruct ancient diet.

Core: A chunk of raw material or a blank that is struck purposefully to remove flakes in the process of making stone tools.

Culture: The central concept of anthropology; refers to the complex, integrated system of learned behaviors that is the basis of the adaptation of human societies. Using remains, archaeologists reconstruct cultural systems, including their technological, social, and ideological subsystems. See **Archaeological culture**.

Culture area: A geographical area identified as distinct in that the peoples who lived there shared features of culture and were more like each other than like peoples in adjacent regions. Examples include the Andean Culture Area, Mesoamerica, the Subarctic, and (in the United States) the Southwest, the Eastern Woodlands, the Plains, and California.

Differentiated roles: Social roles (especially sex roles) that are nonoverlapping: women and men perform different activities and have different goals.

Direct historical approach: A method for inferring some features of an extinct culture by analogy with historic cultures when sociocultural continuity is presumed between the two. A form of **Ethnographic analogy**.

Division of labor: The process by which tasks are assigned to individuals depending on their sex, age, or specialization. In societies with a simple division of labor, all members classified in a particular broad category (by sex or age) perform about the same activities. In societies with a complex division of labor, there are a greater number of specialist categories beyond those of sex and age. See **Specialization**.

Domestic mode of production: The organization of labor and productive activities at the level of the household.

Early Horizon: In Peruvian archaeology, the period of time marked by the spread of Chavín iconography and other aspects of culture, including the use of hallucinogenic drugs in ritual, the heddle loom, and gold metallurgy.

Early Intermediate Period: In Peruvian archaeology, the time between the end of direct Chavín influence and the first appearance of Huari iconography. The major cultures at this time included the Moche, Recuay, and Nazca.

Economy: The cultural subsystem that involves the production of goods and their distribution and consumption.

Elites: Individuals in ranked societies who have greater access to prestige, power, and/or wealth. They may belong to an upper class or to highly ranked lineages.

Emic: Focused on the internal functioning of cultural systems as seen from the viewpoint of participants in the systems and not from outside. Contrast the etic perspective of scientific observers.

Endogamy: A social system in which a person marries a member of her own kin or social group, however defined. Compare **Exogamy**.

Engender: (a neologism) To introduce the dimension of gender, or to take real women and men into consideration in any discourse.

Epigraphy: The study and interpretation of ancient inscriptions.

Ethnoarchaeology: The study of contemporary cultures with the goal of understanding the relationship between behavior and material culture.

Ethnocentrism: The bias that assumes that one's own way of thinking or doing or being is natural, universal, normal, immutable, and inherently superior.

Ethnographic analogy: A method for inferring certain features of an extinct culture by using ethnographic evidence from a group whose culture can be shown to be analogous to the extinct one in some ways.

Ethnography: The study of living social groups and the description of their cultural patterns.

Ethnohistory: A field of study related to anthropology that endeavors to reconstruct societies and their cultures from historical documents written early in the period of a people's contact with Europeans.

Ethnology: The use of ethnographic evidence for the comparative study of human societies.

Exogamy: A system in which people tend to marry outside their own group. Compare **Endogamy**.

Extended family: A social unit composed of individuals related by blood and marriage in which several generations are represented and in which the members exhibit more degrees of relationship than do the members of a **Nuclear family**.

Family: Fundamental social group composed of people related by blood and marriage, often defined for archaeological purposes as the coresidential domestic group. See **Nuclear family** and **Extended family**.

Feminism: A doctrine and movement that advocates rights for women in political and economic spheres and that encourages scholars to include women and their domains of experience in research and interpretation.

Feminist archaeology: The scientific and humanistic study of the past through its material remains that uses contemporary feminist theory to critique androcentric research and to produce prehistoric interpretations that include gender, and that redresses the imbalance of previous research by focusing on women.

Feminist theory: A set of ideas that guides research and interpretation (in anthropology, sociology, history, and philosophy), that is critical of ideologies that have attributed certain characteristics to women and others to men, and that seeks to include the dimension of gender in developing understanding of both history and contemporary sociocultural systems.

Flakes: The sharp-edged byproducts of working stone that are removed when a flint-knapper applies force to a core of raw material. When flakes are removed expediently, the toolmaker invests a minimum of labor and skill and the resulting core and flakes are less controlled with respect to shape and size.

Fluted bifacial point: A chipped stone artifact that was used as a projectile point or knife by some Paleoindians and is distinguished by one or two longitudinal, flutelike flake scars. Examples include Clovis and Folsom points.

Food production: A kind of subsistence system that involves the cultivation of domesticated plant and/or animal species. Pastoralists, agriculturalists, and horticulturalists all produce food.

Foraging: An efficient mode of acquisition under conditions of low population density involving the harvest of wild resources using low-technology hunting and gathering strategies. Broad-spectrum foraging is the acquisition of a wide variety of resources using low-technology hunting and collecting strategies. Compare with specialized foraging, which focuses on one principal resource or prey species.

Formative: A period in New World prehistory characterized by food production and village life. Equivalent to the Neolithic of the Old World.

Gender: A dimension of social life involving the classification of people into two (or more) categories defined loosely on the basis of sexual differences, but involving a large number of socially ascribed characteristics.

Gender attribution: The way individuals are identified as males, females, or members of another culturally defined gender category, e.g., berdache or transsexual. For archaeologists, the processes of identifying particular kinds of material remains with one sex or another.

Gender complementarity: A cultural ideal that conceptualizes female and male as different and incomplete such that only together can they create harmony and balance.

Gender hierarchy: A feature of social organization that involves the members of one gender group exercising power and having authority over another (usually men over women). Also called gender stratification or sexual stratification.

Gender ideology: That aspect of thought and worldview that expresses the meaning of male, female, masculine, feminine, sex, and reproduction in any given culture, and that includes rules for appropriate male and female behavior, and expectations about public and private gender relations.

Gender role: What women and men are expected to do in a sociocultural setting; their prescribed activity patterns, social relations, and behaviors.

Gender system: The parts of a sociocultural system that involve customary female-male relations and the roles of women, men, and sometimes other genders.

Gynocentric: Focused on females and their activities and values, and favoring these above the activities and values of other social categories of people (males and other genders). See **Androcentric**.

Habitation site or **living site:** Place where people resided and left the remains of their activities.

Heterarchy: A postmodern idea about an organization in which the members are unranked or have the potential for being ranked in a number of different ways (see Ehrenreich et al. 1995). In such organizations, power is exercised from many loci and in multiple contexts. Compare **Hierarchy**.

Hierarchy: A kind of organization in which rulers hold power over ranks of subordinates; power is exercised from the apex of the organization.

Historic Period: Span of time (varying in length in different geographical regions) for which there are written records on which to base scholarly study. History is the narrative constructed about that period. Compare **Prehistoric Period.**

Horticulture: Plant cultivation using no power except human muscle and simple tools. Compare **Agriculture**.

Household: A group of people who reside together who may or may not be kin to each other.

Household cluster: The archaeological remains of a house and associated spaces and structures where residents carried out activities.

Hunter-gatherers: Human groups that subsist by exploiting wild plant and animal resources and that share a number of social and cultural features. See **Foraging**.

Ideology: That aspect of human cultural behavior that involves thought habits and includes beliefs about the nature of human beings, the structure of the world and the cosmos, and the supernatural realm. Includes gender ideology, political ideology, religious ideology, etc.

Kiva: An underground ceremonial room (used by men in historic times) characteristic of some prehistoric and ethnographic Puebloan peoples of the Southwest.

Late Intermediate Period: In Peruvian archaeology, the time between the cessation of direct Huari influence and the Inca conquest of the coastal cultures.

Lineage: A corporate group of kin whose members claim descent from a common ancestor in either the female or male line.

Masculine: That which is associated with the male sex in the norms of a particular social group.

Material culture: All the physical products of people, including artifacts and architecture.

Matriarchy: A hypothetical kind of social organization dominated by women in which female leaders have authority over men. No examples are known from history or ethnography. See **Patriarchy**.

Matrifocal: Refers to the centrality of mothers or adult females in the structure and functioning of a social unit, such as a family.

Matrilineal organization: A form of social organization in which an individual's descent is figured through his or her mother and female relatives. The social system is based on matrilineages. Compare **Patrilineal organization.**

Matrilocal residence: A pattern of postmarital residence in which the married couple resides with the family of the wife's mother. Compare **Patrilocal residence**.

Maya: Contemporary indigenous people of southern Mexico and northern Central America whose ancestors, the ancient Maya of the Preclassic and Classic Periods, left impressive archaeological remains and written texts.

Mealing bin: A structure, characteristic of the North American Southwest, designed to contain meal (processed grain) as it is being ground by hand.

Megafauna: Large species of animals, such as horse, elephant (mastodon and mammoth), ground sloth, bison, etc., that flourished during the last Ice Age. These species became extinct with the arrival of modern climatic regimes and, it is argued, from overhunting by Paleoindians.

Mesoamerica: That portion of Mexico and Central America where prehistoric peoples shared certain cultural features including hieroglyphic writing; a distinctive calendar; folding books; a religious system involving a ceremonial ball game and blood sacrifice; three-stone hearths; and a distinctive cuisine based on maize, squash, and beans. See **Culture area**.

Metate: Mesoamerican name for a shaped stone slab employed in combination with a hand stone, called a mano, for grinding grain and other materials.

Microsocial perspective: The idea that social analysis can focus on real individuals—men, women, and families—units that usually do not figure in interpretations generated by archaeologists. This perspective is often missing when societies are treated as systems.

Midden: The accumulated refuse and debris resulting from human activity.

Middle Horizon: In Peruvian archaeology, the period when influences from the Huari culture are visible in material culture throughout much of Peru.

Mimbres: The archaeological culture of a group of Mogollon people who lived along the Mimbres River in New Mexico and crafted distinctive ceramic vessels.

Model: A theoretical construct designed to describe the form and function of a real set of data or phenomena, which facilitates the understanding and explanation of those data or phenomena.

Nuclear family: A group of kin composed of an adult female, an adult male, and their biological offspring. See **Extended family**.

Paleoindian: The earliest known inhabitants of the New World, who occupied America in the late Pleistocene.

Paleolithic: The long archaeological period in the Old World that ended with the Pleistocene Epoch (about 12,000 years ago) and was characterized by cultures known principally from stone tools.

Paleopathology: The study of disease patterns in ancient human remains.

Patriarchy: A social organization in which men dominate society and hold positions of authority.

Patrilineal organization: A form of social organization in which an individual's descent is figured through his or her father and male relatives. The social system is based on patrilineages. Compare **Matrilineal organization**.

Patrilocal residence: A pattern of postmarital residence in which the married couple resides with the family of the husband's father. Compare **Matrilocal residence**.

Phytolith analysis: A method for studying microscopic silica skeletons of plant cells found in the soil and reconstructing the inventory of plants used by ancient people.

Pollen analysis: A method for studying the microscopic pollen grains found in archaeological soil and reconstructing the inventory of plants used by ancient people.

Polyandry: Marriage involving one woman and several men (husbands).

Polygamy: Marriage involving multiple spouses.

Polygyny: Marriage involving one man and several women (wives).

Postclassic Period: In Mesoamerica, the latest prehistoric period, dominated by the Aztec and known as a time of major political change.

Postmodern theory: An approach in anthropology in which practitioners reject the possibility of objectivity in the comparative study of peoples and cultures; they are aware of their own political and social biases, and they view culture as a dynamic system in which meanings and relationships are constantly negotiated by the interacting members of communities.

Power: The ability of one individual or group to affect the behavior of others.

Preceramic: A period of culture history (in a particular region) before the adoption of pottery.

Preclassic Period: In Mesoamerica, the time (also known as the Formative) when farming villages with ceramic industries were established and when the Olmec, Zapotec, and Teotihuacán states first emerged.

Prehistoric Period: That span of time (varying in length across geographical space) for which scholars have no written records.

Prehistory: The narratives constructed about the cultures of the prehistoric period based on the archaeological record.

Priestess or **priest:** A religious specialist who operates in a bureaucratically arranged religious institution in a complex society or state and who manages the cult of a deity.

Primary burial: The interment of a human being directly into the earth so that the skeleton is found in an anatomically correct position. Compare **Secondary burial**.

Projectile point: A bifacially flaked stone artifact with a point capable of piercing the hide of an animal and designed for hafting on a shaft.

Pueblo (Puebloan): One of the major indigenous cultural traditions of the Southwest. Modern Pueblo Indians (including Hopi and Zuni) are the descendants of the ancient Anasazi. In this tradition, people reside in communal masonry dwellings called pueblos.

Rank: Differential prestige and social position, often based on birth. Egalitarian societies were replaced by ranked societies later in prehistory.

Regional Developmental Period: In Ecuador, the period that embraced regional cultures and ceramic styles such as Guangala, Bahía, Jama-Coaque, and La Tolita, all derived from the Chorrera tradition.

Religion: A subsystem of culture and aspect of human behavior that involves the spiritual and/or supernatural realms.

Rites of passage: Ceremonial activities that mark the induction of an individual into a new social status. Commonly, people celebrate birth, puberty, marriage, and death.

Role: The customary behavior expected of an individual occupying a certain status.

Secondary Burial: The interment of human bones from which the soft tissue has disappeared or been removed before burial, so that the skeleton is not articulated. See **Primary burial**.

Sedentism: The practice of reducing group mobility and inhabiting a living site on a permanent or near-permanent basis.

Sex: The biological identification of an individual as female or male (or one of several androgynous combinations of female and male genes and genitalia).

Shaman: A female or male intermediary between humans and the spirit world who is often responsible for spiritual healing and who may interact with spiritual beings during trance. Compare **Priestess**.

Site: A discrete cluster of the remains of human behavior; a place where ancient activities occurred.

Social: Having to do with the organization of people in groups. This is distinct from "cultural," which refers to the learned behavior of people organized in a group.

Society: A group of people organized and held together by a common set of customs and values. **Culture** refers to systems of ideas and customs that organize social life.

Specialization: The social processes that result in a multiplication of roles and statuses and a complex division of labor. When individuals specialize in performing a particular task, they satisfy their needs by exchanging the fruits of their labor with other specialists. See **Division of labor**.

State: A territorial, sociopolitical organization characterized by hierarchically arranged governing institutions, and distinct social strata (in which some people are separated from others by birth and privilege); kinship is not a principal organizing feature of political life.

Status: The relative position (or social standing) of an individual in society, implying certain customary behavior (see **Role**). In some societies statuses are ranked, and status may refer to prestige or high social standing.

Stratified society: An integrated group of human beings in which some subgroups are accorded differential treatment, and in which some groups have power over others. See **Gender hierarchy**.

System: A kind of organization in which all the constituent parts (including subsystems) are interdependent and interact dynamically such that alterations in any part will result in coordinated changes in other parts. See **Gender system**.

Theory: A body of ideas that is designed to explain phenomena and the relationships among phenomena.

Utilized flakes: Technologically simple stone flakes with patterns of edge damage that suggest they were employed to perform work.

Uxorilocal: Postmarital residence in the household of the wife.

References

Adams, Richard E. W. 1963. A Polychrome Vessel from Altar de Sacrificios, Peten, Guatemala. *Archaeology* 16 (2): 90–92.

———. 1971. *The Ceramics of Altar de Sacrificios*. Papers of the Peabody Museum of American Archaeology and Ethnography 63 (1).

———. 1977. Comments on the Glyphic Texts of the "Altar Vase." In *Social Process in Maya Prehistory: Studies in Honor of Sir Eric Thompson*, ed. Norman Hammond, 409–420. New York: Academic Press.

Adovasio, J. M., Olga Soffer, and Jake Page. 2007. *The Invisible Sex: Uncovering the True Roles of Women in Prehistory*. Washington, DC: Smithsonian Books.

Allison, M. J. 1984. Paleopathology in Peruvian and Chilean Populations. In *Paleopathology at the Origins of Agriculture*, ed. Mark N. Cohen and George J. Armelagos, 515–530. Orlando: Academic Press.

Alva, Walter. 1988. Discovering the New World's Richest Unlooted Tomb. *National Geographic* 174 (4) (April): 510–549.

———. 1990. New Moche Tomb: Royal Splendor in Peru. *National Geographic* 177 (6) (June): 2–16.

Alva, Walter, and Christopher B. Donnan. 1993. *Royal Tombs of Sipán*. Los Angeles: Fowler Museum of Cultural History, University of California.

Anonymous. 1994. New Palenque Tomb Discovered. *Méxicon* 16 (4): 71–72.

Ardren, Traci, ed. 2002. *Ancient Maya Women*. Walnut Creek, CA: AltaMira Press.

Arriaza, Bernardo T. 1995a. Chile's Chinchorro Mummies. *National Geographic* 187 (January): 75–88.

———. 1995b. *Beyond Death: The Chinchorro Mummies of Ancient Chile*. Washington DC: Smithsonian Institution Press.

Arriaza, Bernardo T., Marvin Allison, and E. Gerszt. 1988. Maternal Mortality in the Pre-Columbian Indians of Arica. *American Journal of Physical Anthropology* 77:35–41.

Arvey, Margaret Campbell. 1988. Women of Ill-Repute in the Florentine Codex. In *The Role of Gender in Precolumbian Art and Architecture*, ed. Virginia E. Miller, 179–204. Lanham, MD: University Press of America.

Auel, Jean M. 1985. *The Mammoth Hunters*. New York: Crown Publishers.

Baird, Ellen. 1993. *Drawings of Sahagún's Primeros Memoriales: Structure and Style.* Norman: University of Oklahoma Press.

Barbour, Warren T. 1976. *The Figurines and Figurine Chronology of Ancient Teotihuacán, Mexico.* Ann Arbor: University Microfilms.

Bárcena, M. 1882. Descripción de un Hueso Labrado, de Llama Fósil, Encontrado en los Terrenos Posteciarios de Tequixquiac. *Anales del Museo Nacional de México* (época 1) 2:439–444.

Barriga, María Cristina. 1994. Malinalli, Malintzin, Doña Marina, y La Llorona: Una Mujer y Cinco Mundos Diferentes. *Southeastern Latin Americanist* 37 (4): 1–4.

Barstow, Anne. 1978. The Uses of Archaeology for Women's History: James Mellaart's Work on the Neolithic Goddess at Çatal Hüyük. *Feminist Studies* 4 (3): 7–18.

Bass, William M. 2005 *Human Osteology: A Field Manual*. Columbia, MO: Missouri Archaeological Society.

Bastien, Joseph W. 1987. *Healers of the Andes: Kallawaya Herbalists and Their Medicinal Plants.* Salt Lake City: University of Utah Press.

Baxter, Jane. 2004. *Gender and the Archaeology of Childhood.* Walnut Creek, CA: AltaMira Press.

Bell, Karen. 2003. Ancient Queens of the Valley of Mexico. In *Ancient Queens: Archaeological Explorations*, ed. Sarah M. Nelson, 137–150. Walnut Creek, CA: AltaMira Press.

Benfer, R. A. 1984. The Challenges and Rewards of Sedentism: The Preceramic Village of Paloma, Peru. In *Paleopathology at the Origins of Agriculture*, ed. Mark N. Cohen and George J. Armelagos, 531–558. Orlando: Academic Press.

———. 1990. The Preceramic Period Site of Paloma, Peru: Bioindications of Improving Adaptation to Sedentism. *Latin American Antiquity* 1 (4): 284–318.

Benson, Elizabeth P. 1988. Women in Mochica Art. In *The Role of Gender in Precolumbian Art and Architecture*, ed. Virginia E. Miller, 63–71. Lanham, MD: University Press of America.

Berlo, Janet Catherine. 1992. Icons and Ideologies at Teotihuacán: The Great Goddess Reconsidered. In *Art, Ideology and the Ancient City of Teotihuacán*, ed. Janet C. Berlo, 129–168. Washington, DC: Dumbarton Oaks.

Berndt, Catherine H. 1981. Interpretations and "Facts" in Aboriginal Australia. In *Woman the Gatherer*, ed. Frances Dahlberg, 153–204. New Haven, CT: Yale University Press.

Berry, David R. 1985. Aspects of Paleodemography at Grasshopper Pueblo, Arizona.

In *Health and Disease in the Prehistoric Southwest*, ed. Charles F. Merbs and Robert J. Miller, 43–64. Anthropological Research Papers No. 34. Tempe: Arizona State University.

Biocca, Ettore. 1971. *Yanoáma: The Story of a White Girl Kidnapped by Amazonian Indians*. New York: E. P. Dutton.

Bird, Carolyn F. M. 1993. Woman the Toolmaker: Evidence for Women's Use and Manufacture of Flaked Stone Tools in Australia and New Guinea. In *Women in Archaeology: A Feminist Critique*, ed. Hilary du Cros and Laurajane Smith, 22–30. Canberra: Australian National University.

Bird, Junius B., and John Hyslop. 1985. *The Preceramic Excavations at the Huaca Prieta, Chicama Valley, Peru*. Anthropological Papers of the American Museum of Natural History 62 (1). New York.

Black, Francis L. 1992. Why Did They Die? *Science* 258 (December 11): 1739–1740.

Blackmore, Chelsea. 2011. How to Queer the Past without Sex: Queer Theory, Feminisms, and the Archaeology of Identity. *Archaeologies: Journal of the World Archaeological Congress*. http://www.scribd.com/doc/52191889/How-to-Queer-the-Past-Without-Sex-Queer-Theory-Feminisms-and-the-Archaeology-of-Identity.

Blaffer Hrdy, Sarah. 1981. Lucy's Husband: What Did He Stand For? *Harvard Magazine* (July–August): 7–9, 46.

Blanton, Richard E., Gary M. Feinman, Stephen A. Kowalewski, and Peter N. Peregrine. 1999. Agency, Ideology, and Power in Archaeological Theory 1: A Dual-Processual Theory for the Evolution of Mesoamerican Civilization. *Current Anthropology* 37 (1): 1–14.

Blower, David. 2001. *It's All in the Stones: Identifying Early Formative Period Transition through the Incised Stone Figurines of Valdivia, Ecuador*. Ann Arbor: University Microfilms.

Bodenhorn, Barbara. 1990. I'm Not the Great Hunter, My Wife Is. *Études/Inuit/Studies* 14 (1–2): 55–74.

Bonnichsen, Robson, and Karen L. Turnmire, eds. 1991. *Clovis: Origins and Adaptations*. Corvallis: Center for the Study of the First Americans, Oregon State University.

Bourget, Steve. 1997. La Colère des Ancêtres: Découverte d'un Site Sacrificiel à la Huaca de la Luna, Vallée de Moche. In *A L'Ombre du Cerro Blanco: Nouvelles Découvertes sur la Culture Moche, Côte Nord du Pérou*, ed. Claude Chapdelaine, 83–100. Les Cahiers d'Anthropologie No. 1. Montreal: Université de Montréal.

Brekhman, I. I., and Y. A. San. 1967. An Ethnopharmacological Investigation of Some Psychoactive Drugs Used by Siberian and Far-Eastern Minority Nationalities of U.S.S.R. In *Ethnopharmacologic Search for Psychoactive Drugs*, ed. Daniel H. Efron, et al., 415. Workshop Series of Pharmacology No. 2, Public Health Service Publication No. 1645. Washington, DC: NIMH.

Bridges, Patricia S. 1991. Skeletal Evidence of Changes in Subsistence Activities between the Archaic and Mississippian Time Periods in Northwestern Alabama. In *What Mean These Bones? Studies in Southeastern Bioarchaeology*, ed. Mary Lucas Powell, Patricia S. Bridges, and Ann Marie Wagner Mires, 89–101. Tuscaloosa: University of Alabama Press.

Brown, Betty Ann. 1983. Seen but Not Heard: Women in Aztec Ritual—The Sahagún Texts. In *Text and Image in Pre-Columbian Art*, ed. Janet Catherine Berlo, 119–154. BAR International Series 180. Oxford.

Browne, David M., Helaine Silverman, and Rubén Garcia. 1993. A Cache of 48 Nasca Trophy Heads from Cerro Carapo, Peru. *Latin American Antiquity* 4:274–294.

Bruhns, Karen Olsen. 1988. Yesterday the Queen Wore . . . an Analysis of Women and Costume in the Public Art of the Late Classic Maya. In *The Role of Gender in Precolumbian Art and Architecture*, ed. Virginia E. Miller, 105–134. Lanham, MD: University Press of America.

———. 1991. Sexual Activities: Some Thoughts on the Sexual Division of Labor and Archaeological Interpretation. In *The Archaeology of Gender: Proceedings of the 22nd Annual Chacmool Conference*, ed. Dale Walde and Noreen D. Willows, 420–429. Calgary: Archaeological Association of the University of Calgary.

———. 1999. The Olmec Queens. *Yumtzilob* 11 (2): 163–189.

Brumbach, Hetty Jo, and Robert Jarvenpa. 1997. Woman the Hunter: Ethnoarchaeological Lessons from Chipewyan Life-Cycle Dynamics. In *Women in Prehistory: North America and Mesoamerica*, ed. Cheryl Claassen and Rosemary Joyce, 17–32. Philadelphia: University of Pennsylvania Press.

Brumbach, Hetty Jo, Robert Jarvenpa, and Clifford Buell. 1982. An Ethnoarchaeological Approach to Chipewyan Adaptations in the Late Fur Trade Period. *Arctic Anthropology* 19:1–49.

Brumfiel, Elizabeth M. 1991. Weaving and Cooking: Women's Production in Aztec Mexico. In *Engendering Archaeology: Women in Prehistory*, ed. Joan M. Gero and Margaret W. Conkey, 224–251. London: Basil Blackwell.

———. 1996a. Comments on Agency, Ideology, and Power. *Current Anthropology* 37 (1): 48–50.

———. 1996b. The Quality of Tribute Cloth: The Place of Evidence in Archaeological Argument. *American Antiquity* 61 (3): 453–462.

Buikstra, Jane E. 1984. The Lower Illinois River Region: A Prehistoric Context for the Study of Ancient Diet and Health. In *Paleopathology at the Origins of Agriculture*, ed. Mark N. Cohen and George R. Armelagos, 215–234. Orlando: Academic Press.

Buikstra, Jane E., T. Douglas, Lori E. Wright, and James A. Burton. 2004. Tombs from the Copán Acropolis: A Life-History Approach. In *Understanding Early Classic Copán*, ed. Ellen E. Bell, Marcello A. Canuto, and Robert J. Sharer, 191–212.

Philadelphia: University of Pennsylvania Museum of Archaeology and Anthropology.

Buikstra, Jane E., Lyle W. Konigsberg, and Jill Bullington. 1986. Fertility and the Development of Agriculture in the Prehistoric Midwest. *American Antiquity* 51 (3): 528–546.

Burkhart, Louise M. 1997. Mexica Women on the Home Front: Housework and Religion in Aztec Mexico. In *Indian Women of Early Mexico*, ed. Susan Schroeder, Stephanie Wood, and Robert Haskett, 25–54. Norman: University of Oklahoma Press.

Butler, Judith. 1993. *Bodies That Matter*. New York: Routledge.

Cabello Valvoa, Miguel. [1576–1586] 1951. *Miscelánea Antártica. Una Historia del Perú Antiguo*. Lima: Facultad de Letras, Instituto de Etnología, Universidad Mayor de San Marcos.

Caillavet, Chantal. 1996. Antropofagía y Frontera: El Caso de los Andes Septentrionales. In *Frontera y Poblamiento: Estudios de Historia y Antropología de Colombia y Ecuador*, ed. Chantal Caillavet and Ximena Pachón, 57–109. Bogotá: Institut Français de Etudes Andines, Instituto Amazónico de Investigaciones Científicas, and Departamento de Antropología, Universidad de los Andes.

Cardale Schrimpff, Marianne, ed. 2005. *Calima and Malagana: Art and Archaeology in Southwestern Colombia*. Bogotá: Pro Calima Foundation.

Carrasco, Pedro. 1984. Royal Marriages in Ancient Mexico. In *Explorations in Ethnohistory: Indians of Central Mexico in the 16th Century*, ed. H. R. Harvey and Hanns J. Prem, 41–81. Albuquerque: University of New Mexico Press.

———. 1997. Indian-Spanish Marriages in the First Century of the Colony. In *Indian Women of Early Mexico*, ed. Susan Schroeder, Stephanie Wood, and Robert Haskett, 87–104. Norman: University of Oklahoma Press.

Caso, Alfonso. 1964. *Interpretación del Códice Selden 3135 (A.2)*. Mexico: Sociedad Mexicana de Antropología.

———. 1969. *El Tesoro de Monte Albán*. Mexico: Instituto Nacional de Antropología e Historia (INAH).

Cassidy, Claire Monod. 1987. Skeletal Evidence for Prehistoric Subsistence Adaptation in the Central Ohio Valley. In *Paleopathology at the Origins of Agriculture*, ed. Mark N. Cohen and George R. Armelagos, 307–345. Orlando: Academic Press.

Castaño Uribe, Carlos. 1985. *Secuencias y Correlaciones Cronológicas en el Río de la Miel*. Bogotá: Fundación de Investigaciones Arqueológicas Nacionales.

———. 1987. La Vivienda y el Enterramiento como Unidades de Interpretación: Anatomía de Dos Casos de Transición del Modelo de Cacicazgo. In *Chiefdoms in the Americas*, ed. Robert D. Drennan and Carlos Castaño Uribe, 231–248. Lanham, MD: University Press of America.

Chadwick-Hawkes, Sonia, and Calvin Wells. 1975. Crime and Punishment in an Anglo-Saxon Cemetery? *Antiquity* 49:118–122.

Chandler-Ezell, Karol, Deborah M. Pearsall, and James A. Zeidler. 2006. Root and Tuber Phytoliths and Starch Grains Document Manioc (*Manihot esculenta*), Arrowroot (*Maranta arundinacea*), and Lléren (*Calathea* sp.) at the Real Alto Site, Ecuador. *Economic Botany* 60 (2): 103–120.

Cheal, David. 1987. Strategies of Resource Management in Household Economies: Moral Responsibility or Political Economy. In *The Household Economy: Reconsidering the Domestic Mode of Production*, ed. Richard R. Wilk, 11–22. Boulder, CO: Westview Press.

Chipman, Donald. 2005. *Moctezuma's Children: Aztec Royalty under Spanish Rule 1520–1700*. Austin: University of Texas Press.

Cieza de León, Pedro de. [1553] 1984. *Crónica del Perú, Primera Parte*. Lima: Pontificia Universidad Católica del Perú, Fondo Editorial.

Claassen, Cheryl P. 1991. Gender, Shellfishing, and the Shell Mound Archaic. In *Engendering Archaeology: Women in Prehistory*, ed. Joan M. Gero and W. Margaret Conkey, 276–300. London: Basil Blackwell.

———. 2002. Mothers' Workloads and Children's Labor during the Woodland Period. In *In Pursuit of Gender: Worldwide Archaeological Approaches*, ed. Sarah Milledge Nelson and Myriam Rosen-Ayalon, 225–234. Walnut Creek, CA: AltaMira Press.

Claassen, Cheryl, and Rosemary A. Joyce, eds. 1997. *Women in Prehistory: North America and Mesoamerica*. Philadelphia: University of Pennsylvania Press.

Clarkson, Persis B. 1978. Classic Maya Pictorial Ceramics: A Survey of Content and Theme. In *Papers on the Economy and Architecture of the Ancient Maya*, ed. Raymond Sidrys, 86–141. Institute of Archaeology, Monograph 7. Los Angeles: University of California.

Closs, Michael P. 1992. I Am a Kahal; My Parents Were Scribes: Soy un Kahal; Mis Padres Fueron Escribas. *Research Reports on Ancient Maya Writing* 38 (7): 7–22.

Cobo, Bernabé. [1653] 1990. *Inca Religion and Customs*. Translated and edited by Rowland Hamilton. Austin: University of Texas Press.

Code, Lorraine. 1991. *What Can She Know? Feminist Theory and the Construction of Knowledge*. Ithaca: Cornell University Press.

Collins, Michael B. 2002. The Gault Site, Texas, and Clovis Research. *Athena Review* 3 (2): 24–36.

Conkey, Margaret W. 2001. Epilogue: Thinking about Gender with Theory and Method. In *Gender in Pre-Hispanic America*, ed. Cecilia Klein and Jeffrey R. Quilter, 341–362. Washington, DC: Dumbarton Oaks.

Conkey, Margaret W., and Joan M. Gero. 1997. Programme to Practice: Gender and Feminism in Archaeology. *Annual Review of Anthropology* 26:411–437.

Conkey, Margaret W., and Ruth E. Tringham. 1995. Archaeology and the Goddess: Exploring the Contours of Feminist Archaeology. In *Feminisms in the Academy*, ed. Donna C. Stanton and Abigail J. Stewart, 199–234. Ann Arbor: University of Michigan Press.

Conlee, Cristina A. 2007. Decapitation and Rebirth: A Headless Burial from Nasca, Peru. *Current Anthropology* 48 (3): 438–442.

Connolly, Thomas J., Jon M. Erlandson, and Susan E. Norris. 1995. Early Holocene Basketry and Cordage from Daisy Cave, San Miguel Island, California. *American Antiquity* 60 (2): 309–318.

Conyers, Lawrence B. 1996. Archaeological Evidence for Dating the Loma Caldera Eruption, Ceren, El Salvador. *Geoarchaeology* 11 (5): 377–391.

Cook, Della Collins. 1984. Subsistence and Health in the Lower Illinois Valley: Osteological Evidence. In *Paleopathology at the Origins of Agriculture*, ed. Mark N. Cohen and George R. Armelagos, 235–269. Orlando: Academic Press.

Correal Urrego, Gonzalo, and Thomas van der Hammen. 1977. *Investigaciones Arqueológicas en los Abrigos Rocosos del Tequendama. 12.000 Años de Historia del Hombre y Su Medio Ambiente en la Altiplanacie de Bogotá*. Bogotá: Fondo de Promoción de la Cultura del Banco Popular.

Costin, Cathy Lynne. 1996. Exploring the Relationship between Gender and Craft in Complex Societies: Methodological and Theoretical Issues of Gender Attribution. In *Gender and Archaeology*, ed. Rita P. Wright, 111–142. Philadelphia: University of Pennsylvania Press.

———. 1998. Housewives, Chosen Women, Skilled Men: Cloth Production and Social Identity in the Late Prehispanic Andes. In *Craft and Social Identity*, ed. Cathy Lynne Costin and Rita P. Wright, 123–144. Archaeological Papers of the American Anthropological Association No. 8. Washington, DC.

Cowgill, George L. 1992. Social Differentiation at Teotihuacán. In *Mesoamerican Elites: An Archaeological Assessment*, ed. Diane Z. Chase and Arlen F. Chase, 206–220. Norman: University of Oklahoma Press.

———. 1997. State and Society at Teotihuacán, Mexico. *Annual Reviews in Anthropology* 26:129–161.

Crown, Patricia L., and Suzanne K. Fish. 1996. Gender and Status in the Hohokam Pre-Classic to Classic Transition. *American Anthropologist* 98 (4): 803–817.

Crown, Patricia L., and W. H. Wills. 1995. The Origins of Southwestern Ceramic Containers: Women's Time Allocation and Economic Intensification. *Journal of Anthropological Research* 51:173–186.

Crumley, Carole L. 1995. Heterarchy and the Analysis of Complex Societies. In *Heterarchy and the Analysis of Complex Societies*, ed. Robert M. Ehrenreich, Carole L. Crumley, and Janet E. Levy, 1–7. Washington DC: Archaeological Papers of the American Anthropological Association No. 6.

Cummins, Thomas. 1991. We Are the Other: Colonial Portraits of Kurakakuna. In *Translating Encounters*, ed. K. Andrien and Rolena Adorno, 203–231. Berkeley: University of California Press.

———. 1992. Tradition in Ecuadorian Pre-Hispanic Art: The Ceramics of Chorrera and Jama-Coaque. In *Amerindian Signs: 5000 Years of Precolumbian Art in Ecuador*, ed. Francisco Váldez and Diego Veintimilla, 63–82. Quito: Dinediciones.

———. 2003. Nature as Culture's Representation: A Change of Focus in Late Formative Iconography. In *Archaeology of Formative Ecuador*, ed. J. Scott Raymond and Richard L. Burger, 423–464. Washington, DC: Dumbarton Oaks.

Cyphers Guillén, Ann. 1984. The Possible Role of a Woman in Formative Exchange. In *Trade and Exchange in Early Mesoamerica*, ed. Kenneth Hirth, 115–123. Albuquerque: University of New Mexico Press.

———. 1993. Women, Rituals, and Social Dynamics at Ancient Chalcatzingo. *Latin American Antiquity* 4 (3): 209–224.

———. 1994. Las Mujeres de Chalcatzingo. *Arqueología Mexicana* 2 (7) (April–May): 70–73.

Dahlberg, Frances, ed. 1981. *Woman the Gatherer*. New Haven, CT: Yale University Press.

Damp, Jonathan E. 1979. *Better Homes and Gardens: The Life and Death of the Early Valdivia Community*. Ann Arbor: University Microfilms.

———. 1984. Architecture of the Early Valdivia Village. *American Antiquity* 49 (3): 573–585.

Davis, Leslie B. 1993. Paleo-Indian Archaeology in the High Plains and Rocky Mountains of Montana. In *From Kostenki to Clovis: Upper Paleolithic-Paleoindian Adaptations*, ed. Olga Soffer and N. D. Praslov, 263–277. New York: Plenum Press.

Davis-Kimball, Jeannine. 2002. *Warrior Women: An Archaeologist's Search for History's Hidden Heroines*. New York: Warner Books.

DeBoer, Warren R. 2001. Of Dice and Women: Gambling and Exchange in Native North America. *Journal of Archaeological Method and Theory* 8 (1): 215–268.

Demarrais, Elizabeth, Luis Jaime Castillo, and Timothy Earle. 1996. Agency, Ideology, and Power in Archaeological Theory 2: Ideology, Materialization, and Power Strategies. *Current Anthropology* 37 (1): 15–32.

Di Capua, Costanza. 1994. Valdivia Figurines and Puberty Rituals. *Andean Past* 4:229–279.

Dickel, David N., P. D. Schultz, and H. M. McHenry. 1984. Central California Prehistoric Subsistence and Health. In *Paleopathology at the Origins of Agriculture*, ed. Mark N. Cohen and George G. Armelagos, 439–462. Orlando: Academic Press.

Diehl, Michael W. 1996. The Intensity of Maize Processing and Production in Upland Mogollon Pithouse Villages AD 200–1000. *American Antiquity* 61 (1): 102–115.

Dillehay, Tom D. 1992. Keeping Outsiders Out: Public Ceremony, Resource Rights, and Hierarchy in Historic and Contemporary Mapuche Society. In *Wealth and Hierarchy in the Intermediate Area*, ed. Frederick W. Lange, 379–422. Washington DC: Dumbarton Oaks.

————, ed. 1995. *Tombs for the Living: Andean Mortuary Practices*. Washington, DC: Dumbarton Oaks.

————. 1996. *Monte Verde: A Late Pleistocene Settlement in Chile*. Vol. 2, *The Archaeological Context*. Washington, DC: Smithsonian Institution Press.

————. 2000. *The Settlement of the Americas: A New Prehistory*. New York: Basic Books.

Donnan, Christopher B. 1975. The Thematic Approach to Iconography. *Journal of Latin American Lore* 1 (2): 147–162.

————. 1982. Dance in Moche Art. *Ñawpa Pacha* 20:97–120.

————. 2004. *Moche Portraits of Ancient Peru*. Austin: University of Texas Press.

Donnan, Christopher B., and Luis Jaime Castillo. 1992. Finding the Tomb of a Moche Priestess. *Archaeology* 45 (6): 38–42.

————. 1994. Excavaciones de Tumbas de Sacerdotisas Moche en San José de Moro, Jequetepeque. In *Moche: Propuestas y Perspectivas*, ed. Santiago Uceda and Elías Mujica, 415–424. Travaux de L'Institut Français d'Etudes Andines 79. Lima: Universidad Nacional de la Libertad, Instituto Francés de Estudios Andinos, and Asociación Peruana para el Fomento de las Ciencias Sociales.

Donnan, Christopher B., and Donna McClelland. 1979. *The Burial Theme in Moche Iconography*. Studies in Pre-Columbian Art and Archaeology No. 21. Washington, DC: Dumbarton Oaks.

Drennan, Robert D. 1976. *Religion and Social Evolution: Formative Mesoamerica*. Orlando: Academic Press.

Drooker, Penelope Ballard. 1992. *Mississippian Village Textiles at Wickliffe*. Tuscaloosa: University of Alabama Press.

Duke, Philip, and Michael C. Wilson, eds. 1995. *Beyond Subsistence: Plains Archaeology and the Postprocessual Critique*. Tuscaloosa: University of Alabama Press.

Duviols, Pierre. 1976. La Capacocha: Mecanismo y Función del Sacrificio Humano. *Allpanchis Phuturinga* 9:11–57.

Ehrenreich, Barbara, and Deirdre English. 2010. *Witches, Midwives, and Nurses: A History of Women Healers*. 2nd ed. New York: Feminist Press at CUNY.

Ehrenreich, Robert M., Carole L. Crumley, and Janet E. Levy, eds. 1995. *Heterarchy and the Analysis of Complex Societies*. Archaeological Papers of the American Anthropological Association No. 6. Washington, DC.

Eisenberg, Leslie E. 1988. Mississippian Cultural Terminations in Middle Tennessee: What the Bioarchaeological Evidence Can Tell Us. In *What Mean These Bones? Studies in Southeastern Bioarchaeology*, ed. Mary Lucas Powell, Patricia S. Bridges, and Ann Marie Wagner Mires, 70–88. Tuscaloosa: University of Alabama Press.

Eller, Cynthia. 2000. *The Myth of Matriarchal Prehistory: Why an Invented Past Won't Give Women a Future*. Boston: Beacon Press.

Espenshade, Christoper B. 1997. Mimbres Pottery, Births, and Gender: A Reconsideration. *American Antiquity* 62 (4): 733–736.

Espinosa, Gaspar de. [1519] 1873. Relación y Proceso quel Licenciado Gaspar

Despinosa, Alcalde Mayor, Hizo en el Viaje. . . . desde esta Ciudad de Panamá a las Provincias de Paris e Natá, e a las Otras Provincias Comarcanas. *Documentos Inéditos de Colombia* 20:5–119.

Espinosa Soriano, Waldemar. 1976. Las Mujeres Secundarias de Huayna Capac: Dos Casos de Señorialismo Feudal en el Imperio Inca. *Revista del Museo Nacional* 42:248–296.

Ewers, John C. 1994. Women's Roles in Plains Indian Warfare. In *Skeletal Biology of the Great Plains: Migration, Warfare, Health, and Subsistence*, ed. Douglas W. Owsley and Richard L. Janz, 325–332. Washington, DC: Smithsonian Institution Press.

Ezzo, Joseph A. 1993. *Human Adaptation at Grasshopper Pueblo, Arizona: Social and Ecological Perspectives*. International Monographs in Prehistory, Archaeological Series No. 4.

Faux, Jennifer L. 2012. Hail the Conquering Gods: Ritual Sacrifice of Children in Inca Society. *Journal of Contemporary Anthropology* 3 (1). http://docs.lib.purdue.edu/cgi/viewcontent.cgi?article=1017&context=jca.

Ferguson, R. Brian. 1992. A Savage Encounter: Western Contact and the Yanomami War Complex. In *War in the Tribal Zone: Expanding States and Indigenous Warfare*, ed. R. Brian Ferguson and Neil L. Whitehead, 199–298. School of American Research Advanced Seminar Series. Seattle: University of Washington Press.

———. 1995. *Yanomami Warfare: A Political History*. Santa Fe, NM: School of American Research.

Fernández Distel, A. 1975. Restos Vegetales de Etapas Arcaicas en Yacimientos del N.O. de la República Argentina (Pcia. de Jujuy). *Etnia* 22:11–24.

Finerma, Ruthbeth. 1989. The Forgotten Healers: Women as Family Healers in an Andean Indian Community. In *Women as Healers: Cross-Cultural Perspectives*, ed. Carol Shepherd McClain, 24–41. New Brunswick, NJ: Rutgers University Press.

Flannery, Kent V. 1968. Archaeological Systems Theory and Early Mesoamerica. In *Anthropological Archaeology in the Americas*, ed. Betty J. Meggers, 67–87. Washington, DC: Anthropological Society of Washington.

———. 1976. Interregional Exchange Networks. In *The Early Mesoamerican Village*, ed. Kent V. Flannery, 283–286. Orlando: Academic Press.

———, ed. 1986. *Guila Naquitz: Archaic Foraging and Early Agriculture in Oaxaca, Mexico*. Orlando: Academic Press.

Flannery, Kent V., and Marcus C. Winter. 1976. Analyzing Household Activities. In *The Early Mesoamerican Village*, ed. Kent V. Flannery, 34–48. Orlando: Academic Press.

Follensbee, Billie J. A. 2000. *Sex and Gender in Olmec Art and Archaeology*. PhD diss., University of Maryland, College Park.

Freidel, David, and Linda Schele. 1993. Royal Women: A Lesson in Precolumbian History. In *Gender in Cross-Cultural Perspective*, ed. Caroline B. Brettell and Carolyn F. Sargent, 59–63. Upper Saddle River, NJ: Prentice Hall.

Freidel, David, and Stanley Guenter. 2003. Bearers of War and Creation. *Archaeology Archive*. http://archive.archaeology.org/online/features/siteq2/.

Frink, Lisa. 2005. Gender and the Hide Production Process in Colonial Western Alaska. In *Gender and Hide Production*, ed. Lisa Frink and Kathryn Weedman, 89–105. Walnut Creek, CA: AltaMira Press.

Frison, George C. 1993. North American High Plains Paleo-Indian Hunting Strategies and Weaponry Assemblages. In *From Kostenki to Clovis: Upper Paleolithic-Paleoindian Adaptations*, ed. Olga Soffer and N. D. Praslov, 237–249. New York: Plenum Press.

Frison, George C., R. L. Andrews, J. M. Adovasio, R. C. Carlisle, and Robert Edgar. 1986. A Late Paleoindian Animal Trapping Net from Northern Wyoming. *American Antiquity* 51 (2): 352–360.

Furst, Peter T. 1965. West Mexican Tomb Sculpture as Evidence for Shamanism in Prehispanic Mesoamerica. *Antropológica* 15 (December): 29–60.

———. 1974. Morning Glory and Mother Goddess at Tepantitla: Iconography and Analogy in Pre-Columbian Art. In *Mesoamerican Archaeology: New Approaches*, ed. Norman Hammond, 187–217. Austin: University of Texas Press.

———. 1976. *Hallucinogens and Culture*. San Francisco: Chandler and Sharp.

———. 1978. *The Ninth Level: Funerary Art from Ancient Mesoamerica*. Iowa City: University of Iowa Museum of Art.

———. 1996. *People of the Peyote: Huichol Indian History, Religion and Survival*. Albuquerque: University of New Mexico Press.

Galloway, Anne. n.d. Archaeological Evidence for Textile Production at Tarmatambo, an Inca Administrative Center in the Peruvian Central Highlands. Unpublished manuscript in the possession of the author.

Galloway, Patricia. 1997. Where Have All the Menstrual Huts Gone? The Invisibility of Menstrual Seclusion in the Late Prehistoric Southwest. In *Women in Prehistory: North America and Mesoamerica*, ed. Cheryl Claassen and Rosemary A. Joyce, 47–64. Philadelphia: University of Pennsylvania Press.

Garcilaso de la Vega, El Inka. [1609] 1945. *Comentarios Reales de los Incas*. Buenos Aires: Emecé Editores.

———. [1605] 1951. *The Florida of the Inca*. Translated and edited by John G. and Jeannette J. Varner. Austin: University of Texas Press.

———. [1609] 1961. *The Incas: The Royal Commentaries of the Inca Garcilaso de la Vega*. Translated by María Jolas. Edited and introduction by Alain Gheerbrandt. New York: Avon Books.

Gero, Joan M. 1990. Pottery, Power and Parties at Queyash Alto. *Archaeology* 43 (2): 52–56.

———. 1991. Genderlithics: Women's Roles in Stone Tool Production. In *Engendering Archaeology: Women in Prehistory*, ed. Joan M. Gero and Margaret W. Conkey, 163–193. London: Basil Blackwell.

————. 1992. Feasts and Females: Gender Ideology and Political Meals in the Andes. *Norwegian Archaeological Review* 25 (1): 15–30.

————. 1993. The Social World of Prehistoric Facts: Gender and Power in Paleoindian Research. In *Women in Archaeology*, ed. Hilary du Cros and Laurajane Smith, 31–40. Canberra: Australian National University.

————. 1999. La Iconografía Recuay y el Estudio de Genero. *Gaceta Arqueológica Andina* 25:23–44.

————. 2000. Troubled Travels in Agency and Feminism. In *Agency in Archaeology*, ed. Marcia-Anne Dobres and John Robb, 34–39. London: Routledge.

————. 2004. Sex Pots of Ancient Peru: Post-Gender Reflections. In *Combining the Past and the Present: Archaeological Perspectives on Society*, ed. Terje Oestigaard, Nils Anfinset, and Tore Saetersdal, 3–22. BAR International Series 1210. Oxford.

Gero, Joan M., and M. Cristina Scattolin. 2002. Beyond Complementarity and Hierarchy: New Definitions for Archaeological Gender Relations. In *Pursuit of Gender: Worldwide Archaeological Approaches*, ed. Sarah Milledge Nelson and Myriam Rosen-Ayalon, 155–171. Walnut Creek, CA: AltaMira Press.

Gifford-Gonzalez, Diane. 1995. The Drudge on the Hide. *Archaeology* 48 (2) (May–June): 84.

Gilchrist, Roberta. 1999. *Gender and Archaeology: Contesting the Past*. London: Routledge.

Gillespie, Susan D. 1989. *The Aztec Kings: The Construction of Rulership in Mexica History*. Tucson: University of Arizona Press.

Gillespie, Susan D., and Rosemary A. Joyce. 1997. Gendered Goods: The Symbolism of Maya Hierarchical Exchange Relations. In *Women in Prehistory: North America and Mesoamerica*, ed. Cheryl Claassen and Rosemary A. Joyce, 189–210. Philadelphia: University of Pennsylvania Press.

Gilmore, David D. 1990. *Manhood in the Making: Cultural Concepts of Masculinity*. New Haven, CT: Yale University Press.

Gimbutas, Marija. 1991. *The Civilization of the Goddess: The World of Old Europe*. San Francisco: Harper Collins.

Glass-Coffin, Bonnie. 1998. *The Gift of Life: Female Spirituality and Healing in Northern Peru*. Albuquerque: University of New Mexico Press.

Goldstein, Marilyn. 1988. Gesture, Role, and Gender in West Mexican Sculpture. In *The Role of Gender in Precolumbian Art and Architecture*, ed. Virginia E. Miller, 53–62. Lanham, MD: University Press of America.

González Cruz, Arnoldo. 2011. *La reina roja: una tumba real de Palenque*. Mexico: Consejo Nacional para la Cultura y las Artes, Instituto Nacional de Antropología e Historia.

Graham, Elizabeth. 1991. Women and Gender in Maya Prehistory. In *The Archaeology of Gender: Proceedings of the 22nd Annual Chacmool Conference*, ed. Dale Walde and Noreen D. Willows, 470–478. Calgary: Archaeological Association of the University of Calgary.

Graham, Mark M. 1992. Art-Tools and the Language of Power in the Early Art of the Atlantic Watershed of Costa Rica. In *Wealth and Hierarchy in the Intermediate Area*, ed. Frederick W. Lange, 165–206. Washington, DC: Dumbarton Oaks.

Grange, Jr., Roger T. 1979. An Archaeological View of Pawnee Origins. *Nebraska History* 60:134–160.

Graulich, Michel. 1992. Las Brujas de las Peregrinaciones Aztecas. *Estudios de Cultura Náhuatl* 22:87–98.

Green, Thomas J., Bruce Cochran, Todd W. Fenton, James C. Woods, Gene L. Titmus, Larry Tieszen, Mary Anne Davis, and Susanne J. Miller. 1998. The Buhl Burial: A Paleoindian Woman from Southern Idaho. *American Antiquity* 63 (3): 437–456.

Grove, David C. 1984. *Chalcatzingo: Excavations on the Olmec Frontier*. London: Thames and Hudson.

Grove, David C., and Susan D. Gillespie. 1984. Chalcatzingo's Portrait Figurines and the Cult of the Ruler. *Archaeology* 37 (4): 20–26.

Guaman Poma de Ayala, Felipe de. [1615] 1936. *Nueva Corónica y Buen Gobierno*. Codex Peruvien Ilustre. Traveaux et Memoires de l'Institut d'Ethnologie 23. Paris: Institut d'Ethnologie, Université de Paris.

Guillén, Sonia Elizabeth. 1992. *The Chinchorro Culture: Mummies and Crania in the Reconstruction of Preceramic Coastal Adaptation in the South Central Andes*. Ann Arbor: University Microfilms.

Guillén Guillén, Edmundo. 1983. El Enigma de las Momias Incas. *Boletín de Lima* 28:29–42.

Guinea, Mercedes. 2004. Los Símbolos del Poder o el Poder de los Símbolos. In *Simbolismo y Ritual en los Andes Septentrionales*, ed. Mercedes Guinea, 9–50. Quito: Ediciones Abya-Yala.

Hadingham, Evan. 1980. *Secrets of the Ice Age: The World of the Cave Artists*. London: Heineman.

Hammond, Norman, and Theya Molleson. 1994. Huguenot Weavers and Maya Kings: Anthropological Assessment versus Documentary Record of Age at Death. *Méxicon* 16 (4): 75–77.

Hanmann, Bryon. 1997. Weaving and the Iconography of Prestige: Lord 5 Flower's / Lady 4 Rabbit's Family. In *Women in Prehistory: North America and Mesoamerica*, ed. Cheryl Claassen and Rosemary A. Joyce, 153–172. Philadelphia: University of Pennsylvania Press.

Harvey, Herbert R. 1986. Household and Family Structure in Early Colonial Tepetlaoztoc. *Estudios de Cultura Náhuatl* 18:275–294.

Hassig, Ross. 1988. *Aztec Warfare: Imperial Expansion and Legal Control*. Norman: University of Oklahoma Press.

Hastorf, Christine. 1990. The Effect of the Inka State on Sausa Agricultural Production and Crop Consumption. *American Antiquity* 55 (2): 262–290.

———. 1991. Gender, Space, and Food in Prehistory. In *Engendering Archaeology: Women in Prehistory*, ed. Joan M. Gero and Margaret W. Conkey, 132–159. London: Basil Blackwell.

———. 1993. *Agriculture and the Onset of Political Inequality before the Inca*. Cambridge: Cambridge University Press.

Haviland, William A. 1997. The Rise and Fall of Sexual Inequality: Death and Gender at Tikal, Guatemala. *Ancient Mesoamerica* 8 (1): 1–12.

Hawkes, Kristin, James F. O'Connell, and Nigel G. Blurton-Jones. 1997. Women's Time Allocation, Offspring Provisioning, and the Evolution of Long Postmenopausal Life Span. *Current Anthropology* 38 (4): 551–577.

Hayden, Brian A. 1986. Old Europe: Sacred Matriarchy or Complementary Opposition. In *Archaeology and Fertility Cult in the Ancient Mediterranean*, ed. Antonio Bonnano, 17–30. Amsterdam: Gruner.

———. 1992. Contrasting Expectations in Theories of Domestication: Models of Domestication. In *The Transition to Agriculture in Prehistory*, ed. A. B. Gebauer and T. D. Price, 11–20. Madison, WI: Prehistory Press.

Hayden, Brian A., Cannon Deal, and J. Casey. 1986. Ecological Determinants of Women's Status among Hunter/Gatherers. *Human Evolution* 1 (5): 449–474.

Hayden, Brian A., Edward Bakewell, and Rob Gargett. 1996. The World's Longest-Lived Corporate Group: Lithic Analysis Reveals Prehistoric Social Organization near Lillooet, British Columbia. *American Antiquity* 61 (2): 341–356.

Hays-Gilpin, Kelley, and David S. Whitley. 1998. *Reader in Gender Archaeology*. London: Routledge.

Hegmon, Michelle, and Wenda R. Trevathan. 1996. Gender, Anatomical Knowledge, and Pottery Production: Implications of an Anatomically Unusual Birth Depicted on Mimbres Pottery from Southwestern New Mexico. *American Antiquity* 61 (4): 747–754.

———. 1997. Response to Comments by LeBlanc, Espenshade, and Shaffer et al. *American Antiquity* 62 (4): 737–739.

Hendon, Julia A. 1996. Archaeological Approaches to the Organization of Domestic Labor: Household Practices and Domestic Relations. *Annual Review of Anthropology* 25:45–62.

———. 1997. Women's Work, Women's Space, and Women's Status among the Classic-Period Maya Elite of the Copan Valley. In *Women in Prehistory: North America and Mesoamerica*, ed. Cheryl Claassen and Rosemary A. Joyce, 33–46. Philadelphia: University of Pennsylvania Press.

Hernández Príncipe, Rodrigo. [1622] 1923. Mitología Andina: Idolatrías de Recuay. *Revista Inca* 1 (1): 25–78.

Herr, Rebecca Lynn. 1987. *Women of Yaxchilán and Naranjo: A Study of Classic Texts and Contexts*. MA thesis, University of Texas, Austin.

Heth, Charlotte, ed. 1992. *Native American Dance: Ceremonies and Social Traditions*. Washington DC: National Museum of the American Indian, Smithsonian Institution, and Starwood Publishing.

Hewitt, Erika A. 1999. What's in a Name? Gender, Power, and Classic Maya Women Rulers. *Ancient Mesoamerica* 10 (2): 251–252.

Hickmann, Ellen. 1986. Instrumentos Musicales del Museo Antropológico del Banco Central del Ecuador, Guayaquil. *Miscelánea Antropológica Ecuatoriana* 6:117–141.

———. 1987. Instrumentos Musicales del Museo Antropológico del Banco Central del Ecuador, Guayaquil II. *Miscelánea Antropológica Ecuatoriana* 7:7–30.

Hirschkind, Lynn. 1995. History of the Indian Population of Cañar. *Colonial Latin American Historical Review* 4:311–342.

Historia de los Mexicanos por sus Pinturas. 1988. Paris: Asociación Oxomoco y Cipactonal.

Hocquenghem, Anne Marie. 1977a. Un "Vase Portrait" de Femme Mochica. *Ñawpa Pacha* 15:123–130.

———. 1977b. Les Représentations de Chamans dans l'Iconographie Mochica. *Ñawpa Pacha* 15:123–131.

Hocquenghem, Anne Marie, and Patricia J. Lyon. 1980. A Class of Anthropomorphic Supernatural Females in Moche Iconography. *Ñawpa Pacha* 18:27–48.

Hollimon, Sandra E. 1997. The Third Gender in Native California: Two-Spirit Undertakers among the Chumash and Their Neighbors. In *Women in Prehistory: North America and Mesoamerica*, ed. Cheryl Claassen and Rosemary Joyce, 173–188. Philadelphia: University of Pennsylvania Press.

———. 2005. Infancy, Personhood, and Mortuary Treatment: European Constructs and Their Effect on Archaeological Contexts in Nineteenth Century San Francisco. Paper presented at the Annual Meetings of the Society for California Archaeology, Sacramento.

Holmquist Pachas, Ulla Sarela. 1992. *El Personaje Mítico Feminino de la Iconografía Mochica*. Memoria para Obtener de Grado de Bachiller en Humanidades con Mención en Arqueología. Lima: Facultad de Letras y Ciencias Humanas, Pontificia Universidad Católica del Perú.

Hooton, Earnest A. 1940. Skeletons from the Cenote of Sacrifice at Chichén Itzá. In *The Maya and Their Neighbors*, ed. Clarence L. Hay, et al., 272–280. New York: Appleton-Century.

Howell, Todd L. 1995. Tracking Zuni Gender and Leadership Roles across the Contact Period. *Journal of Anthropological Research* 51 (2): 125–147.

Howell, Todd L., and Keith W. Kintigh. 1996. Archaeological Identification of Kin Groups Using Mortuary and Biological Data: An Example from the American Southwest. *American Antiquity* 61 (3): 537–554.

Idrovo Urigüen, Jaime. 1995. La Tumba de una Yana Aclla en Pumapungo, Tome-bamba. *Caspicara* 3 (8): 3–5.

Instituto Nacional Indigenista. 1994. *Atlas de las Plantas de la Medicina Tradicional Mexicana*. 3 vols. Mexico City: INC.

Jackson, Thomas L. 1991. Pounding Acorn: Women's Production as Social and Economic Focus. In *Engendering Archaeology: Women in Prehistory*, ed. Joan M. Gero and Margaret W. Conkey, 301–325. London: Basil Blackwell.

Jansen, Maarten. 1990. The Search for History in the Mixtec Codices. *Ancient Mesoamerica* 1 (1): 99–112.

Jarvenpa, Robert. 1987. The Hudson's Bay Company, the Roman Catholic Church, and the Chipewayan in the Late Fur Trade Period. In *Le Castor Fait Tout: Selected Papers of the Fifth North American Fur Trade Conference, 1985*, ed. Bruce Trigger, T. Morantz, and L. Duchene, 485–517. Montreal: St. Louis Historical Society.

Johnson, Eileen. 1991. Late Pleistocene Cultural Occupation on the Southern Plains. In *Clovis: Origins and Adaptation*, ed. Robson Bonnichsen and Karen L. Turnmire, 215–236. Corvallis: Center for the Study of the First Americans, Oregon State University.

Jolie, Edward A., Thomas F. Lynch, Phil R. Greib, and J. M. Adovasio. 2011. Cordage, Textiles and the Late Pleistocene Peopling of the Andes. *Current Anthropology* 52 (2): 285–296.

Joyce, Rosemary A. 1992. Images of Gender and Labor Organization in Classic Maya Society. In *Exploring Gender through Archaeology: Selected Papers from the 1991 Boone Conference*, ed. Cheryl Claassen, 63–70. Madison, WI: Prehistory Press.

———. 1993. Women's Work: Images of Production and Reproduction in Pre-Hispanic Southern Central America. *Current Anthropology* 34 (3): 255–273.

———. 1996. The Construction of Gender in Classic Maya Monuments. In *Gender and Archaeology*, ed. Rita Wright, 167–195. Philadelphia: University of Pennsylvania Press.

———. 2000. *Gender and Power in Prehispanic Mesoamerica*. Austin: University of Texas Press.

———. 2001. Negotiating Sex and Gender in Classic Maya Society. In *Gender in Pre-Hispanic America*, ed. Cecelia F. Klein, 109–142. Washington, DC: Dumbarton Oaks.

———. 2002. Beauty, Sexuality, Body Ornamentation, and Gender in Ancient Meso-America. In *In Pursuit of Gender: Worldwide Archaeological Approaches*, ed. Sarah Milledge Nelson and Myriam Rosen-Ayalon, 81–92. Walnut Creek, CA: AltaMira Press.

———. 2005. Archaeology of the Body. *Annual Reviews in Anthropology* 34:139–158.

———. 2008. *Ancient Bodies, Ancient Lives: Sex, Gender, and Archaeology*. New York: Thames and Hudson.

Joyce, Rosemary A., and Cheryl Claassen. 1997. Women in the Ancient Americas:

Archaeologists, Gender, and the Making of Prehistory. In *Women in Prehistory: North America and Mesoamerica*, ed. Cheryl Claassen and Rosemary A. Joyce, 1–14. Philadelphia: University of Pennsylvania Press.

Karttunen, Frances. 1997. Rethinking Malinche. In *Indian Women of Early Mexico*, ed. Susan Schroeder, Stephanie Wood, and Robert Haskett, 291–312. Norman: University of Oklahoma Press.

Kato, Yasutake. 1993. Resultados de las Excavaciones en Kuntur Wasi, Cajamarca. In *El Mundo Ceremonial Andino*, ed. Luis Millones and Yoshio Onuki, 203–228. Senri Ethnological Studies No. 37. Osaka: National Museum of Anthropology.

Katterman, Grace L., and Francis A. Riddell. 1994. A Cache of Textiles from Rodadero, Acarí Valley, Peru. *Andean Past* 4:141–167.

Kauffman Doig, Frederico. 1978. *Comportamiento Sexual en el Antiguo Peru*. Lima: Kompactos.

Kehoe, Alice B. 1970. The Function of Ceremonial Sexual Intercourse among the Northern Plains Indians. *Plains Anthropologist* 15:99–103.

———. 1987. Points and Lines. In *Powers of Observation: Alternative Views in Archaeology*, ed. Sarah M. Nelson and Alice B. Kehoe, 23–37. Washington, DC: American Anthropological Association.

———. 1995. Processual and Postprocessual Archaeology: A Brief Critical Review. In *Beyond Subsistence: Plains Archaeology and the Postprocessual Critique*, ed. Philip Duke and Michael C. Wilson, 19–27. Tuscaloosa: University of Alabama Press.

———. 2000. *Shamans and Religion: An Anthropological Exploration in Critical Thinking*. Long Grove, IL: Waveland Press.

———. 2005. Hideworking and Changes in Women's Status among the Arikara 1700–1862. In *Gender and Hide Production*, ed. Lisa Frink and Kathryn B. Weedman, eds., 77–89. Walnut Creek, CA: AltaMira Press.

Kellogg, Susan. 1984. Aztec Women in Early Colonial Courts: Structure and Strategy in a Legal Context. In *Five Centuries of Law and Politics in Central Mexico*, ed. Ronald Spores and Ross Hassig, 25–38. Publications in Anthropology No. 30. Nashville: Vanderbilt University.

———. 1995. *Law and the Transformation of Aztec Culture, 1500–1700*. Norman: University of Oklahoma Press.

———. 1997. From Parallel and Equivalent to Separate but Unequal: Tenochca Mexica Women, 1500–1700. In *Indian Women of Early Mexico*, ed. Susan Schroeder, Stephanie Wood, and Robert Haskett, 105–122. Norman: University of Oklahoma Press.

———. 2005. *Weaving the Past: A History of Latin America's Indigenous Women from the Prehispanic Period to the Present*. Oxford: Oxford University Press.

Kent, Susan. 1984. *Analyzing Activity Areas: An Ethnoarchaeological Study of the Use of Space*. Albuquerque: University of New Mexico Press.

———, ed. 1998. *Gender in African Prehistory*. Walnut Creek, CA: AltaMira Press.

Klein, Cecilia F., and Jeffrey R. Quilter, eds. 2001. *Gender in Pre-Hispanic America*. Washington, DC: Dumbarton Oaks.

Koehler, Lyle. 1997. Earth Mothers, Warriors, Horticulturalists, Artists, and Chiefs: Women among the Mississippian and Mississippian-Oneota Peoples, A.D. 1211 to 1750. In *Women in Prehistory: North America and Mesoamerica*, ed. Cheryl Claassen and Rosemary A. Joyce, 211–226. Philadelphia: University of Pennsylvania Press.

Koontz, Rex. 2009. Investiture and Violence at El Tajín and Cacaxtla. In *Blood and Beauty: Organized Violence in the Art and Archaeology of Mesoamerica and Central America*, ed. Heather Orr and Rex Koontz, 73–95. Los Angeles: Cotsen Institute of Archaeology Press, University of California at Los Angeles.

Lackey, Louana M. 1982. *The Pottery of Acatlán: A Changing Mexican Tradition*. Norman: University of Oklahoma Press.

Landa, Diego de. [1566] 1978. *Yucatan Before and After the Conquest*. Translated by William Gates. New York: Dover.

Langdon, Jean Matteson. 1992. Introduction: Shamanism and Anthropology. In *Portals of Power: Shamanism in South America*, ed. E. J. M. Langdon and Gerhard Baer, 1–24. Albuquerque: University of New Mexico Press.

Larco Hoyle, Rafael. 1965. *Checan: Essay on Erotic Elements in Peruvian Art*. Geneva: Nagel Publishers.

Larsen, Clark Spencer. 1984. Health and Disease in Prehistoric Georgia: The Transition to Agriculture. In *Paleopathology at the Origins of Agriculture*, ed. Mark N. Cohen and George R. Armelagos, 367–392. Orlando: Academic Press.

Larsen, Clark S., and C. B. Ruff. 1991. Biomechanical Adaptation and Behavior on the Prehistoric Georgia Coast. In *What Mean These Bones? Studies in Southeastern Bioarchaeology*, ed. Mary Lucas Powell, Patricia S. Bridges, and Ann Marie Wagner Mires, 102–113. Tuscaloosa: University of Alabama Press.

Lathrap, Donald W., Jorge G. Marcos, and James Zeidler. 1977. Real Alto: An Ancient Ceremonial Center. *Archaeology* 30 (1): 2–13.

LeBlanc, Stephen A. 1997. A Comment on Hegmon and Trevathan's "Gender, Anatomical Knowledge, and Pottery Production." *American Antiquity* 62 (4): 723–726.

Lee, Richard B. 1976. *Kalahari Hunter-Gatherers: Studies of the !Kung San and Their Neighbors*. Cambridge, MA: Harvard University Press.

Lee, Richard B., and Irven Devore, eds. 1968. *Man the Hunter*. Chicago: Aldine.

Lepper, Bradley T., and David J. Meltzer. 1991. Late Pleistocene Human Occupation of the Eastern United States. In *Clovis: Origins and Adaptations*, ed. Robson Bonnichsen and Karen L. Turnmire, 175–184. Corvallis: Center for the Study of the First Americans, Oregon State University.

Levy, Janet E. 2006. Gender, Heterarchy, and Hierarchy. In *Handbook of Gender in Archaeology*, ed. Sarah M. Nelson, 219–247. Lanham MD: AltaMira Press.

Lewis, Oscar. 1941. Manly-Hearted Women among the Northern Peigan. *American Anthropologist* 39 (2): 173–187.

Lockhart, James. 1992. *The Nahuas after the Spanish Conquest: A Social and Cultural History of the Indians of Central Mexico, Sixteenth through Eighteenth Centuries.* Stanford, CA: Stanford University Press.

López Reyes, Erick. 1996. Las Venus Valdivia Gigantes de Río Chico (OMJPLP-170A): Costa Sur de la Provincia de Manabí, Ecuador. *Boletín Arqueológico* 5:157–174.

Lumbreras, Luis Guillermo. 1989. *Chavín de Huántar en el Nacimiento de la Civilización Andina.* Lima: Ediciones INDEA.

Lyon, Patricia J. 1978. Female Supernaturals in Ancient Peru. *Ñawpa Pacha* 16:94–140.

MacAnulty Quilter, Sarah. 1976. Report on the Fiber Objects and Construction of Paloma, a Preceramic Archaeological Site. Unpublished paper in the possession of the author.

Mackey, Carol. 2002. Los Dioses que Perdieron los Colmillos. In *Los Dioses del Antiguo Perú, Tomo 2,* ed. Krzysztof Makowski Hanula. Lima: Banco del Crédito del Perú.

Manzanilla, Linda. 1996. Corporate Groups and Domestic Activities at Teotihuacán. *Latin American Antiquity* 7 (3): 228–246.

Marcos, Jorge G. 1988. *Real Alto: La Historia de un Centro Ceremonial Valdivia.* Biblioteca Ecuatoriana de Arqueología, vols. 4 and 5. Quito: Corporación Editora Nacional.

Marcus, Joyce. 1983. Rethinking the Zapotec Urn. In *The Cloud People: The Divergent Evolution of the Zapotec and Mixtec Civilizations,* ed. Kent V. Flannery and Joyce Marcus, 144–148. New York: Academic Press.

———. 1998. *Women's Ritual in Formative Oaxaca: Figurine-Making, Divination, Death and the Ancestors.* Memoirs of the Museum of Anthropology 33. Ann Arbor: Museum of Anthropology, University of Michigan.

Marcus, Joyce, and Kent V. Flannery. 1996. *Zapotec Civilization: How Urban Society Evolved in Mexico's Oaxaca Valley.* London: Thames and Hudson.

Martin, Paul S. 1973. The Discovery of America. *Science* 179 (4077): 969–974.

Martin, Simon. 2000. *Chronicles of the Kings and Queens: Deciphering the Dynasties of the Ancient Maya.* London: Thames and Hudson.

Matisoo-Smith, Elizabeth, and K. Ann Horsburgh. 2012. *DNA for Archaeologists.* Walnut Creek, CA: Left Coast Press.

Mazel, Aron David. 1989. People Making History: The Last Ten Thousand Years of Hunter-Gatherer Communities in the Thukela Basin. *Natal Museum Journal of Humanities* 1:1–158.

McAnany, Patricia A., and Shannon Plank. 2001. Perspectives on Actors, Gender Roles, and Architecture at Classic Maya Courts and Households. In *Royal Courts of the Ancient Maya*. Vol. 1, *Theory, Comparison, and Synthesis*, ed. Takeshi Inomata and Stephen D. Houston, 84–129. Boulder, CO: Westview Press.

McCafferty, Geoffrey G., and Sharisse McCafferty. 2003. Questioning a Queen? A Gender-Informed Evaluation of Monte Alban's Tomb 7. In *Ancient Queens: Archaeological Explorations*, ed. Sarah Milledge Nelson, 41–58. Lanham, MD: AltaMira Press.

McCafferty, Sharisse D., and Geoffrey G. McCafferty. 1988. Powerful Women and the Myth of Male Dominance in Aztec Society. *Archaeological Review from Cambridge* 7 (1): 45–59.

——. 1991. Spinning and Weaving as Female Gender Identity in Post-Classic Mexico. In *Textile Traditions of Mesoamerica and the Andes: An Anthropology*, ed. Margot Blum Schevill, Janet Catherine Berlo, and Edward B. Dwyer, 19–44. New York: Garland Press.

——. 1994a. The Conquered Women of Cacaxtla. Gender Identity or Gender Ideology? *Ancient Mesoamerica* 5:159–172.

——. 1994b. Engendering Tomb 7 at Monte Albán: Respinning an Old Yarn. *Current Anthropology* 35 (2): 143–166.

——. 1999. The Metamorphosis of Xochiquetzal: A Window on Womanhood in Pre- and Post-Conquest Mexico. In *Manifesting Power, Gender and Interpretation in Archaeology*, ed. Tracy L. Sweely, 103–125. London: Routledge.

McGuire, Randall H. 1992. *Death, Society, and Ideology in a Hohokam Community*. Boulder, CO: Westview Press.

McGuire, Randall, and Dean J. Saitta. 1996. Although They Have Petty Captains, They Obey Them Badly: The Dialectics of Prehispanic Western Pueblo Social Organization. *American Antiquity* 61 (2): 197–216.

McNett, Jr., Charles W. 1985. *Shawnee Minisink: A Stratified Paleoindian-Archaic Site in the Upper Delaware Valley of Pennsylvania*. Orlando: Academic Press.

Medicine, Beatrice. 1983. "Warrior Women"—Sex Role Alternatives for Plains Indian Women. In *The Hidden Half: Studies of Plains Indian Women*, ed. Patricia C. Albers and Beatrice Medicine, 267–280. Lanham, MD: University Press of America.

Meisch, Lynn A. 2002. *Andean Entrepreneurs: Otavalo Merchants and Musicians in the Global Arena*. Austin: University of Texas Press.

Merbs, Charles, and Ellen Vestergaard. 1985. The Paleopathology of Sundown, a Prehistoric Site near Prescott, AZ. In *Health and Disease in the Prehistoric Southwest*, ed. Charles F. Merbs and Robert J. Miller, 85–103. Anthropological Research Papers No. 34. Tempe: Arizona State University.

Milbrath, Susan. 1988. Birth Images in Mixteca-Puebla Art. In *The Role of Gender in Precolumbian Art and Architecture*, ed. Virginia E. Miller, 153–178. Lanham, MD: University Press of America.

Miller, Mary Ellen. 1986. *The Murals of Bonampak*. Princeton, NJ: Princeton University Press.

———. 2001. Life at Court: The View from Bonampak. In *Royal Courts of the Ancient Maya*. Vol. 2, *Data and Case Studies*, ed. Takeshi Inomata and Stephen D. Houston, 201–222. Boulder, CO: Westview Press.

Millon, René. 1973. *Urbanization at Teotihuacán, Mexico*. Vol. 1, *The Teotihuacán Map. Part I. Text*. Austin: University of Texas Press.

Milner, George R., Eve Anderson, and Virginia G. Smith. 1991. Warfare in Late Prehistoric West Central Illinois. *American Antiquity* 56 (4): 581–603.

Minnis, Paul E. 1984. Earliest Plant Cultivation in the Desert Borderlands of North America. In *The Origins of Agriculture: An Evolutionary Perspective*, ed. David Rindos, 121–142. Orlando: Academic Press.

———. 1985. Domesticating People and Plants in the Greater Southwest. In *Prehistoric Food Production in North America*, ed. Richard Ford, 309–339. Anthropological Paper No. 75. Ann Arbor: Museum of Anthropology, University of Michigan.

Mitchell, Douglas R. 1991. An Investigation of Two Classic Period Hohokam Cemeteries. *North American Archaeologist* 12 (2): 109–127.

Mock, Shirley Boteler. 2011 Portable Rock Art of the Lower Pecos Canyonlands: The Symbolic Work of Women. *American Indian Rock Art* 37:115–132.

Molloy, John P., and William L. Rathje. 1974. Sexploitation among the Late Classic Maya. In *Mesoamerican Archaeology: New Approaches*, ed. Norman Hammond, 431–444. Austin: University of Texas Press.

Moseley, Michael E., Carol J. Mackey, and David Brill. 1973. Peru's Ancient City of Kings. *National Geographic Magazine* 143 (3): 318–345.

Murdock, George P., et al. 1950. *Outline of Cultural Materials*. New Haven, CT: Human Relations Area Files.

Nelson, Sarah Milledge. 1987. Diversity of the Upper Paleolithic "Venus" Figurines and Archaeological Mythology. In *Powers of Observation: Alternative Views in Archaeology*, ed. Sarah M. Nelson and Alice B. Kehoe, 11–22. Archaeological Papers of the American Anthropological Association No. 2. Washington, DC.

———. 2004. *Gender in Archaeology: Analyzing Power and Prestige*. 2nd ed. Walnut Creek, CA: AltaMira Press.

Netting, Robert McC. 1987. Small Holders, Householders, Freeholders: Why the Family Farm Works Well Worldwide. In *The Household Economy: Reconsidering the Domestic Mode of Production*, ed. Richard R. Wilk, 221–244, Boulder, CO: Westview Press.

O'Brian, Patricia J. 1990. Evidence for the Antiquity of Gender Roles in the Central Plains Tradition. In *Powers of Observation: Alternative Views in Archaeology*, ed. Sarah M. Nelson and Alice B. Kehoe, 61–72. Archaeological Papers of the American Anthropological Association No. 2. Washington, DC.

Ortiz de Montellano, Bernard R. 1990. *Aztec Medicine, Health, and Nutrition*. New Brunswick, NJ: Rutgers University Press.

Ortner, Donald T. 2003. *The Identification of Pathological Conditions in Human Skeletal Remains*. 2nd ed. Orlando: Academic Press.

Osgood, Cornelius. 1940. *Ingalik Material Culture*. Publications in Anthropology No. 22. New Haven, CT: Yale University Press.

Owen, James. 2012. Tomb of Maya Queen Found—"Lady Snake Lord" Ruled the Centipede Kingdom. *National Geographic Daily News*, October 4, 2012. http://www.nationalgeographic.com.

Owsley, Douglas W. 1994. Warfare in Coalescent Tradition Populations of the Northern Plains. In *Skeletal Biology in the Great Plains: Migration, Warfare, Health, and Subsistence*, ed. Douglas W. Owsley and Richard R. Janz, 333–343. Washington, DC: Smithsonian Institution Press.

Oyuela-Caycedo, Augusto. 1998. Ideology, Temples and Priests: Change and Continuity in the House Societies of the Sierra Nevada de Santa Marta. In *Recent Advances in the Archaeology of the Northern Andes: In Memory of Gerardo Reichel-Dolmatoff*, ed. Augusto Oyuela-Caycedo and J. Scott Raymond, 39–53. Institute of Archaeology, Monograph 39. Los Angeles: University of California.

Pasztory, Esther. 1976. *The Murals of Tepantitla, Teotihuacán*. New York: Garland Press.

———. 1988. A Reinterpretation of Teotihuacán and Its Mural Painting Tradition. In *Feathered Serpents and Flowering Trees: Reconstructing the Murals of Teotihuacán*, ed. Kathleen Berrin, 45–77. San Francisco: Fine Arts Museums of San Francisco.

Pasztory, Esther, and Kathleen Berrin, eds. 1993. *Teotihuacán: Art from the City of the Gods*. New York: Thames and Hudson.

Paul, Lois, and Benjamin D. Paul. 1975. The Maya Midwife as Sacred Specialist: A Guatemala Case. *American Ethnologist* 2 (4): 707–726.

Paulinyi, Zoltán. 2006. The "Great Goddess" of Teotihuacan: Fiction or Reality? *Ancient Mesoamerica* 17 (1): 1–15.

Pearsall, Deborah Marie. 1988. *La Producción de Alimentos en Real Alto*. Guayaquil, Ecuador: Biblioteca Ecuatoriana de Arqueología, Corporación Editora Nacional.

———. 2003. Plant Food Resources of the Ecuadorian Formative: An Overview and Comparison to the Central Andes. In *Archaeology of Formative Ecuador*, ed. J. Scott Raymond and Richard L. Burger, 213–257. Washington, DC: Dumbarton Oaks.

Perls, Thomas T. 2004. The Oldest Old. *Scientific American* 14 (3): 6–11.

Piña Chan, Román. 1968. *Jaina: La Casa en el Agua*. Mexico: Instituto Nacional de Antropología e Historia.

Pohl, John M. D., and Bruce E. Byland. 1990. Mixtec Landscape Perception and Archaeological Settlement Patterns. *Ancient Mesoamerica* 1 (1): 113–131.

Powell, Mary Lucas. 1988. *Status and Health in Prehistory: A Case Study of the Mound-ville Chiefdom.* Washington, DC: Smithsonian Institution Press.

Powledge, Tabitha M., and Mark Rose. 1996. The Great DNA Hunt. *Archaeology* 49 (5): 36–44.

Prezzano, Susan. 1997. Warfare, Women, and Households: The Development of Iroquois Culture. In *Women in Prehistory: North America and Mesoamerica,* ed. Cheryl Claassen and Rosemary A. Joyce, 88–99. Philadelphia: University of Pennsylvania Press.

Price, T. Douglas, Linda Manzanilla, and William D. Middleton. 2000. Immigration and the Ancient City of Teotihuacán in Mexico: a Study Using Strontium Isotope Ratios in Human Bone and Teeth. *Journal of Archaeological Science* 27:903–913.

Pringle, Heather. 1998. New Women of the Ice Age. *Discover* 19 (4): 62–69.

Proskouriakoff, Tatiana. 1960. Historical Implications of a Pattern of Dates at Piedras Negras, Guatemala. *American Antiquity* 25 (4): 454–475.

———. 1961. Portraits of Women in Maya Art. In *Essays in Pre-Columbian Art and Archaeology,* ed. S. K. Lothrop, et al., 81–99. Cambridge, MA: Harvard University Press.

Pyburn, Anne K. 1999. Repudiating Witchcraft. In *Manifesting Power: Gender and the Interpretation of Power in Archaeology,* ed. Tracy L. Sweely, 190–197. London: Routledge.

———. 2004. *Ungendering Civilization.* New York: Routledge.

Quilter, Jeffrey. 1989. *Life and Death at La Paloma.* Iowa City: University of Iowa Press.

Rapp, Rayna. 1987. Women, Religion, and Archaic Civilizations: An Introduction. *Feminist Studies* 4 (3): 1–6.

Raymond, J. Scott. 2003. Social Formations in the Western Lowlands of Ecuador during the Early Formative. In *Archaeology of Formative Ecuador,* ed. J. Scott Raymond and Richard L. Burger, 33–68. Washington DC: Dumbarton Oaks.

Redder, Albert J., and John W. Fox. 1988. Excavation and Positioning of the Horn Shelter's Burial and Grave Goods. *Central Texas Archeologist* 11:1–10.

Redmond, Elsa M. 1994. *Tribal and Chiefly Warfare in South America.* Memoirs of the Museum of Anthropology 28. Ann Arbor: Museum of Anthropology, University of Michigan.

Reichel-Dolmatoff, Gerardo. 1961. Anthropomorphic Figurines from Colombia: Their Magic and Art. In *Essays in Pre-Columbian Art and Archaeology,* ed. Samuel K. Lothrop, et al., 229–241. Cambridge, MA: Harvard University Press.

———. 1965. Los Kogi: Una Tribu Indígena de la Sierra Nevada de Santa Marta. *Revista del Instituto Etnológico Nacional* 4 (1/2).

Reid, J. J., and S. M. Whittlesey. 1982. Households at Grasshopper Pueblo. *American Behavioral Scientist* 25 (6): 687–703.

Reinhard, Johan. 2006. *Ice Maiden: Inca Mummies, Mountain Gods, and Sacred Sites in the Andes*. Washington, DC: National Geographic Society.

Rice, Prudence. 1981. Prehistoric Venuses: Symbols of Motherhood or Womanhood? *Journal of Anthropological Research* 37 (4): 402–416.

Richards, Cara B. 1957. Matriarchy or Mistake: The Role of Iroquois Women through Time. In *Cultural Stability and Cultural Change*, ed. Verne F. Ray, 36–45. Seattle: American Ethnological Society, University of Washington Press.

Riddle, John M. 1992. *Contraception and Abortion from the Ancient World to the Renaissance*. Cambridge, MA: Harvard University Press.

Rivera, Mario A. 1995. The Preceramic Chinchorro Mummy Complex of Northern Chile: Context, Style, and Purpose. In *Tombs for the Living: Andean Mortuary Practices*, ed. Tom D. Dillehay, 43–78. Washington, DC: Dumbarton Oaks.

Romanowicz, Janet V., and Rita P. Wright. 1996. Gendered Perspectives in the Classroom. In *Gender and Archaeology*, ed. Rita P. Wright, 199–223. Philadelphia: University of Pennsylvania Press.

Rowe, Ann Pollard. 1979. Textile Evidence for Huari Music. *Textile Museum Journal* 18:5–18.

Rowe, John Howland. 1948. The Kingdom of Chimor. *Acta Americana* 6:219–246.

Russell, Pamela. 1991. Men Only? The Myths about European Paleolithic Artists. In *The Archaeology of Gender: Proceedings of the 22nd Annual Chacmool Conference*, ed. Dale Walde and Noreen D. Willows, 346–351. Calgary: Archaeological Association of the University of Calgary.

Saénz Samper, Juanita. 1993. Mujeres de Barro: Estudio de las Figurinas Cerámicas de Montelíbano. *Boletín de Museo del Oro* 34–35:77–110.

Sahagún, Bernadino de. [1579] 1979. *General History of the Things of New Spain: Florentine Codex*. 13 vols. Translated by Arthur J. O. Anderson and Charles F. Dibble. Santa Fe, NM: School of American Research.

Sarmiento de Gamboa, Pedro. [1572] 1943. *Historia de los Incas*. 2nd ed. Buenos Aires: Emecé Editores.

Sassaman, Kenneth E. 1992a. Lithic Technology and the Hunter-Gatherer Sexual Division of Labor. *North American Archaeologist* 13 (3): 249–262.

———. 1992b. Gender and Technology at the Archaic-Woodland Transition. In *Exploring Gender through Archaeology: Selected Papers from the 1991 Boone Conference*, ed. Cheryl Claassen, 71–80. Madison, WI: Prehistory Press.

Saul, Frank P. 1972. *The Human Skeletal Remains of Altar de Sacrificios: An Osteobiographic Analysis*. Papers of the Peabody Museum of American Archaeology and Ethnography 63:2. Cambridge, MA.

Schlegel, Alice. 1972. *Male Dominance and Female Autonomy: Domestic Authority in Matrilineal Societies*. New Haven, CT: Human Relations Area Files.

Schmidt, Robert A., and Barbara L. Voss, eds. 2000. *Archaeologies of Sexuality*. London: Routledge.

Schroeder, Susan.1992. The Noblewomen of Chalco. *Estudios de Cultura Náhuatl* 22:45–86.

Scott, John F. 1978. *The Danzantes of Monte Albán.* 2 vols. Studies in Pre-Columbian Art and Archaeology No. 19. Washington DC: Dumbarton Oaks.

Seeman, Mark F. 1979. Feasting with the Dead: Ohio Hopewell Charnel House Ritual as a Context for Redistribution. In *Hopewell Archaeology: The Chillicothe Conference,* ed. David S. Brose and N'omi Greber, 39–46. Kent, OH: Kent State University Press.

Sempowski, Martha L., and Michael W. Spence. 1994. *Mortuary Practices and Skeletal Remains at Teotihuacán.* Salt Lake City: University of Utah Press.

Serra Puche, Mari Carmen. 2001. The Concept of Feminine Places in Mesoamerica: The Case of Xochetécatl, Tlaxcala, Mexico. In *Gender in Pre-Hispanic America,* ed. Cecelia Klein and Jeffrey R. Quilter, 255–284. Washington DC: Dumbarton Oaks.

Shady, Ruth, and Carlos Leyva, eds. 2003. *La Ciudad Sagrada de Caral-Supe: Los Orígenes de la Civilización Andina y la Formación del Estado Prístino en el Antiguo Perú.* Lima: Proyecto Especial Arqueológico Caral-Supe.

Shafer, Harry J. 1986. *Ancient Texans: Rock Art and Lifeways along the Lower Pecos.* Dallas: Texas Monthly Press.

Shaffer, Brian S., Karen M. Gardner, and Harry J. Shafer. 1997. An Unusual Birth Depicted in Mimbres Pottery: Not Cracked Up to What It Is Supposed to Be. *American Antiquity* 62 (4): 727–732.

Sharon, Douglas, and Christopher B. Donnan. 1974. Shamanism in Moche Iconography. In *Ethnoarchaeology,* ed. Christopher B. Donnan and C. William Clewlow, Jr., 51–80. Institute of Archaeology, Monograph 4. Los Angeles: University of California.

Sheets, Payson D. 1992. *The Cerén Site: A Prehistoric Village Buried by Volcanic Ash in Central America.* New York: Harcourt Brace Jovanovich.

Sheets, Payson D., et al. 1990. Household Archaeology at Cerén, El Salvador. *Ancient Mesoamerica* 1:81–90.

Shimada, Izumi, Stephen Epstein, and Alan K. Craig. 1983. The Metallurgical Process in Ancient North Peru. *Archaeology* 36 (5): 38–45.

Silverblatt, Irene M. 1978. Andean Women in Inca Society. *Feminist Studies* 4 (3): 37–61.

———. 1980. The Universe Has Turned Inside Out . . . There Is No Justice for Us Here: Andean Women under Spanish Rule. In *Women and Colonization: Anthropological Perspectives,* ed. Mona Etienne and Eleanor Leacock, 149–195. New York: Praeger.

———. 1987. *Moon, Sun, and Witches: Gender Ideologies and Class in Inca and Colonial Peru.* Princeton, NJ: Princeton University Press.

———. 1988. Women in States. *Annual Review of Anthropology* 17:427–460.

Simon, Arleyn W., and John C. Ravesloot. 1995. Salado Ceramic Burial Offerings: A Consideration of Gender and Social Organization. *Journal of Anthropological Research* 51:103–123.

Smith, Augustus Ledyard. 1972. *Excavations at Altar de Sacrificios: Architecture, Settlement, Burials, and Caches*. Papers of the Peabody Museum of American Archaeology and Ethnography 62 (2). Cambridge, MA.

Smith, Kevin E. 1991. The Mississippian Figurine Complex and Symbolic Systems of the Southeastern United States. In *The New World Figurine Project*. Vol. 1, ed. Terry Stocker, 125–126. Provo, UT: Research Press.

Snow, Dean R. 1994. *The Iroquois*. London: Basil Blackwell.

———. 1995. Migration in Prehistory: The Northern Iroquoian Case. *American Antiquity* 60 (1): 59–79.

Sobolik, Kristin D., Kristin J. Gremillion, Patricia L. Whitten, and Patty Jo Watson. 1996. Technical Note: Sex Determination of Prehistoric Human Paleofeces. *American Journal of Physical Anthropology* 101:283–290.

Sofaer Derevenski, Joanna. 1997. Engendering Children, Engendering Archaeology. In *Invisible People and Processes*, ed. J. Moore and E. Scott, 192–202. Leicester, UK: University of Leicester Press.

Solís, Felipe. 1992. El Temalacatl-Cuauhxicalli de Moctezuma Ilhuicamina. In *Azteca-Mixteca*, ed. José Alcina Franch, Miguel León-Portilla, and Eduardo Matos Moctezuma, 225–232. Madrid.

Soustelle, Jacques. 1961. *Daily Life of the Aztecs on the Eve of the Spanish Conquest*. Stanford, CA: Stanford University Press.

Spence, Michael W. 1974. Residential Practices and the Distribution of Skeletal Traits in Teotihuacán, Mexico. *Man* 9:262–273.

Spencer-Wood, Suzanne M. 1996. Feminist Historical Archaeology and the Transformation of American Culture by Domestic Reform Movements, 1840–1925. In *Historical Archaeology and the Study of American Culture*, ed. L. A. De Cunzo and B. L. Herman, 397–446. Knoxville: Winterthur Museum and University of Tennessee Press.

———. 2011. Feminist Theories and Archaeology. In The Impact of Feminist Theories on Archaeology, ed. Suzanne M. Spencer-Wood and Laurajane Smith, special issue. *Archaeologies: Journal of the World Archaeological Congress* 7 (1): 1–34.

Spielmann, Katherine A. 1995. Glimpses of Gender in the Prehistoric Southwest. *Journal of Anthropological Research* 51 (2): 91–102.

Spores, Ronald. 1974. Marital Alliance in the Political Integration of Mixtec Kingdoms. *American Anthropologist* 76 (2): 297–311.

Staden, Hans. [1557] 1963. *The Captivity of Hans Staden of Hesse in A.D. 1547–1555 among the Wild Tribes of Eastern Brazil*. Translated by Albert Tootal. New York: Burt Franklin.

Staller, John Edward. 2001. The Jelí Phase Complex at La Emerenciana, a Late Valdivia Site in Southern El Oro Province, Ecuador. *Andean Past* 6:117–174.

Stone, Andrea. 1988 Sacrifice and Sexuality: Some Structural Relationships in Classic Maya Art. In *The Role of Gender in Precolumbian Art and Architecture*, ed. Virginia E. Miller, 63–74. Lanham, MD: University Press of America.

Storck, Peter L. 1991. Imperialists without a State: The Cultural Dynamics of Early Paleoindian Colonization as Seen from the Great Lakes Region. In *Clovis: Origins and Adaptations*, ed. Robson Bonnichsen and Karen L. Turnmire, 153–162. Corvallis: Center for the Study of the First Americans, Oregon State University.

Storey, Rebecca. 1985. An Estimate of Mortality in a Pre-Columbian Urban Population. *American Anthropologist* 87:519–535.

———. 1986. Prenatal Mortality at Pre-Columbian Teotihuacán. *American Journal of Physical Anthropology* 69:541–548.

———. 1992. *Life and Death in the Ancient City of Teotihuacán: A Modern Paleodemographic Synthesis*. Tuscaloosa: University of Alabama Press.

Stothert, Karen E. 1985. The Preceramic Las Vegas Culture of Coastal Ecuador. *American Antiquity* 50 (3): 613–637.

———. 1988. *La Prehistoria Temprana de la Peninsula de Santa Elena: Cultura Las Vegas*. Miscelánea Antropológica Ecuatoriana, Serie Monográfica 10. Guayaquil: Museos del Banco Central del Ecuador.

———. 1997. Fundición Tradicional Campesina en la Costa del Ecuador. *Boletín de Museo del Oro* 43:89–117.

———. 2003. Expression of Ideology in the Formative Period of Ecuador. In *Archaeology of Formative Ecuador*, ed. J. Scott Raymond and Richard L. Burger, 337–421. Washington, DC: Dumbarton Oaks.

Stothert, Karen E., and Iván Cruz Cevallos. 2007. Art in the Centers of Power. In *Ecuador: The Secret Art of Precolumbian Ecuador*, ed. Daniel Klein and Iván Cruz Cevallos, 107–195. Milan: 5 Continents Editions.

Stothert, Karen E., Dolores R. Piperno, and Thomas C. Andres. 2003. Terminal Pleistocene/Early Holocene Human Adaptation in Coastal Ecuador: The Las Vegas Evidence. *Quaternary International* 109–110:23–43.

Sued Badillo, Jalil. 1985. Las Cacicas Indoantillanas. *Revista del Instituto Puertorriqueño* 87:17–26.

Sullivan, Thelma D. 1966. Pregnancy, Childbirth, and the Deification of the Women Who Died in Childbirth. *Estudios de Cultura Náhuatl* 6:63–95.

Surovell, Todd A. 2000. Early Paleoindian Women, Children, Fertility and Mobility. *American Antiquity* 65 (3): 493–508.

Sweely, Tracy L., ed. 1999. *Manifesting Power: Gender and the Interpretation of Power*. London: Routledge.

Tate, Carolyn E. 1992. *Yaxchilán: The Design of a Maya Ceremonial City*. Austin: University of Texas Press.

Taube, Karl A. 1983. The Teotihuacán Spider Woman. *Journal of Latin American Lore* 9 (2): 107–189.

Taylor, Timothy. 1996. *The Prehistory of Sex: Four Million Years of Human Sexual Culture*. New York: Bantam.

Tello, Julio C. 1956. *Arqueología del Valle de Casma*. Publicación Antropológica del Archivo "Julio C. Tello," vol. 1. Lima: Universidad Nacional Mayor de San Marcos.

Thomas, Elizabeth Marshall. 1987. *Reindeer Moon*. Boston: Houghton Mifflin.

Tiesler, V., A. Cucina, and A. Romano Pacheco. 2004. Who Was the Red Queen? *Journal of Comparative Human Biology* 55 (1–2): 65–76.

Topic, John R., and Theresa Lange Topic. 1997. Hacia una Comprensión Conceptual de la Guerra Andina. In *Arqueología, Antropología, e Historia: Homenaje a María Rostworowski*, ed. Rafael Varón Gabai and Javier Flores Espinoza, 567–590. Lima: Instituto de Estudios Peruanos/Banco Central de la Reserva del Perú.

Topic, Theresa Lange. 2002. The Mobility of Women in the Inca Empire and in the Spanish Colony of Peru. In *The Archaeology of Contact: Processes and Consequences*, 458–467. Proceedings of the 25th Annual Conference of the Archaeological Association of the University of Calgary.

Trexler, Richard C. 1995. *Sex and Conquest: Gendered Violence, Political Order, and the European Conquest of the Americas*. Ithaca: Cornell University Press.

Trigger, Bruce G. 1989. *A History of Archaeological Thought*. Cambridge: Cambridge University Press.

Trocolli, Ruth. 1992. Colonization and Women's Production: The Timacua of Florida. In *Exploring Gender through Archaeology: Selected Papers from the 1991 Boone Conference*, ed. Cheryl Claassen, 95–102. Madison, WI: Prehistory Press.

———. 1999. Women Leaders in Native North American Societies: Invisible Women of Power. In *Manifesting Power: Gender and the Interpretation of Power in Archaeology*, ed. Tracy L. Sweely, 49–61. London: Routledge.

———. 2002. Mississippian Chiefs: Women and Men of Power. In *The Dynamics of Power*, ed. Maria O'Donovan, 168–187. Center for Archaeological Investigations, Occasional Paper No. 30. Carbondale: Southern Illinois University.

Tung, Tiffany A., and Keith J. Knudson. 2010. Childhood Lost: Abductions, Sacrifice, and Trophy Heads of Children in the Wari Empire of the Ancient Andes. *Latin American Antiquity* 21 (1): 44–66.

Ubelaker, Douglas H. 1980. Human Skeletal Remains from Site OGSE-80, a Preceramic Site on the Santa Elena Peninsula, Coastal Ecuador. *Journal of the Washington Academy of Science* 70 (1): 3–24.

———. 1989. *Human Skeletal Remains*. Manuals in Archaeology Series No. 2. Washington, DC: Taraxcum.

———. 2003. Health Issues in the Early Formative of Ecuador: Skeletal Biology of

Real Alto. In *Archaeology of Formative Ecuador*, ed. J. Scott Raymond and Richard L. Burger, 259–287. Washington DC: Dumbarton Oaks.

Uhle, Max. 1903. *Pachacamac. Report of the William Pepper, M.D., L.L.D. Expedition of 1896*. Philadelphia: Dept. of Archaeology, University of Pennsylvania.

Valdez, Francisco. 1992. Symbols, Ideology, and the Expression of Power in La Tolita, Ecuador. In *The Ancient Americas: Art from Sacred Landscapes*, ed. Richard Townsend, 229–243. Chicago: Art Institute of Chicago.

Venables, Robert W. 2010. The Clearings and the Woods: The Haudenosaunee (Iroquois) Landscape—Gendered *and* Balanced. In *The Archaeology and Preservation of Gendered Landscapes*, ed. Sherene Baugher and Suzanne M. Spencer-Wood, 21–57. New York: Springer.

Voss, Barbara L. 2000. Feminisms, Queer Theory and the Archaeological Study of Past Sexualities. *World Archaeology* 32 (2): 180–192.

Washburn, Sherewood L., and Chester S. Lancaster. 1968. The Evolution of Hunting. In *Man the Hunter*, ed. Richard B. Lee and Irven DeVore, 293–304. Piscataway, NJ: Aldine.

Wasson, Gordon. 1974. *María Sabina and Her Mazatec Mushroom Velada*. New York: Harcourt Brace Jovanovich.

Watson, Patty Jo, and Mary C. Kennedy. 1991. The Development of Horticulture in the Eastern Woodlands of North America: Women's Role. In *Engendering Archaeology: Women in Prehistory*, ed. Joan M. Gero and Margaret W. Conkey, 255–275. London: Basil Blackwell.

Weist, Katherine. 1983. Beasts of Burden and Menial Slaves: Nineteenth Century Observations of Northern Plains Indian Women. In *The Hidden Half: Studies of Plains Indian Women*, ed. Patricia C. Albers and Beatrice Medicine, 29–52. Lanham, MD: University Press of America.

White, Tim D. 1992. *Prehistoric Cannibalism at Mancos, 5MTUMR-2346*. Princeton, NJ: Princeton University Press.

Whiting, Beatrice B. 1993. *Six Cultures: Studies of Child Rearing*. New York: Wiley.

Whitten, Dorothea S., and Norman E. Whitten, Jr. 1988. *From Myth to Creation: Art from Amazonian Ecuador*. Urbana: University of Illinois Press.

Widmer, Randolph J., and Rebecca Storey. 1993. Social Organization and Household Structure of a Teotihuacán Apartment Compound: S3W1:33 of the Tlajinga Barrio. In *Prehispanic Domestic Units in Ancient Mesoamerica*, ed. Robert S. Santley and Kenneth G. Hirth, 47–104. Boca Raton: CRC Press.

Williams, Ann R. 2006. Mystery of the Tattooed Mummy. *National Geographic Magazine* 209 (6): 70–83.

Williams, Nigel. 1995. Ancient DNA: The Trials and Tribulations of Cracking the Prehistoric Code. *Science* 269 (August 18): 923–924.

Wilson, Diane. 1997. Gender, Diet, Health, and Social Status in the Mississippian Powers Phase Turner Cemetery Population. In *Women in Prehistory: North*

America and Mesoamerica, ed. Cheryl Claassen and Rosemary A. Joyce, 119–135. Philadelphia: University of Pennsylvania Press.

Wilson, Samuel. 1990. *Hispaniola: Caribbean Chiefdoms in the Age of Columbus*. Tuscaloosa: University of Alabama Press.

Winter, Marcus. 1997. Who Was Lady 12N? *News from the Center* 5 (1): 1–3, Center for Latin American Art and Archaeology, Denver Art Museum.

Wylie, Alison. 1991. Gender Theory and the Archaeological Record: Why Is There No Archaeology of Gender? In *Engendering Archaeology: Women and Prehistory*, ed. Joan M. Gero and Margaret W. Conkey, 31–54. Oxford: Basil Blackwell.

Zeidler, James A. 1984. *Social Space in Valdivia Society: Community Patterning and Domestic Structure at Real Alto, 3000–2000 B.C.* Ann Arbor: University Microfilms.

———. 2000. Gender, Status, and Community in Early Formative Valdivia Society. In *The Archaeology of Communities: A New World Perspective*, ed. Marcello A. Canuto and Jason Yeager, 161–181. New York: Routledge.

Zuidema, R. Tom. 1977–1978. Shaft Tombs and the Inca Empire. In *Prehistoric Contact Between Mesoamerica and South America: New Data and Interpretations. Journal of the Steward Anthropological Society* 9. Urbana, IL.

———. 1992. The Tairona of Ancient Colombia. In *The Ancient Americas: Art from Sacred Landscapes*, ed. Richard F. Townsend, 245–257. Chicago: Art Institute of Chicago.

Index

Page numbers in italics refer to illustrations.

Mayas, 19, 21, 23, 112–13, 145–47, 200–201, 223, 229
McGuire, Randal H., 93, 190, 192
Medicine, Beatrice, 218
Midwives, 112, 144
Military activities, 162, 194, 215, 220, 223, 226
Milner, George R., 227
Mimbres bowl, 4, 5, 144
Mistress of Fishes, 160
Mitchell, Douglas R., 94
Mitimas, 230
Mixtec Codices, 144
Mixtec people, 25–26, 169–70, 201–204, 208–209
Moche people, 25–26, 166–69, 226
Moctezuma, *135*, 204, 206
Moctezuma II, 206
Mogollon people, 91–92, 120, 229
Monte Verde site, *46*, 46–47, 50
Moon-boat, 160
Morro de Arica site, 59–60
Moundville site, 216
Mummies, 59–60, 156, 185–86
Mural, "Paradise of Tlaloc," 164
Mural, "Temple of Agriculture," 164

Navajo hogans, 108
Nelson, Sarah Milledge, 11, 13
Nine Grass Death, Lady, *169*, 171, 203
Nine Wind Flint Quequechmetl, Lady, 202
Noble Lady Scribe-Sky. *See* Jaguar Lord, Lady

Oaxaca, 47–49, 171, 199, 201
O'Brian, Patricia J., 184
Ochpaniztli, 166
Old Lord of Sipán, 208
Olmecs, 197, 199
Ortiz de Montellano, Bernard R., 143–44
Osgood, Cornelius, 38–39
Osteoarthritis, 62, 89
Osteoporosis, 59

Outline of Cultural Materials, 5
Owasco people, 116–17
Owl Woman, 26

Pacal (Palenque ruler), 200
Pachacamac, 160, 186, *187*
Pachacuti (Inca ruler), 211
Paget's Disease, 170
Palenque, 200
Paloma site, 61–65
Parita, Chief, 184
Pañamarca, 167
Patrilineal descent, 124–25, 200, 210
Pearsall, Deborah Marie, 108
Peigan people, 219
Piedras Negras site, 23
Polyandry, 63, 102
Polygyny, 102, 115–16, 136, 195, 234
Postprocessual archaeology, 12
Pottery. *See* Ceramics
Primogeniture, 211
Proskouriakoff, Tatiana, 23, 25
Prostitutes, 142–43
Pyburn, Anne K., 28

Quechua, 230
Queens, 135, 199–202, 209, 223
Queyash Alto site, 207
Quichua people, 151–52
Quilter, Jeffrey, 11, 61–62, 64
Quimbaya people, 184

Radiocarbon dating, 51
Rapp, Rayna, 245
Real Alto site, 97–98, 105–106, 108–109, 174
Recuay culture, 207–208, *208*
Redder, Albert J., 51
Reichert, Raphael X., 208
Reid, J. J., 120–21
Rivera, Mario A., 60
Roman alphabet, speed of transition to, 146

Wilson, Diane, 12
Witches, 143–44, 156, 235–36
Woman the Gatherer, 36
Wycliffe site, 133–34

Xoc, Lady, 24, 147
Xochitécatl shrine, 223

Yanomami (Yanoami), 224–25
Yaxchilán site, 182, 223
Yax Kuk Mo'o (Copan king), 200
Yutopian site, 130

Zak Kuk (Palenque queen), 200
Zapotec people, 145, 201
Zeidler, James A., 97–98, 105–109, 174

CPSIA information can be obtained at www.ICGtesting.com
Printed in the USA
LVOW06s1457230714

395346LV00003BA/4/P